W9-CMO-411

STRANGE
RITES

STRANGE
RITES

New Religions for a Godless World

Tara Isabella Burton

PUBLICAFFAIRS

NEW YORK

Copyright © 2020 by Tara Isabella Burton
Cover design by Faceout Studio, Tim Green
Cover copyright © 2020 Hachette Book Group, Inc.

Hachette Book Group supports the right to free expression and the value of copyright. The purpose of copyright is to encourage writers and artists to produce the creative works that enrich our culture.

The scanning, uploading, and distribution of this book without permission is a theft of the author's intellectual property. If you would like permission to use material from the book (other than for review purposes), please contact permissions@hbgusa.com. Thank you for your support of the author's rights.

PublicAffairs
Hachette Book Group
1290 Avenue of the Americas, New York, NY 10104
www.publicaffairsbooks.com
@Public_Affairs

Printed in the United States of America
First Edition: May 2020

Published by PublicAffairs, an imprint of Perseus Books, LLC, a subsidiary of Hachette Book Group, Inc. The PublicAffairs name and logo is a trademark of the Hachette Book Group.

The Hachette Speakers Bureau provides a wide range of authors for speaking events. To find out more, go to www.hachettespeakersbureau.com or call (866) 376-6591.

The publisher is not responsible for websites (or their content) that are not owned by the publisher.

Print book interior design by Linda Mark.

Library of Congress Cataloging-in-Publication Data
Names: Burton, Tara Isabella, author.
Title: Strange rites : new religions for a godless world / Tara Isabella Burton.
Identifiers: LCCN 2019050895 | ISBN 9781541762534 (hardback) |
  ISBN 9781541762510 (epub)
Subjects: LCSH: Spirituality—United States—History—21st century. | United
  States—Religion—21st century. | Non-church-affiliated people—United States. |
  Capitalism—Religious aspects.
Classification: LCC BL624 .B884 2020 | DDC 200.973/09051—dc23
LC record available at https://lccn.loc.gov/2019050895

ISBNs: 978-1-5417-6253-4 (hardcover), 978-1-5417-6251-0 (ebook)

LSC-C

10 9 8 7 6 5 4 3 2 1

To the women who helped me belong:
Kayla, Susannah, Erin, Simone, Alexandra, Allison, Ari, & Zelma

To explore the womb, or tomb, or dreams; all these are usual
Pastimes and drugs, and features of the press:
And always will be, some of them especially
When there is distress of nations and perplexity
Whether on the shores of Asia, or in the Edgware Road

T.S. ELIOT, "The Dry Salvages"

CONTENTS

NOTES FROM A
SO-CALLED SECULAR AGE

IT's THE END OF 2018. THREE IN THE MORNING. IN THE MIDDLE of a rave. We're in the McKittrick Hotel, equal parts warehouse, performance art space, bar, and party venue in the heart of Manhattan's Chelsea neighborhood. Ten or twenty years ago, this used to be a different sort of nightclub—populated by "freaks and crackheads," as one regular put it, in the heart of New York City's Club Row.[1] The sort of place where people did coke in the bathroom line, had sex in the stalls, ended up on *Page Six*. "We'd find people passed out in the bathroom," one former employee of a West 27th Street club said. "You would think it was a dead body. Passed out, like scary passed out, like smack them, pick them up, they're like Jell-O, like someone took their spine out. And on the street. You would literally see people face down in the gutter." Someone else called the neighborhood "a Disneyland for drunks."[2]

But the place is different now. You might even say a little bit more sacred.

It's still a party. People are still drunk. One or two may still be having sex in the bathrooms. Some are definitely making out on the dance floor. One of the performers onstage, dressed in a baroque costume that's equal parts Marie Antoinette and diabolical siren, is singing "God Is a Woman," and everyone is screaming along in joyous collective effervescence, because they, and she, really believe this. The theme of the party is vaguely inspired by *The Odyssey*, and by sirens and their call to self-defeating decadence. Because of this there is candy everywhere, streaming from the false-cobwebbed candelabras, for guests to eat: a playful riff on the idea, ubiquitous from the Greek myth of Persephone to the book of Genesis, that eating something illicit traps you in the world of death. Almost every single person in this building—and there are about a thousand—is taking a selfie.

But in the middle of all this revelry is something profound. Whether its participants are fully aware of it or not, they are in the middle of a religious ritual. More than that, it is one of the most *representative* religious rituals of our so-called secular age: a place where faith and fantasy, art and irony, capitalism and creation converge. We are at the holy of holies for the religiously unaffiliated—the fastest-growing religious demographic in America—the spiritual but not religious, the religious mix and matches, the theologically bi- and tri-curious who attend Shabbat services but also do yoga, who cleanse with sage but also sing "Silent Night" at Christmastime. Throughout America, already the religiously unaffiliated make up about a quarter of the population—and almost 40 percent of young millennials. Here, in the middle of hipster New York, those numbers are wildly higher.

BUT HERE, AT THIS RAVE, WE AREN'T JUST WATCHING THE "RISE OF THE Nones," as this phenomenon is often called. Rather, it's a collective celebration—what the sociologist Émile Durkheim once termed the "collective effervescence" that defines religion—of a new, eclectic, chaotic, and thoroughly, quintessentially American religion. A religion of emotive intuition, of aestheticized and commodified experience, of self-creation and self-improvement and, yes, selfies. A religion for a new generation of Americans raised to think of themselves both as capitalist consumers and as content creators. A religion decoupled from institutions, from creeds, from metaphysical truth-claims about God or the universe or the Way Things Are, but that still seeks—in various and varying ways—to provide us with the pillars of what religion always has: meaning, purpose, community, ritual.

Let me explain: Back in 2011, you see, the British theater company Punchdrunk took over the space that would become the McKittrick. They transformed the lattice of warehouse rooms into a 1930s hotel, a forest, a cemetery, a speakeasy. Dead flowers hang from the walls of an apothecary. Taxidermy moose heads overlook teak floors. Most of the time, the space serves as the home of *Sleep No More*, the company's near-wordless, dance-based, Hitchcock-inflected retelling of *Macbeth*. Masked audience members are free to wander the space in silence: rummaging through drawers, prowling around corners. If you're lucky, you might be singled out for a "one-on-one"—a coveted, intimate, often sexually charged encounter with a character in one of the production's secret locked rooms. (Lady Macduff, for example, might ask you to pray with her for the fate of her imperiled son; she'll whisper Bible verses into your ear and press salt into your palms as a good luck charm. The sultry witch Hecate might try to seduce you on a mission to reclaim a lost magical ring and leave a diabolical kiss on your mask, or even your neck.) It's equal parts video game, voyeurism, and religious pilgrimage.

You're encouraged to look around, to explore, to find hidden connections. To figure out how it all *fits together*: What the mysterious nurses in the insane asylum on the fifth floor (where Lady Macbeth tries to scrub out, of course, that damn spot) have to do with the lonely taxidermist on floor two. How Hecate and her three subservient witches who hail Macbeth as a would-be king—presaging his prideful downfall—have left their mark (or lipstick kiss) on nearly every room. The McKittrick—as even the elevator bellhops remind you on your way in—is an enchanted place.

Everything here, you see, has meaning. The show's creators have gone on record as claiming that *every single line* of *Macbeth* is "embedded" in the production's design, somewhere or other.[3] There's still an orgy, nightly, at the McKittrick, but this time it's a *blood orgy*: in the script, repeated three times per show. Techno music blares. Strobe lights flare. (Epileptics are not encouraged.) Hecate's witches strip bare. They fling blood—chocolate sauce, actually—on the crowd. The music is so loud that it's impossible to tell whether or not audience members—let alone Hecate—are screaming along.

Ostensibly, it's a reimagining of the famous prophecy scene from *Macbeth*'s act 4, in which Hecate and her witches tell Macbeth all the different ways he might be killed. Only this time, if you follow the characters, you might get to participate. You see moments of vulnerability and pain. You become part of the ritual. You might help the fully nude Boy Witch, shaken from the intensity of his revels, put his clothes back on—if he makes eye contact with you, invites you to come closer, you might even get to touch him. You might get to comfort him in his pain. Sometimes, *sometimes*, he hugs you.

Back in 2011, *Sleep No More* got a rapturous critical response. "The show infects your dreams," *New York* said.[4] The *New York Times* crowed about the erotic element of the show's immersivity, calling it "a voyeur's delight, with all the creepy, shameful pleasures that entails."[5] The show seemed destined to have a long, profitable run as a must-see, delightfully provocative New York tourist attraction, if nothing else. It augured a hunger, in New York and London alike, for immersive theater pieces: not art but *experience*.

But then something unexpected happened. The show developed fans. Not *fans* as in people who tweeted about it once or twice, but full-on, rapturous, devoted *fanatics*. (I should know. Reporting on the phenomenon, back in 2012–2013, I ultimately became one.) People came back ten, twenty, fifty, one hundred times—spending about $100 a ticket, and that's before you get to the coat check, the drinks, the cab home. Several communities sprang up on the blogging platform Tumblr devoted to painstakingly recapping trips to the show, sharing tips and tricks for garnering secret one-on-ones, and trying to predict the constantly changing cast. Blogging friends became real-life friends, or at the very least financial supporters: one well-known Tumblr user, whose *Sleep No More* viewings easily ranked in the hundreds, raised $2,000 from well-wishers on GoFundMe to attend the final performance of Punchdrunk's similarly structured London show, *The Drowned Man*, which he'd already seen dozens of times. Some self-proclaimed superfans came three hundred times or more.

Fandom is nothing new, of course. But *Sleep No More* was different. You didn't just watch a show or read a book or even write a blog. You got to *participate*. You got to touch people. You got to go inside a magical world, discover symbolic connections, find meaning. Almost unanimously, the superfans I interviewed cited the power of living— even for a few hours at a time—in an enchanted place: a world where everything, even the design of a room or the arrangement of dead flowers or the cards on a table, had symbolic weight. They cited the sense of profound intimacy they got from those coveted one-on-one interactions with characters. "It's like a switch went off and the power of this art form became clear," one fan told me. "Your first personal interaction is the catalyst. It feels like the story is choosing you to be a part of it."[6] "I'd never seen or felt anything like it," said another. "I felt I was both an observer and a part of the story being told."[7] Her husband, who told me they'd spent at least $17,000 on the show in the past couple years, added: "We didn't travel, go out, even go to movies. We pretty much only spent money on this one thing for a couple of years." But that was fine. Because, his wife told me, "every time I come out the end of the [entry] maze into that beautiful red light, I break into the biggest smile. It feels like I've come home."

And the McKittrick *was* a home. And a therapy session. And a bordello. And, yes, a church. Fans would go to celebrate a birthday. They'd go when they were sad, when they needed to be alone in a dark room with a mask to hide their tears. They'd go when they were lonely and wanted a moment of intimacy with the Porter—who pined for the male member of Hecate's triad of witches—or with Hecate herself. They'd go to feel tears—actors in one-on-ones often really cried—on their cheeks.

They'd forge personal relationships with Annabella, a folk-witch character (conceived and created by Punchdrunk actress Ava Lee Scott, who told me once that she "studied every night and day" and that she "disappeared in living this role") who sat in the show's bar—the only place outside the one-on-ones where talking was acceptable. At the bar, performers interact consistently with audience members, like NPCs in a video game, listening to their problems, concocting magical potions and charms, and giving life advice. (One fan attributes his decision to leave his day job and become a full-time artist to Annabella's advice.) Fans would speak fondly of Max, the bar's flirtatious MC, or Calloway, another bar local, as if they were personal friends.

The enthusiasts have expanded the world of the McKittrick. At private parties—including those I attended as a fan, and ultimately as a friend—we would write our own one-on-ones: bonding with friends by creating intimate, ritualistic spaces and expressions just for us. One fan created his own special coin to "tip" the bellhop who escorts guests from the bar into the show proper. Another developed his own costumed character—a lumberjack named Clyde—and took to haunting the McKittrick's (non-ticketed) rooftop garden bar while studying for his university exams, delighting in the fact that most people never quite figured out whether he was really part of the show.

As *Sleep No More* got more popular, the idea of the immersive experience started to get bigger and more commercial. Immersive theater productions in New York—often just repackaged sexy nightclub acts—all but outnumbered their fourth-wall-preserving counterparts. As of 2019, there was even immersive theater for babies.[8] In the decade since *Sleep No More* opened, the pop-up experience—a capitalist reimagining of immersive theater as Instagram bait—became an essential base of any worthwhile brand's marketing strategy. As exhausted critic Amanda Hess wrote on the rise of the "Instagrammable pop-up" in 2018 for the *New York Times*, "The 'experience' has emerged as among the defining fads of a generation. There have been New York experiences centered on tea, dreams, eggs, illusions and cereal. Soon the Museum of Pizza, 'the world's first and only immersive art experience celebrating pizza,' will open. There's one for dogs now, too: Human's Best Friend, which offers 20 'photo moments' for your pet to endure."[9] (Punchdrunk today does as much, if not more, advertorial work as independent creative projects, producing immersive ad campaigns for the beer company Stella Artois, the tech giant Samsung, and, of all people, Rihanna.)

Meanwhile, the McKittrick expanded. *Sleep No More* opened a second outpost in Shanghai: the McKinnon Hotel. Meanwhile, the New York McKittrick opened restaurants, extra performance space, and concert venues. It started throwing public ticketed raves on holidays like Halloween and New Year's Eve. It created an expanded universe for its characters: the pageantry of its parties was often filled with clues, likely to sail over the head of novices or party-only guests, as to characters' backstories. It encouraged attendees to come in themed costume. Inevitably, a slate of finance bros would arrive in half-hearted black with drugstore masks, while superfans would often spend months preparing intricate costumes based on characters from the show or on oblique references to lines of Shakespeare hidden in that enchanted world. Whether you were a superfan or just a Halloween reveler, these parties were, like the religious festivals they mimicked, *rituals*: ways of marking the passing of time through a carnival atmosphere of transcendence. They were invitations, not just to enter this world of witchcraft and magic that one British theater company had, via Shakespeare, created, but also to celebrate a very particular, if informally codified, worldview. A worldview that celebrated not *evil*, exactly, but subversion. A wholesale *fuck you* to repression, to patriarchy, to rules, to order, to the petty offices of men.

Whether you were a superfan or a novice at one of the McKittrick parties, you'd notice a recurring theme embedded in the dance numbers, songs, stories, and exclusive one-on-ones specially designed for each event. The McKittrick had a distinct and consistent ideological system underpinning its plays and parties alike: The world was a darkly magical place. Hecate and her witches were pulling the strings. They'd seduce uptight virgins and make them into maenads. They'd eat their hearts and lick the bones. The witches were evil, sure, but they were also *fun*. The way Milton's Satan was fun. Hecate's signature appearance—the reveal, at almost every party, that she and her witchy acolytes were behind some incident or another—engendered applause, not offense.

After all, Hecate is *cool*. In the world of the show, at least, she stands for personal freedom, for bodily autonomy, for sexual agency and empowerment, for unabashed, unapologetic *being*. She doesn't just break the rules, she makes her own. She tricks that silly, haughty Macbeth (ironically, the actual Macbeths feature little in the fandom) into throwing away his life on a futile power quest. She wears a bias-cut red dress with black ostrich trim. She is *sexy*. She's living her best life. We're supposed to side with the witches, at least secretly. When we celebrate Hecate and her witches, when we scream along as confetti pours down from the warehouse roof, we're celebrating her agency—*our* agency—to live freely.

Which brings me back to our rave, and the decision made by one particular member of the *Sleep No More* fandom, a woman I know socially but not well whom I'll call Shelley. Shelley decided to come to this party dressed not as a character from the show itself but as the Virgin Mary, flanked by a retinue of similarly costumed saints. Shelley had designed her own one-on-one: an interaction that specifically spoke both to the McKittrick's celebration of subversion and to the culture of creativity it had fostered. Over the course of the evening, her confidence bolstered by the party's open bar, Shelley made eye contact not just with fellow superfans but with total strangers. She brought them to her. Like the professional *Sleep No More* actors she was mimicking, she got spine-tinglingly, erotically close to them, her lips tickling their ear. (She later told me she'd had a special bespoke perfume manufactured for the occasion.) She whispered them prayers. She fed them candies. Then, the reveal. The Virgin Mary was Hecate all along. The audience member had been tricked into a deal with the devil. And, more often than not, they loved it.

But it wasn't just the superfans who got excited. The casual partygoers, too, got in on the action. Nearly everyone Shelley made eye contact with wanted to participate, fully, in the ritual. While a few people got offended, most embraced her. Some, Shelley told me later, thanked her profusely. "We asked people to confess their sins—and some people really did." One man, apparently a newlywed, admitted that his greatest sin was that he had no idea how to be a good husband.

"We wanted people to have an intimate experience with strangers or heavenly creatures," Shelley told me. "To feel like they were special and blessed in an otherwise crowded and anonymous party. We wanted them to leave feeling some sense of wonder and delight." She used the words "private performance" and "blessing" interchangeably. "We wanted them to wonder why they were picked." To feel, in other words, chosen.

FROM ONE VANTAGE POINT, SHELLEY'S ACT WAS QUITE SIMPLE. SHE WAS a fan playing around with the themes of her favorite media property—not so different from dressing as a character from *Star Trek* or *Buffy* at Comic-Con (although even these, as we'll see, are deeply imbued with religious significance). But, seen another way, what Shelley was doing was, well, *extremely 2019*. At three in the morning, at the heart of a $100 ticketed rave dedicated to celebrating the sexual subversion and empowering potential of witchcraft, at a theater space that started a national craze for experiential, enchanted, and Instagrammable performances, bolstered by an Internet-fueled fan culture obsessed with creating newer and ever-more-elaborate symbolic rituals in search of intimacy and meaning and homecoming, flanked by a close-knit community of superfans who have devoted tens of thousands of dollars to uncovering the mysteries of this enchantment, Shelley created a religious-but-not-really-but-actually-kind-of-yes ritual that spoke to what people really needed. She "blessed the sinners," in her words. And the sinners embraced her.

SURE, MOST OF US DON'T ATTEND PARTIES AT THE MCKITTRICK HOTEL. And, even if we do, we don't pal around with women pretending to be Hecate pretending to be the Virgin Mary. But the story of Shelley and the McKittrick and its superfans, however seemingly fringe and specific, is also the story of the religious sensibility of a whole generation. It's the story not just of the religious "Nones," but of an even broader category: those who aren't rejecting religion, but rather remixing it. It's the story of how more and more Americans—and particularly how more and more millennials—envision themselves as creators of their own bespoke religions, mixing and matching spiritual and aesthetic and experiential and philosophical traditions. The Remixed hunger for the same things human beings have always longed for: a sense of meaning in the world and personal purpose within that meaning, a community to share that experience with, and rituals to bring the power of that experience into achievable, everyday life. But they're doing it differently. (Or, at least, they *think* they are. More on that in the coming chapters.)

Today's Remixed reject authority, institution, creed, and moral universalism. They value intuition, personal feeling, and experiences. They demand to rewrite their own scripts about how the universe, and human beings, operate. Shaped by the twin forces of a creative-communicative Internet and consumer capitalism, today's Remixed don't want to receive doctrine, to assent automatically to a creed. They want to choose—and, more often than not, *purchase*—the spiritual path that feels more authentic, more meaningful, to them. They prioritize intuitional spirituality over institutional religion. And they want, when available institutional options fail to suit their needs, the freedom to mix and match, to create their own daily rituals and practices and belief systems.

FROM SOULCYCLE TO CONTEMPORARY OCCULTISM, FROM OBSESSIVE fan culture to the polyamorous and kink-based intentional communities of our new sexual revolution, from wellness culture to the reactionary, atavist alt-right, today's American religious landscape is teeming with new claimants to our sense of meaning, our social place, our time, and our wallets.

If you've ever been to a yoga studio or a CrossFit class, ever practiced "self-care" with a ten-step Korean beauty routine or a Gwyneth Paltrow–sanctioned juice cleanse, ever written or read Internet fan fiction, ever compared your spiritual outlook to a Dungeons and Dragons classification ("lawful good, chaotic evil") or your personal temperament to that of a Hogwarts house, ever channeled your sense of cosmic purpose into social justice activism, ever tried to "bio-hack" yourself or used a meditation app like Headspace, ever negotiated "personal relationship rules"—be they kink or ethical nonmonogamy—with a partner, ever cleansed a house with sage, or ever been wary of a person's "toxic energy," you've participated in some of these trends. There are more. Just you wait. We'll get to that.

Scholars of religion often claim that it's impossible to separate out the invention of the printing press from the Protestant Reformation. The technology that gave us the ability to sit with a text in the privacy of our own home and internalize and interpret its message for ourselves gave us at once a profound sense of agency and a retraction of the boundaries of a public sphere. Protestantism is, perhaps, the ultimate religion of the printed book. The Remixed religions we're about to explore are the religions of the Internet.

But first, a caveat.

As you've probably noticed, I cannot write about the McKittrick, or *Sleep No More*, or what it means to find a church in a secular place, from a standpoint of total journalistic objectivity.

I am not just a fly on the wall.

I started going to the McKittrick regularly as a reporter around 2013—I'd been once before, as a casual viewer, and been entranced by both the show's artistic intensity and, after a subsequent frenzied Google search ("what the fuck was that all about?"), its fan culture. I started interviewing fans in New York, where I was from, as well as fans of *The Drowned Man* in London, near where I was living. I told myself, at first, that my interest was purely intellectual—why do these people love this show so much?—as well as artistic (I'd briefly considered becoming a theater director). So many ironies were lost on me. I was a lonely academic theologian in my midtwenties, uncertain about graduate school, about my future, about what I believed about the world, about what was beyond it. I studied God, but I had no idea what I actually believed. I knew, only, that I wanted *more*.

And, for a time, I found what I was looking for at the McKittrick. I made my own fan blog. I made friends—first online, then off—some of whom remain pals to this day. I had a *community*, an *identity*. I went to the show thirteen times (a paltry number compared to many of the people I knew). I went annually to its Halloween and New Year's parties. There was a time in my midtwenties when I could show up at the McKittrick's Manderley Bar and be all but certain that someone I knew would be there. I remember, vividly, sneaking awkwardly and still sober out of a literary journal party next door on West 27th Street, where I knew nobody, only to all but sob with relief when I entered that red room. I, like my initial interview subjects, had found a place I felt "at home."

I remember telling myself that I wanted to *live* in the McKittrick, in this place where everything seemed meaningful, where everything mattered. A place that—although, despite nearly a decade of academic study, I did not have the language for it yet—was sacred.

Long before ever thinking about writing this book, long before I made a career out of my fascination with intense subcultures and the communities they foster—out of my search for meaning in what seems at times to be an astoundingly unenchanted world—I, too, fell under Hecate's spell.

She was wearing a red dress, a diamanté belt. She had black hair. She was swaying. She looked me straight in the eye and was lip-synching to a distorted cover of that old Peggy Lee song "Is That All There Is?"

The narrator of that song—which I later learned recurs throughout *Sleep No More*'s soundtrack—suffers from profound ennui. Nothing—not a fire that destroys her childhood home, not the excitement of a circus she attends as a teenager, not the heartbreak of lost love, not even death itself, that "final disappointment"—can shake her conviction that the world is a fundamentally meaningless place: a random kaleidoscope of atoms and mistakes.

"If that's all there is, my friends," she sings, "then let's keep dancing / Let's break out the booze and have a ball."

WE DO NOT KNOW FOR CERTAIN WHETHER *THIS* IS, WELL, ALL THERE IS. But that night in 2012, watching Hecate sing for the first time, overwhelmed by the magic—and, yes, it was a kind of magic—of the space, I remember both the wrenching terror that this was, in fact, *all there is* and the hope that maybe there was something more. That promise of something more was what brought me back to the McKittrick, and, through my love for the McKittrick and the friends I'd made there, to so many of the worlds explored here. (And, through that, to faith—but that's a story for a different book.)

This book is, in large part, about charlatans. It's about capitalism and corporations and the new, cutthroat Silicon Valley of spirituality. It's about people who want to sell us meaning, brand our purpose, custom-produce community, tailor-make rituals, and commodify our very humanity. It's about how the Internet and consumer capitalism alike have produced experientially satiating substitutes—many, though not all of them, poor—for well-developed ethical, moral, and metaphysical systems. It's about the denatured selfishness of self-care, and the way in which "call-out culture," at its worst, serves as psychic methadone, providing us with a brief and illusory hit of moral belonging.

But this book is also about the hunger and hope I felt that first night at the McKittrick. It is about the Americans who don't know if this is all there is, or what *all* means, or *there*, or even *is*. It is about our quest for knowing, for belonging, and for meaning: the pilgrimage none of us can get out of.

one

WHO ARE THE RELIGIOUSLY REMIXED (AND WHAT IS A RELIGION, ANYWAY)?

STRANGE BEDFELLOWS SEEM TO AGREE THAT WE LIVE IN A godless world. Back in 2001, right after the terrorist attacks of 9/11, pastor Jerry Falwell—among the most influential evangelical architects of the right-leaning political movement known as the Moral Majority—blamed the fall of the twin towers on the fact that America had turned its back on God. Speaking on the Christian talk show *The 700 Club*, Falwell told interviewer Pat Robertson that America was a godless nation. "The abortionists have got to bear some burden for this," Falwell said, speaking of the attacks, "because God will not be mocked. And when we destroy 40 million little innocent babies, we make God mad. I really believe that the pagans, and the abortions, and the feminists, and the gays and the lesbians, who are actively trying to make that an alternative lifestyle, the ACLU, People for the American Way, all of them who have tried to secularize America. I point the finger in their face and say 'You helped this happen.'"[1]

Five years later, in a 2006 interview with *Wired* magazine, author Sam Harris—widely known as one of the Four Horsemen of the New Atheist movement, alongside Richard Dawkins, Daniel Dennett, and

Christopher Hitchens—lauded the contemporary rise of secularism as a kind of apocalyptic triumph: a battle won by the shining forces of Reason and Truth over Irrationality and Superstition. Comparing belief in God to the legitimization of slavery, Harris told interviewer Gary Wolf that "the most intelligent, sophisticated people used to accept that you could kidnap whole families, force them to work for you, and sell their children. That looks ridiculous to us today. We're going to look back and be amazed that we approached the asymptote of destructive capacity while allowing ourselves to be balkanized by fantasy. . . . At some point . . . it's just going to be too embarrassing to believe in God."[2]

Falwell and Harris agreed on almost nothing when it came to religion or politics. But on this point, at least, they were in accord. The country we're living in now—as opposed to the America of sixty or a hundred or three hundred years ago—is secular, and only getting more so. We're hurtling at top speed through a tunnel, heading straight for that blinding light—be it zenith or nadir—of a world without God.

The numbers seem to bear this out. Back in 2007, 15 percent of Americans called themselves religiously unaffiliated, meaning that they didn't consider themselves to be members of any traditional organized religion. By 2012, that number had risen to 20 percent, and to 30 percent when it came to adults under thirty.[3] Now, those numbers are higher still. About a quarter of American adults say they have no religion.[4] And when you look at young millennials—those born after 1990—those numbers reach almost 40 percent.

In fact, the religious Nones, as they are often known, are the single biggest religious demographic in America, as well as the fastest-growing one. As a political unit, the Nones significantly outnumber white evangelicals, a group traditionally considered among the most influential voting blocs in America, but whose numbers are now dwindling to just 15 percent of the population.[5]

In 2009, 41 percent of American weddings were held in houses of worship.[6] By 2017, that number had plummeted to just 22 percent. Almost 30 percent of Americans do not anticipate having a religious funeral when they die.[7]

At first glance, the story both Falwell and Harris tell seems like a plausible one. America is getting less religious. America's *youth*—its future—are more irreligious still. The gays and the abortionists and the ACLU have won. The secularists have emerged, victorious, from the culture wars and salted the earth behind them. We're all Nones now. Or, at least, eighty-one million of us are.

But let's look a little closer.

While more and more Americans are saying that they don't belong to an organized religion, that doesn't necessarily mean that they aren't spiritual—or even that they don't believe in a Judeo-Christian God. Only around 7 percent of Americans identify outright as "atheist" or even "agnostic"—most just say they're "nothing in particular."

A full 72 percent of the Nones say they believe in, if not the God of the Bible, at least *something*. According to a 2018 Pew Research Center study, 55 percent of the religiously unaffiliated believe in a higher power or spiritual force distinct from that described in the Judeo-Christian Bible.[8] Furthermore, an additional 17 percent of the unaffiliated said that they believed precisely *in the God of the Abrahamic Bible*.[9]

Forty-six percent of those Nones talk to God, or this higher power, regularly, and 13 percent say that God talks back. Forty-eight percent of them think that a higher power has protected them throughout life. Forty-one percent say that it has rewarded them. Twenty-eight percent say it has punished them. Forty percent experience a sense of "spiritual peace and well-being" at least once a week—a percentage that actually increased by five points between 2007 and 2014.[10] Forty-seven percent believe in the presence of "spiritual energy" in physical objects. Forty percent believe in psychics. Thirty-eight percent in reincarnation. Thirty-two percent in astrology. And 62 percent, it turns out, in at least one of those four.[11]

In other words, our Nones may not be traditionally religious, in the sense that either Jerry Falwell or Sam Harris is used to. But they're not exactly *secular*, either.

The story of the rise of the religious Nones in America, it turns out, isn't really about Nones at all. Rather, it's about three distinct and complicated groups of people, people whose spiritual lives, sense of meaning, community, and rituals are a blend of what you might call traditional religious practices and personal, intuitional spirituality: privileging feelings and experiences over institutions and creeds.

It's a blend we see among the officially religiously unaffiliated— people who call themselves spiritual but not religious, or people who self-report as Nones but also say they believe in psychics or practice prayer. But it's a blend we also see among the millions more people who officially identify as one religion—checking the census box for Episcopalian or Jewish, attending services on High Holidays or Christmas and Easter—but whose actual beliefs, practices, and sources of meaning vary widely and incorporate a much more diverse range of traditions. To truly comprehend America's changing, dynamic religious landscape, we need to understand not only the Nones but also a significantly larger group: the Remixed. Now, it's difficult to calculate precisely how many Remixed there are in America. Polling data on the religiously unaffiliated and the spiritual but not religious is pretty scant as is. But, by looking at three distinct groups of Remixed Americans, we can get a sense of just how widespread Remixed culture is in American religious life.

THE FIRST GROUP THAT MAKES UP OUR REMIXED IS THE MOST STRAIGHT-forward. They're the spiritual but not religious, a designation that—according to at least one 2017 Pew study—consists of a full 27 percent of Americans.[12]

This in itself is a striking increase from years past. Back in 2012, for comparison, polls using the same methodology found that just 19 percent of Americans felt the same way. During that period, the study found, the percentage of Americans who identified as spiritual *and* religious significantly declined—from 59 percent to 48 percent—while the percentage of Americans who identified as *neither* religious nor spiritual rose very slightly, from 16 to 18 percent. (Meanwhile, the number of Americans who identified as religious but *not* spiritual remained static at a perplexing 6 percent.) In other words, the marked rise in "spirituality" as distinct from religion tracks directly with a decline in organized religious affiliation. Only a tiny percentage of people are moving away from spirituality altogether.

So, who are these self-proclaimed spiritual but not religious (let's call them the SBNRs)? The Pew poll also found them to be slightly whiter and significantly more left leaning than average, as well as more likely to identify as politically independent—not a surprising conclusion, given that they tend to feel comfortable questioning institutional hierarchies and creedal policies in other areas. They're also a staggering six points more likely than the average American to have a college degree.

The study also found that women were slightly more likely than men to embrace the SBNR label, even though the converse is true among both self-proclaimed atheists and the unaffiliated more broadly. SBNRs are also not necessarily religiously unaffiliated. In fact, only about 37 percent say they are, with about an equal percentage describing themselves as Protestant (14 percent call themselves Catholic).

This apparent contradiction—what does it mean to be spiritual but not religious and yet identify with a given religion?—points to a much wider and more serious problem, which is how difficult it is to define what a religion actually *is*. Is it about identity—the box we check on a form, or the way we describe our cultural heritage? Is it about community—the family and friends we gather with at regular festivals? Is it about rituals and practices—attending weekly services at a church or synagogue, or fasting during Ramadan? Or is it about belief—what people actually think and feel about the metaphysics of the world around them and the transcendent beyond? One of the biggest difficulties that we'll return to, again and again, in numbering America's religiously Remixed is that it's not so easy to pin down what we're remixing. Among the SBNRs, at least, it seems that religious affiliation plays some role in many of their lives—be it social or cultural, for example, perfunctory Christmas Mass attendance or a sense of Catholic identity divorced from religious faith as such—but that their primary sources of what we might call meaning-making, their sense of purpose, their source of wonder at the world, come from outside their religious traditions.

Often, they come from the so-called secular world.

A 2017 survey of self-identified spiritual Americans (both religious and not), for example, found that the most significant spiritual experience they had undergone in the past week was not prayer or meditation but rather music. Seventy-one percent of spiritual Americans reported having been inspired or moved by a piece of music or a song (compared to just 43 percent of nonspiritual Americans).[13]

For Dain Quentin Gore, for example, an artist in Arizona who grew up Southern Baptist but now considers himself an SBNR, that sense of purpose comes from his artistic practice. For Gore, organized religion is "obtuse and hopelessly convoluted." But when he creates, he feels closer to the divine. "Ceremonies, to me, have now become my puppet shows," Gore told me back in 2017.[14] "All of these things are the closest I get to 'religious experience' these days. Making art and puppetry are my transcendent moments." Likewise, New Yorker Megan Ribar, who worked at a yoga studio, finds purpose in meditation and yoga, as well as personal rituals. Although she's not sure how she feels about a higher power, she sets apart a space in her apartment as an "altar"—filled with objects that have personal significance to her. "The practices I consider spiritual," she told me, "are the things I do to care for myself in a deep way, to calm myself when I'm distressed, to create meaning out of the experiences of my life."[15]

THE SECOND GROUP OF OUR REMIXED ARE WHAT WE MIGHT CALL THE "faithful Nones," the self-proclaimed religiously unaffiliated whose behavior patterns and poll responses nevertheless suggest a belief in, and a hunger for, something bigger. These are the 72 percent of Nones who, as we've already discussed, say they believe in a higher power (maybe even the Judeo-Christian God); they're about 18 percent of Americans overall. They're pretty similar to the SBNRs (many faithful Nones would also self-describe as spiritual but not religious), with one major difference: they by definition don't see themselves as belonging to a religious community or having a religious identity in any way. While they have a personal spiritual tradition of some kind, which may or may not involve interfacing with organized religion, religious institutions are unlikely to provide them with a sense of community. When it comes to, say, dealing with a major life change or a personal catastrophe, faithful Nones don't necessarily have access to the kind of structural and institutional support that a synagogue, church, or similar community might offer. They—perhaps even more than SBNRs, many of whom still have access to those spaces—often seek out other forms of community life, finding and creating rituals with a chosen family of like-minded people who may or may not share their metaphysical example.

Take, for example, the case of a New York social worker named Iris. Iris was a self-described "lax Jew" married to a queer man whose primary spiritual interest was in the occult. When she was suddenly and unexpectedly widowed, she found herself at a loss for how to best commemorate the life of her husband. She declined to attend the memorial service hosted by her husband's family in their hometown—they were born-again Christians, uncomfortable with both her husband's sexuality and his interest in the occult—and she felt that the service they chose would not honor his memory (she circulated an email to attendees asking them to donate to Planned Parenthood). Instead, she and her friends threw an eclectic ceremony in New York: one that incorporated everything from the Jewish mourner's Kaddish to the theme song from *The Legend of Zelda*, her husband's favorite video game. And when she struggled with mourning in the months after his death, Iris found comfort in a perhaps unlikely institution: that same gamer culture. She and her husband had often played a game called *Destiny* together. She hadn't particularly enjoyed it, but she'd liked spending time with him. But when its sequel came out after his death, Iris found that connecting with other *Destiny 2* players helped her make sense of her grief.[16] (Months after our interview, she joyfully sent me a screenshot of the moment she finished the game.)

THE REMIXED CATEGORY ALSO INCORPORATES A THIRD GROUP, A GROUP that might not necessarily show up in polls in the same way that the faithful Nones and SBNRs do. These are the "religious hybrids": People who say they belong to a given religion, and believe or practice a portion of it. But they also feel free to disregard elements that don't necessarily suit them, or to supplement their official practice with spiritual or ritualistic elements, not to mention beliefs, from other traditions.

To better explain this particular phenomenon, let's go back to the poll we looked at earlier about the prevalence of New Age beliefs, defined by Pew as astrology, reincarnation, psychics, and spiritual energy located in physical objects. About 60 percent of the religiously unaffiliated believed in at least one of these phenomena. But what is most striking about the poll is that *so did an almost identical percentage of Christians*. A full 29 percent of them said they believed in reincarnation, which any scholar of Christianity would agree is fundamentally incompatible with orthodox Christian doctrine. (About a third of the US public at large says the same thing.) In other words, the personal beliefs and practices of self-identifying Christians are themselves increasingly varied.

About a third of Americans say they've attended services in multiple different houses of worship, and that doesn't include people who have, for example, attended an interfaith wedding or funeral. One in eight Americans say their spiritual life has been influenced by Buddhism. (For comparison, just 1 percent of Americans actually identify as Buddhist.)[17]

Just look at religion professor Paul F. Knitter, who in 2009 published his syncretic manifesto, *Without Buddha I Could Not Be a Christian*, which argued for his own hybrid religious identity. "Has my dialogue with Buddhism made me a Buddhist Christian?" he asks, using language like "InterBeing" and "Connecting Spirit" to refer to the Christian God. "Or [am I] a Christian Buddhist? Am I a Christian who has understood his own identity more deeply with the help of Buddhism? Or have I become a Buddhist who still retains a stock of Christian leftovers?"[18]

While Knitter's explicit hybridism might be an extreme example, he reflects our increasing willingness to blur the boundaries of religious traditions, and to pick and choose what suits us. NBA player Joakim Noah—profiled in Duane R. Bidwell's book on the "spiritually fluid"—regularly sports a Christian crucifix, Muslim prayer beads, and Tibetan Buddhist stones and says "I'm a little bit of everything."[19] Bidwell describes himself as spiritually fluid and is both a Presbyterian minister and a Buddhist, and, like many of his interview subjects, he characterizes spiritual fluidity as the preferable status of the legitimately spiritually curious: people who are "restless until they rest in a combination of spiritual thought and practice—a combination that speaks to and engages their entire being."[20]

Of course, spiritual fluidity is nothing new. Syncretism has long been a hallmark of American immigrant traditions—particularly those of nonwhite Americans. Just look, for example, at the practice of voodoo or other Afro-Caribbean folk religions in places like New Orleans, or the ubiquity of Mexican folk traditions among otherwise orthodox Latinx Catholics. But what we're seeing now isn't just an increase in culturally specific syncretism, but religious fluidity on a personal level.

We're witnessing the phenomenon that Harvard Divinity scholars Casper ter Kuile and Angie Thurston have called "unbundling": the rise of bespoke religious identities. The more individualized our religious identities become, the more willing we are to mix and match ideas and practices outside our primary religious affiliation.

"In an Internet-defined generation," ter Kuile told me last year, "we're used to finding our own sources of information, and mixing it together with eight different perspectives. We want to contribute in the comments section; we want to engage with it in a more discursive way." In an increasingly multicultural society, "people's identities and relationships become mixed. Maybe they have a Buddhist practice. Maybe they use a tarot deck."[21]

Scholars have been tracking this phenomenon for decades. As early as 2000, academics Steven Sutcliffe and Marion Bowman were commenting on how, "in our fin de siècle emporium, Irish Catholic nuns are enhancing their devotions with Buddhist meditation, Anglicans are learning spiral dances and Druids are teaching Neuro Linguistic Programming."[22] Sociologists Stef Aupers and Dick Houtman, likewise, wrote in 2007 of the rise of "bricolage" religion, inextricably connected to modern consumer capitalism and the room it has created for a robust spiritual marketplace. The "erosion of the Christian monopoly," they write, has created a "market" where "religious consumers construct strictly personal packages of meaning, based on individual tastes and preferences."[23]

But the contemporary rise of the Internet—and in particular of the self-creating power of social media—has only intensified that trend. The idea that our lives can and should be customized to our personal interests and wants and needs has bled into the way we construct our religious identities. As scholar and psychologist Phil Zuckerman, author of *Living the Secular Life*, told me: "We want to curate our own Facebook page. Why wouldn't we want to curate our own funeral?"[24] More and more people hunger for a spiritual identity and surrounding community that *precisely* reflects their values, their moral and social intuitions, their lived experience, and their sense of self.

As we increasingly consume our religious information the way we do the rest of our media—curated, like our Facebook feeds—so, too, does our religious "feed" become increasingly bespoke. More and more of us, even among the religiously affiliated, are religious hybrids: willing to incorporate non-Western or New Age spiritual traditions, or sources of spiritual energy, or regular meditative rituals within our spiritual diets. Concepts like "mindfulness"—a secularized version of principles associated with Zen Buddhism—have become ubiquitous in our workplaces, while the onetime meditation practice of yoga—associated with both Hinduism and Buddhism—has now become a $16 billion a year empire in the United States, as much associated with wellness culture and fitness as with spirituality proper.[25]

IT'S DIFFICULT TO ASCERTAIN EXACTLY WHAT PERCENTAGE OF AMERICA is Remixed. If, by rough estimation, we consider separately the SBNRs who *technically* profess a faith (65 percent of SBNRs), we get about 18 percent of Americans. If we add in the faithful Nones (72 percent of Nones, or another 18 percent of Americans overall), we get about 36 percent of Americans, already a pretty significant proportion. Adding in the religious hybrids is difficult, because they are harder to quantify. But even at an overly conservative estimate (say, exclusively looking at the 29 percent of self-proclaimed Christians who say they believe in something as counter to orthodox doctrine as reincarnation—or about 21 percent of Americans overall), combining the religious hybrids with the SBNRs and faithful Nones gets easily to over 50 percent of the population. At least half of America—and likely far more—is either a faithful None, an SBNR, or a religiously flexible hybrid.

But Remixed culture transcends its practitioners to become an embedded part of our environment. None of us—atheist, SBNR, hybrid, or orthodox Christian—can escape it entirely. Remixed culture is ubiquitous, in what high street stores and workout studios offer us, in the spiritualized language of advertising we see on billboards and street signs (halfway through writing this book, I noticed a giant sign at my local bus stop assuring me that YOU MADE IT TO THIS VERY SPOT AT THIS VERY MOMENT. THERE IS A REASON FOR EVERYTHING. It was a billboard trying to sell me oat milk). It's in the mindfulness training we go through at work, and the meditation apps on our iPhones. It's in the techno-utopian culture of Silicon Valley—equal parts messianic and libertarian—that shapes our daily life more than we know, as well as in the political narratives of both social justice and reactionary atavism that are battling it out as our new civil religions.

We may not all be Remixed, but we all live in a Remixed nation.

AT THIS POINT, YOU MIGHT BE LOOKING UP FROM THIS BOOK IN PERTURBATION. *Come on*, you may say. *SoulCycle, a religion? Really?* Sure, New Age stuff may be "weird" or "unconventional," but at least it makes metaphysical truth-claims about the world and the magical "energy" around us. But CrossFit?

Before we can get into these new religions, therefore, we should talk a little about what, exactly, a religion is. Now, I'm not looking to provide a thoroughgoing definition of religion, as anthropologists, sociologists, and other scholars of religion have been disagreeing about that for centuries. But, in briefly touching upon some of these debates and the different ways in which scholars have tried to pin down what religion is, I'll be focusing primarily on what a religion does: the way in which it functions both individually and societally to give us a sense of our world, our place in it, and our relationships to the people around us. Functions that today's religions—whether or not they make claims about God or the Supreme Being or the Interconnecting Energy That Runs Through Us All—fulfill.

TRADITIONALLY, WE (OR AT LEAST THOSE OF US WHO AREN'T ANTHRO-pologists or sociologists or scholars of religion) think of religion as straightforward: a box you can tick on a form. People are Christian, or Jewish, or Hindu, or Buddhist. Those are all "real" religions. But that doesn't tell us what a religion is, just what society has considered to be a legitimate and institutionalized form of one. Are newer religious categories, such as the New Age movement or Scientology, not religions? Any account that privileges merely size and history when defining a legitimate religion rests on academically shaky ground. (Again, we're not making claims about whether a religion is *true*, just how it can be defined.) While it's possible to knee-jerk categorize some practices into "real religions" and others into "cults," it's far more difficult to ascertain why, or what the precise differences are between religions and cults other than size or historical convention. Indeed, scholars tend to avoid the label "cult" altogether as unnecessarily pejorative, preferring the more ambiguous "new religious movements." Is religion, therefore, just faith in God? Or, at least, a codified or organized faith in God? That's what many of the earliest nineteenth-century scholars of religion—such as Edward Tylor and James Frazer—believed. They defined religion as a faith in a higher power. But, if so, then what does that make certain branches of Confucianism or Zen Buddhism, which are popularly acknowledged religions that don't formally hold to truth-claims about the divine?

Is religion about believing a certain set of principles? If so, what does that mean for those people whose internal beliefs don't track 100 percent with the external doctrines of their faith? How do we distinguish the people who *profess* beliefs—reciting the Nicene Creed in church, for example—from those who *really* believe? And are people only religious during periods of their life when they're surer of God, even when their personal feelings and intuitions fluctuate? Even the Catholic saint Mother Teresa grappled with yearlong terrors about whether God, in fact, existed. Was she only Catholic on the days she experienced security in her faith and atheist on the days she did not?

For the sociologist Émile Durkheim (1858–1917), often considered the founder of the field of sociology of religion, religion wasn't about belief, or really *content* at all. Rather, it was about how a given society cohered. In his 1911 book *The Elementary Forms of Religious Life*, Durkheim argues that religion is basically the glue that keeps a society together: a set of rituals and beliefs that people affirm in order to strengthen their identity as a group. Religion, he writes, is a "unified system of beliefs and practices which unite in one single moral community called a Church all those who adhere to them."[26] This church, furthermore, is sustained not through a top-down hierarchy, or through some invisible spirit, but rather through the collective energy of its adherents, a process he calls "collective effervescence," a shared intoxication participants experience when they join together in a symbolically significant, socially cohesive action. Collective effervescence is both a result and a cause of the church: each time it happens, participants renew, reiterate, and reify their experience of being members of that church.

But Durkheim doesn't specify an object for that effervescence. For him, the metaphysics and the ideas being expressed don't really matter. The ultimate object of worship he sees in a society's church is society itself. "God," he writes in *Elementary Forms*, "and society are one of the same. . . . The god of the clan can be none other than the clan itself, but the clan transfigured and imagined" as a totem, be it plant, animal, or deity. "Religious force," he ultimately concludes, is "nothing other than the collective and anonymous force of the clan."[27]

By this logic, you can find Durkheimian "churches"—examples of collective effervescence keeping communities together—outside of the venues traditionally constituted as religious. You can find it in the exuberant joy fans experience at a Jonas Brothers concert, or in the intense in-group identity formation you find at a Super Bowl game, or, in its darkest iterations, at a Hitler Youth march. What matters is that participants have a common symbolic object of worship—and that they have rituals and routines to help them solidify their social bonds around that object.

But, other scholars have argued, religion isn't just about social glue. It's also about making sense of the world around us: answering the question *What does it all mean?* Another foundational scholar in the field, Peter Berger, argues that religion is ultimately about creating a coherent and meaningful narrative. In his 1967 book *The Sacred Canopy*, Berger characterizes religion as the way in which humans internalize an orderly picture of the world and how we should act within it: what he calls the "nomos." The nomos, Berger writes, is a "shield against terror," something rooted in a "human craving for meaning." Human beings, he says, "are congenitally compelled to impose a meaningful order on reality."[28] In linking the nomos to a fundamental metaphysical truth, religion serves as the sacred canopy: the only way we feel that we can meaningfully resist anomie, the sense of meaninglessness we experience when we stop to consider the suffering and chaos of existence. The problem of evil and meaninglessness—*Why do bad things happen in the world?*—is too overwhelming for human beings to contemplate without recourse to a God whose wisdom far exceeds our own. Submitting to the "sacred canopy," a kind of self-denial that Berger compares to sexual masochism, is the "intoxication of surrender to another—complete, self-denying, or even self-destroying."[29] The social function of religion comes in the way it gives us a sense of personal and social meaning, allowing us to frame our identities within that of a collective cosmic narrative. "It is not happiness that theodicy primarily provides," Berger ultimately concludes, "but meaning."[30]

By this account, too, Berger's sacred canopy can extend beyond the boundaries of traditional religious doctrine. We can see, for example, that the language of "energies" and "toxins" promoted by contemporary wellness culture—which locates evil and sickness within the pharmaceutical-industrial complex and a society bent on destroying our "natural," "authentic" selves—is, while not dealing with deities as such, nevertheless a foundational theodicy. It explains why there is evil and suffering in the world (or at least in our own bodies) and gives us a series of rituals—exercise, skin care, jade eggs—to help us supposedly counteract them. It transforms the seeming randomness of cell decay, mutation, and death into an illusorily controllable system.

One final foundational definition of religion comes from the anthropologist Clifford Geertz, whose work straddles elements of both Durkheim and Berger. Like Berger, Geertz sees religion as a way of making sense of the world. But, like Durkheim, he emphasizes the social aspect of that meaning-making. Religion, like language, is a way to communicate and emphasize the meaningfulness of the world. Geertz emphasizes the subjective, personal, emotional experience that religions provide. "A religion," he wrote in 1973, "is a system of symbols which act to establish powerful, pervasive, and long-lasting moods in men by formulating concepts of a general order of existence and clothing these conceptions with such an aura of factuality that the moods and motivations seem uniquely realistic."[31]

DURKHEIM, BERGER, AND GEERTZ ARE ONLY A FEW OF THE SCHOLARS who, over the past century or so, have worked to expand our definition of religion beyond "organized faith in a higher power." Taken together, they can help us narrow down four elements of human need that religions function to satisfy. Today's new religions provide their various Remixed flocks with these four elements: meaning, purpose, community, and ritual.

Let's start with **meaning**, which I'm using here to describe something like Berger's nomos: a bigger-picture sense of why the world is the way it is. It's not just about whether there is a God, or an ultimate reality, but about the shape of that reality—and, as Berger rightly points out, about the location of evil. Grand narratives of classical Greco-Roman paganism often saw the world through a fatalistic lens: the destinies of men were determined by internal battles and squabbling among uncaring gods. The grand narrative of Christianity tells us of the struggle we have with sin: how human beings, though created by a good God for good purpose, are nevertheless born in a fundamentally broken world, with a fundamentally broken will—slaves, without the grace of God, to the moral and spiritual phenomenon known as sin. Contemporary grand narratives often locate goodness (or evil) not in a metaphysical *out there*, but within the world itself. Heavily influenced by the political philosophy of Marxism, for example, the progressive civil religion of social justice activism sees ultimate reality as a story about continued power and oppression. Conversely, the grand narrative of reactionary atavism—the kind we see among fans of contemporary gurus like Jordan Peterson—sees history as a process by which feminists and the "politically correct," alongside other insufficiently heroic examples of modern, decaying civilization, have caused us to lose touch with our primal, masculine instincts. The most successful of our modern new religions provide a clear, if nontheistic, account of the meaningfulness of the world.

But meaning is only part of the bigger picture. Religions need to provide an account of what role each individual adherent plays: a sense of personal **purpose** that allows believers to shape their life in accordance with that meaning. Whether it's the call to evangelize the good news of the gospel, or the need to fight in a holy war, or a summons to contemporary political activism, religions provide a framework to link the existential decisions we make in our own lives with the overarching structure of reality. What a wellness junkie who spends days on an expensive juice cleanse to purify her body of toxins shares in common with an "incel" or white supremacist domestic terrorist perpetrating a mass shooting is a sense that their personal decision-making is rooted in a grand narrative about why the world is the way it is—and who (or what) is to blame.

But men are, of course, rarely islands. Religions provide their adherents not just with a personal outlook and purpose but also with a sense of **community**. Traditionally, religions did this in physical spaces: your church, your synagogue, or your mosque was the place where you commemorated major life rituals with like-minded people, where you ate and drank and celebrated and mourned. It was where people would come support you when you were in need, and where you were expected to support them in turn. Members of your religious community were, in many ways, extensions of your own family. A primary function of today's new religions—most of which make use of the geographical irrelevancy of the Internet to foster digital, rather than physical, communal spaces—is to offer alternate sources of community, new forms of chosen family. From the familial bonds of intentional romantic communities exploring kink and nonmonogamy, to the sense of accountability felt by workout-class junkies, to the intense and often toxic reactionary forums that foster alt-right ideologies, one of the most important functions of today's new religions is to provide the sense of social order and place that organized, institutional religion once did. Often, in today's new religions, these makeshift communities—cognizant of their less established status—consciously stress the moral and ideological importance of "rewriting the script" or "remaking the rules" when it comes to societal behavior, rather than adhering to traditional or institutional norms.

As psychologist of secularism Phil Zuckerman told me, "One of the biggest problems for secular culture [is that] you have to cobble together and make it yourself. If you want your kid to have a bar mitzvah, it's all taken care of. You want your kid to go through confirmation class in the Episcopal church? Boom, they're enrolled. If you want to do a secular version of that? Good luck. You're on your own. You have to figure it out, explain it to people, rent the space, find people, figure out how to write up your own program."[32]

And finally, there's **ritual**: the solemnized, formal occasions by which, through activity and participation, adherents achieve collective effervescence, reifying and reaffirming their role in the community and their sense of purpose in the grand narrative religion provides, while communally marking the passage of time. Traditionally, rituals have included sacraments like the Eucharist, or mealtimes like Shabbat dinners, or Friday prayers. But today's rituals include, for example, regular morning workouts at SoulCycle—an integral part of the narrative of self-care so embedded in the cult of wellness—or attending meditation or yoga classes. They include, too, the near-liturgical process of call-out culture in social justice activism, and the even more insidious and abusive "pile-ons" beloved by right-wing Twitter trolls, both of which imbue relatively straightforward actions (clicking away on a keyboard, pressing "send") with cosmic and communal significance.

Taken all together, rituals and a sense of purpose link a community with a wider meaning. Sure, almost anybody can hop on an exercise bike. Or light a candle. Or post on Twitter. But what about when they're sharing energy with a pack in pursuit of eliminating toxins and practicing self-care? Or when they're lighting a candle in contact with thousands of other self-proclaimed witches on Facebook or Instagram in order to collectively hex a despised political figure as a form of performance-art political activism? Or when they're "shitposting" in a political meme war, sharing right-wing talking points and trolling their political enemies as part of a brotherhood devoted to taking down the cathedrals of feminism?

That starts to look a lot more like a religion.

While not every new religion described in this book fulfills all four criteria, they no longer have to: today's mix-and-match culture means that the Remixed can get their sense of community from one place (an intense fandom, say) and their sense of meaning from another (social justice activism, or techno-utopianism). They can practice the rituals associated with wellness culture while seeing their purpose as primarily political. That said, we can see in the rise of today's various new religions a few commonalities.

By and large, today's new cults of and for the Remixed are what I will call "intuitional religions." By this, I mean that their sense of meaning is based in narratives that simultaneously reject clear-cut creedal metaphysical doctrines and institutional hierarchies and place the locus of authority on people's experiential emotions, what you might call gut instinct. Society, institutions, credited authorities, experts, expectations, rules of conduct—all these are generally treated not just as irrelevant, but as sources of active evil. Wellness culture, modern occultism, social justice activism, techno-utopianism, and the modern sexual revolution all share a fundamental distrust, if not outright contempt, for institutions and scripts. Most of these new religions share, too, the grand narrative that oppressive societies and unfairly narrow expectations stymie natural—and sometimes even divine—human potential.

Today's Remixed religions valorize different forms of emotional experience—a person's perceived energy as a clue to their bad character, a modern witch's sense of divine presence during a spell-casting session, a feminist's lived experience as an authoritative account of the world—as the key to interpreting both meaning and purpose. They value, too, authenticity: the idea that one's actions are in harmony with one's emotions. They're less keen on rules, or doctrines, or moral codes that they dismiss as restrictive or outmoded. They're suspicious of moral or truth-claims that don't root themselves in subjective experience. Three-quarters of millennials (and 67 percent of the religious Nones overall) now say they agree with the statement "Whatever is right for your life or works best for you is the only truth you can know," compared with just 39 percent of the elderly, and 47 percent of practicing Christians of all ages.[33] The Remixed demand agency and creative ownership in their spiritual lives, dissatisfied with the narrowness of the options available. Among the most common sayings I heard among the people I interviewed was, "I make my *own* religion."

And the Remixed are willing to put their consumer dollars into pursuing these new religions. If "sex sells" was the unofficial advertising mantra of the *Mad Men* era, then "spirituality sells" is the slogan for post-2016. One "experience management software," for example, promises without a shred of irony that it will "help turn customers into fans/products into obsessions/employees into ambassadors/brands into icons."[34]

The most successful new religions of 2020 and beyond are the ones that have taken this intuitional turn and found ways to make it both communal and—in an increasingly brand-driven age—salable. They're the ones that take the extant consumer-capitalist culture of our age—smartphones, social media, Moon Juice, 4chan boards, oat milk—and make interacting with it into a sacred ritual, an avenue to fulfilling a wider purpose in a meaningful world. They're the ones that alchemize our everyday activities—eating, working out, following the news, posting on social media—and turn them, as Punchdrunk did to the McKittrick Hotel, into strange and sacred rites, not hobbies but rituals. They're the ones that have figured out how to take Twitter, or Instagram, or consumer culture, and enchant it.

For some, this freedom is revelatory, even necessary. For many women who see in organized religion the relics of an oppressive patriarchal culture, or for the nearly 50 percent of queer people—so often marginalized by traditional faiths—who now call themselves religiously unaffiliated, these new religions offer an opportunity to seek out spiritual truth and a connection with the divine, beyond doctrine (and often communities) that would treat them as pariahs.[35]

But, at the same time, the refractory nature of these new intuitional religions—each one, at its core, a religion of the self—risks creating an increasingly balkanized American culture: one in which our desire for personal authenticity and experiential fulfillment takes precedent over our willingness to build coherent ideological systems and functional, sustainable institutions.

When we are all our own high priests, who is willing to kneel?

two

A (BRIEF) HISTORY OF INTUITIONAL RELIGION IN AMERICA

T HE BIRTH OF TODAY'S RELIGIOUSLY REMIXED—AND THE
intuitional religions they practice—is, in many ways, unprecedented. Deeply indebted to both the rise of Internet culture and
the proliferation of consumer capitalism, the development of the Remixed is inextricably of this century, this decade, this administration.

And, yes, this country. The rise of the Nones is happening all over
Western Europe, as is secularism conceived more broadly. But the rise
of the faithful Nones and the spiritual but not religious is a distinctly
American phenomenon. Indeed, according to a 2018 Pew study, American religious Nones score as highly, or higher, on many measures of
religiosity—daily prayer, importance of religion in their lives, and even
stated belief in God—as European self-identified Christians.[1]

But the story of intuitional religion and religious remixing in America isn't just the story of America today. The roots of intuitional religion
go back almost as far as the founding of the country itself. The story of
the American religious landscape has always been a story of the battle for
the American soul: waged between the forces of institutional religion—
organized, orderly, civic-minded—and crazes for its intuitional rivals,

both traditionally Christian and more radically Remixed, that stressed *personal* piety, *personal* experience, and *personal* relationships over the solid but staid offerings from their more established peers.

This battle has historically reflected several of the debates we've already touched on in the previous chapter. Is religion about personal, private spirituality—about our individual practices, our individual faiths, our individual relationship with whatever is out there in the great beyond? Or is religion about community, about society, about bringing people together under a common tent, with easily legible and digestible rules to help them cement their bonds and common ideals?

That debate is encoded in one of the most important founding principles of the United States. I'm talking, of course, about the separation of church and state, which, perhaps more than anything else, has come to define the contours of American religion.

The debate over the separation of church and state is often framed as a debate over secularism: Are we a secular country or a Christian one? But, for our Founding Fathers, the debate wasn't quite so clear-cut. The idea that church and state should be held separate by a governing body wasn't simply an anti-religious stance, it was also a distinctly *theological* one, part of the particular brand of Protestantism that has come to shape America ever since.

The idea that religion should be personal, not social, is encoded in our nation's DNA.

It's an utterly novel idea. Within nearly all other major religious systems in the European West and Middle East—from the civic paganism of ancient Babylon, Greece, and Rome, to the rise of Islam, to medieval Catholicism—the role of religion and the role of society (including government) were intertwined. As historian Sam Haselby writes in *Aeon* magazine, before 1788, "no other modern society had sought to separate law, politics, social life and civic institutions from the divine."[2] From the rich body of Islamic sharia law—which sought to use Koranic principles to govern a disparate people—to the consistent, and consistently wielded, power of the Catholic Holy See as a political as well as religious entity, religion was by and large seen as a civic and communal, rather than private, matter.

Religion itself heralded this transition from the institutional to the individual. But Protestantism—particularly Martin Luther's vision of religion—pioneered a different and far more individualistic path. Luther saw the experience of Christian faith as primarily a personal one; the relationship between the individual and the Bible was one that no outside body or cleric had the authority to encroach upon. (It's worth noting too, here, that integral to the spread of Protestantism was the development of perhaps the most individualizing piece of technology ever created, the printing press, which allowed reformers to disseminate their words and ideas quickly and efficiently to an increasingly literate middle class; likewise, the demand for and proliferation of printing presses was spurred by the viral popularity of Protestant ideas.)[3]

Luther didn't think religion should be absent from politics. Rather, he thought religion should be kept free from political encroachment. And for the (mostly) Protestants who settled the New World, and later founded America, the preservation of the liberty of each individual believer to pursue religion as a private matter, one of conscience rather than of necessity, took shape in the separation of church and state. It was a statement about the personalization of faith.

That does not mean, of course, that America was founded as a Protestant, or even a Christian, nation. The founders of America were a religiously eclectic bunch, with Anglicans and Deists among their numbers. And the separation of church and state the Founding Fathers imagined owed as much to Enlightenment ideals of a formally secular, even atheistic, state—as well as to a growing popular distrust of the American Anglican church, which had largely supported the English during the Revolutionary War—as it did to Protestant individualism. But separation of church and state worked as well as it did in America, in part, because the worldview of so many of its early Protestant settlers laid the cultural groundwork.

From then on, religion in America has been like a pendulum: swinging constantly from the institutional to the intuitional. Fringe religious movements championing personal piety and relationship with a higher power compete with larger, more settled institutional churches. Throughout American history, as large religious institutions fail to meet the needs of their members in a rapidly growing, rapidly diversifying country, new DIY movements appear to fill in the cracks.

Writing about the clash between religious liberals and conservatives in the twentieth century, a representative of the National Council of Churches described a dynamic that could well be applied to Christianity throughout America's history. "Liberals abhor the smugness, the self-righteousness, the absolute certainty, the judgmentalism, the lovelessness of a narrow, dogmatic faith." Meanwhile, conservatives "scorn the fuzzies, the marshmallow convictions, the inclusiveness that makes membership meaningless—the 'anything goes' attitude that views even Scripture as relative."[4]

We saw these same tensions even in the very early days of America's settling. In the world of the Founding Fathers, religion was diffuse and decentered—you might even say Remixed. According to historian Robert Fuller, church attendance was strikingly low in America's early days. In the late seventeenth century, he writes, less than one third of all American adults belonged to a church, a number that dropped to a mere 15 percent by the Revolutionary War.[5]

Plus, Fuller writes, plenty of these self-proclaimed Christians were what we today would consider religious hybrids, supplementing their traditionally religious practices with those that fell between medicine and magic. "Divination, fortune-telling, astrology, witchcraft, and even folk medicine," Fuller writes, "competed with the Christian churches as sources of the colonists' understanding of the supernatural powers that affected their destiny. . . . Fortune-telling was also relied on as a means of gaining supernatural insight into the powers affecting one's life. . . . Astrology, too, was pervasive throughout the colonies. Horoscopes and astrological charts were printed in many of the colonial era's best-selling almanacs, giving wide popular currency to these occult systems for planning one's commercial, agricultural, and romantic affairs."[6] In other words, it's important not to assume that American remixing is an exclusively contemporary phenomenon.

Likewise, you can trace the first great skirmish between institutional and intuitional religion in America to even before the Revolutionary War. The 1730s and 1740s saw the first of what is now known as the Great Awakenings, periods in American history when charismatic reformers and preachers sparked a resurgence in popular piety.

The First Great Awakening—which mirrored movements going on across the Atlantic—saw itinerant preachers like George Whitefield, John Wesley, and Jonathan Edwards travel the country conducting religious revivals, during which they terrified their audiences with the notion that they were nothing better than, to quote Edwards's most famous sermon, "sinners in the hands of an angry God."[7] Frustrated by what they saw as most self-proclaimed Christians' lip-service adherence to Christian traditions without a genuine expression of internal faith, these preachers exhorted their listeners to be "reborn" in Christ. They used powerful, emotive, and cinematic imagery: among Edwards's most abiding images is that of a God "that holds you over the pit of hell, much as one holds a spider, or some loathsome insect over the fire, [and] abhors you, and is dreadfully provoked. . . . He looks upon you as worthy of nothing else, but to be cast into the fire."[8] These preachers irrevocably divided American Christianity, with fervently inspired "New Lights" gleefully advocating wholesale reform of the American church, and "Old Lights" horrified by the energetic upstarts.

The preachers were successful. By the close of this chapter in American history, American Protestant denominations were split between those, like Anglicans and Quakers, who had largely rejected revivalism and those, like Baptists and Methodists, who had embraced it (and those, like Congregationalists and Presbyterians, whose communities had experienced a schism under the weight of controversy).

In this First Great Awakening, we see the broad outline of a dialectic that has come to shape American religious discourse to this day. While the intuitional faiths promoted at the revivals were explicitly

Christian—something that would not be true of crazes like Spiritualism or New Thought a century later—they nevertheless privileged the personal, private, and emotional experience of the believer over public and communal observance. They still had firm doctrine and rules of conduct—these "sinners in the hands of an angry God" weren't exactly being encouraged to "do what feels right to you"—but the emphasis, both practically and theologically, was nevertheless on inward states, not societal structures.

In the wake of the Revolutionary War, religion (and religious observance) in America slumped. Church attendance dropped. The popularity of Enlightenment ideologies like Thomas Jefferson's own preferred religious sentiment, Deism—the idea that there is a God, but that He is little more than an impersonal first cause who created the world then left it largely alone—dominated the cultural milieu of the elites. The evangelical preacher Lyman Beecher bemoaned schools like Princeton and Yale, which were initially founded to train revivalist preachers: "College was in a most ungodly state; the college church was almost extinct. . . . Most of the class before me were infidels and called each other Voltaire, Rousseau, D'Alembert"—all proponents of Enlightenment secularism.[9]

The extremely liberal brand of Christianity known as Unitarianism—with its focus on Jesus as an ethical leader, but not a transcendent one—became more and more popular, with critics bemoaning the proliferation of "deists, nothingarians, and anythingarians" across the American frontier.[10]

Meanwhile, as Fuller points out, the prominence of Freemasonry, which was devoted to supplementing Enlightenment ideals of rationalism and humanism with religious-style ritualism, "can hardly be overestimated." Fifty-two of the fifty-six signers of the Declaration of Independence, Fuller writes, belonged to the Freemasons, while "symbol-laden ceremonies were used both to initiate new members and to mark their progress through successive levels of acquiring Enlightenment beliefs."[11]

Then: another backlash.

The dawn of the nineteenth century saw the second, and potentially the largest, of America's Great Awakenings, alongside the flourishing of dozens of other popular spiritual movements, theistic and not, appealing to a burgeoning middle class: everything from Theosophy to Transcendentalism to New Thought, all designed to provide the average American with a sense of authentic meaning and genuine connection with a higher power, however defined.

In his 1928 book of the same name, the historian Gilbert Seldes referred to the 1800s as the "stammering century," a period of time characterized by "Prohibitionists and . . . Pentecostalists; the diet-faddists and the dealers in mail-order Personality; the play censors and the Fundamentalists; the free-lovers and eugenists; the cranks and possibly the saints. Sects, cults, manias, movements, fads, religious excitements."[12]

New revivalist preachers like Charles Grandison Finney traveled the country, whipping up converts to an apocalyptic, and largely sui generis, version of Christianity that anticipated that Jesus would return to this earth only after a millennium of peace and Christian brotherhood. (In other words: you'd better shape up, fellas!) New York State—the nexus of the revival—was set so aflame by this new brand of religiosity that it became known colloquially as the "burned-over" district. Methodist circuit riders traveled to the western backcountry of the American frontier, holding camp meetings and tent revivals to spark listeners' religious passions. Whole new denominations of Christianity—Churches of Christ, Seventh-Day Adventists—sprang up, while those denominations that had previously embraced New Lights—Methodists, Baptists—continued to swell in number. According to estimates of the time, converts were primarily female—outnumbering their male counterparts three to two—and young, tending toward their teens and early twenties.[13]

Meanwhile, just a few miles away, a young boy named Joseph Smith, raised among the eclectic and intense traditions of the burned-over district, experienced a series of occult visions that led him to—by his own account, at least—uncover a buried collection of golden plates on which a secret American history had been written: a text that would become the Book of Mormon. That text, and the Church of Jesus Christ of Latter-day Saints that Smith founded, is the basis of a faith that almost 2 percent of Americans (and a full 58 percent of Utah residents) practice today.[14]

And then there were the non-Christian movements: the more direct antecedents of today's SBNRs. These intuitional religions didn't just see spiritual piety as a personal or experiential matter, they saw human beings as the source of the divine. Deeply suspicious of organized religion, of society, of rules, and of doctrine, these movements celebrated the spiritual potential of human nature, nature that—if unfettered by the restrictions and prejudices of mediocre bourgeois society—could even produce miracles.

First, there was intuitional religion's intellectual iteration: Transcendentalism, practiced by philosophers like Ralph Waldo Emerson and Henry David Thoreau. It celebrated individual, spiritual experiences, holding that all formal institutions—including organized religion—got in the way of the pure self-expression and "self-reliance" of our true natures. "All that you call the world is the shadow of that substance which you are, the perpetual creation of the powers of thought," Emerson wrote in his 1842 essay "The Transcendentalist."

For the Transcendentalists, the self and society were necessarily at odds. Emerson condemned human society as a "conspiracy against the manhood of every one of its members," a "joint-stock company, in which the members agree . . . to surrender the liberty and culture of the eater."[15] It worked to destabilize our trust in our perceptions, which he deemed "as much a fact as the sun." He called instead for men and women to turn their backs on social norms and cultivate a "greater self-reliance" that "must work a revolution in all the offices and relations of men; in their religion; in their education; in their pursuits; their modes of living."[16]

Transcendentalism may have been the provenance of relatively few intellectuals, mostly clustered in New England. But a few decades later, a different kind of intuitionalism found a broader market in Spiritualism, in which thousands, if not millions, of Americans got swept up in the popular craze for holding séances and talking to the dead.[17] Traveling mediums like the Fox sisters—three young women from the burned-over district who claimed to be able to communicate with the dead through mysterious rapping sounds—became de facto celebrities. The faith healer Andrew Jackson Davis, a self-described clairvoyant and hypnotist who published books like 1847's *The Principles of Nature, Her Divine Revelations, and a Voice to Mankind*, became so well-known that Edgar Allan Poe based one of his more lurid tales, "The Facts in the Case of M. Valdemar," on his visits to Davis's home. "Talking boards," by which Spiritualists could communicate with perceived ghosts, became so popular that, by 1890, a businessman named Elijah Bond decided to patent a version for mass use: today's Ouija board.[18] Spiritualist newspapers like the *Spiritual Telegraph* and *Banner of Light* entered widespread, or even national, circulation, advertising weekly regular lectures and meetings throughout the country for most of the nineteenth century.[19]

And, perhaps most importantly of all, there was New Thought, also known as the "mind-cure" and the "Boston craze," a kind of proto–*The Secret* self-help phenomenon that promised participants that "positive thinking" and "creative visualization" would yield concrete, material results. Its founder, a New Hampshire–born clockmaker, mesmerist, and faith healer named Phineas Parkhurst Quimby, preached a gospel of total psychic self-reliance. There was nothing human beings couldn't do, so long as they believed fully in themselves. The evils of the world, from physical illness to financial ruin, were a direct result of a mind that failed to manifest its own potential: in short, a lack of self-confidence. As we'll see, huge swaths of today's Remixed culture—from self-help to wellness to modern New Age occultism—are heavily and directly reliant on the language of this "mind-cure."

Throughout the late nineteenth and early twentieth centuries, hundreds of thousands of Americans spent their pocket money on dozens of titles promoting differing forms of the New Thought ethos: *your feelings can change the world*. There was Charles Benjamin Newcomb's 1897 *All's Right With the World*, which instructed readers to summon betterment through sheer force of will. ("I am well." "I am opulent." "I have everything." "I do right." "I know.") There was William Walker Atkinson's

1901 *Thought-Force in Business and Everyday Life*. Capitalists like Napoleon Hill advised readers to *Think and Grow Rich* (1937). There was also, via Quimby's former patient Mary Baker Eddy, the Christian version of New Thought: the church that came to be known as Christian Science.

Far fewer Americans in 1900 would have openly identified as a religious None than they do today. But plenty of self-proclaimed American Christians, like today's religious hybrids, were still supplementing their primary (or simply nominal) religious tradition with alternative forms of spirituality. Meanwhile, onetime fringe traditions—from the Church of Latter-day Saints to the Church of Christ, Scientist, to the revivalism of Methodist circuit riders—soon became codified and institutionalized.

But it's in the twentieth century, in particular, that we see the most direct influences on our current Great Awakening. The historian Robert P. Jones writes of an age of "White Christian America": one in which a certain vision of Christianity (and Americanness) held sufficient cultural sway to serve as a de facto civil religion. It was a time that, he writes, "questions like 'And where do you go to church' felt appropriate in casual social interactions or even business exchanges. White Christian America was a place where few gave a second thought to saying 'Merry Christmas!' to strangers on the street. It was a world of shared rhythms that punctuated the week: Wednesday spaghetti suppers and prayer meetings, invocations from local pastors under the Friday night lights and high school football games, and Sunday blue laws that shuttered Main Street for the Sabbath."[20] A time that, for decades at least, conservatives have harkened back to as an example of what America was like before the Remixed got their grubby paws on it.

As we have seen, for most of its history America wasn't exactly like this. But for a brief time, it almost was. The period of relative prosperity, optimism, and tranquility that characterized post–World War II America was, in many ways, the high-water mark of institutional religion in America. The cultural influence of mainline Protestantism—those more socially progressive, often less emotive denominations of Christianity, such as Episcopalianism and Lutheranism, who traced their lineage to European traditions—was at, perhaps, an all-time high.

Part of this flourishing of mainline Protestant institutionalism was due to broader postwar optimism. But it can also be attributed to another Great Awakening, which had emerged at the close of the previous century within mainline Protestantism: the Social Gospel movement called Christians to emulate Jesus Christ in their actions and their ethos. This social justice movement, characterized by its concern for those left behind by the unbridled capitalistic ethos of the post–Civil War Gilded Age, was enormously influential both in terms of shaping mainline Protestant Christianity, particularly in the Northeast, and in sowing the seeds for what would become the United States' labor movement.

As Jones writes of the aftermath of the social gospel movement, "At the beginning of the twentieth century, white mainline Protestants believed that they were on the verge of the 'Christian Century' . . . [in which] Christian principles would finally begin to shape national policy and world events."[21] (Indeed, the flagship magazine of mainline Protestantism, the *Christian Century*, was named with that optimism in mind.)

Whatever the reason, by the time the 1950s rolled around, America (or at least white, non-Catholic America) had something closer to a visible civil religion than ever before. Almost half of all Americans attended church.[22] Prominent mainline theologians, such as the Reformed theologian Reinhold Niebuhr, were regular guests at the White House; Niebuhr was featured on the cover of *Time* magazine.[23] A National Council of Churches—nearly all mainline Protestants—formed in 1950 to jointly advocate and lobby for what were largely socially progressive causes. And mainline Protestants were *powerful*. Among lawyers included in *Marquis Who's Who* in 1950, half listed mainline Protestant affiliations, as did 63 percent of *Who's Who*–listed Fortune 500 directors and executives.[24] (As, of course, had been nearly every single American president up to that point.) Around 30 percent of the population overall identified as part of a mainline Protestant denomination.[25] Mainline Protestantism's cultural traction was due as much to who subscribed to it (wealthy, politically influential white Americans and the news media that covered them) as to how many. Still, the genteel social liberalism of mainline Protestantism came to define the ethos of the American midcentury.

This influential brand of liberal Protestantism did not stress dogma or, in many cases, even metaphysical truth, but rather a utopian vision of what a truly ecumenical, social-justice-focused Christian world would look like. It was a triumph of institutionalism: one that provided its members—whatever their personal beliefs about Christ's divinity or the resurrection—with a blueprint for fostering human brotherhood, and, in so doing, transcending the bloody nationalism that had kindled two world wars. It was—or at least tried to be—the church that influential midcentury theologian Helmut Richard Niebuhr (brother of Reinhold, of *Time* magazine repute) envisioned as "one in which no national allegiance will be suffered to infringe upon the unity of an international fellowship," in which "the vow of love of enemy and neighbor and the practice of non-resistance will need to take their place beside the confession of faith and the rites." He argued that "distinctions between rich and poor will be abrogated by the kind of communism of love which prevailed in the early Jerusalem community," which would "bridge the chasm between the races . . . supplying equality of opportunity."[26]

It seemed, for a few decades at least, that mainline Protestantism could shore up a vision of American civic unity. In 1958, President Dwight D. Eisenhower himself lay the cornerstone for New York City's Interchurch Center, a $20 million monument to religious institutionalism. Thirty-seven historically white, mainline Protestant denominations (as well as some Eastern Orthodox and historically black Protestant denominations) had joined forces to, in the words of Methodist pastor Ralph Sockman, who spoke at the building's ground breaking, "[get] together as races and churches to tackle together our common problems such as moral laxity, juvenile delinquency, and the dangers of war."[27]

For the assembled clergymen, the construction of the Interchurch Center, and its symbolic nature as a space for Protestant ecumenism, represented the cultural triumph of the liberal tradition. And, numerically at least, it did seem a triumph. While in the nineteenth century less than half of Americans were formally affiliated with a local congregation, by the 1950s, between 75 and 80 percent of Americans were.[28]

Still, within Protestant communities, pastors and leaders worried that liberalism was an institution without a theologically consistent center, subject to that long-feared "anything-goes-ism." The *Christian Century's* editor, Disciples of Christ minister Charles Clayton Morrison, expressed concern as early as 1946 that "we have got to ask such questions as these: How seriously do the members of Protestant churches regard their membership? How deep-going are the commitments which the church evokes in the life of its members? How intelligent is the membership with respect to the meaning of the Christian faith? How firm is the bond of loyalty that holds the members together?"[29]

Morrison was right to worry. By the 1960s, the edifice of Interchurch-style institutionalism, and the civic promise it represented, was being assailed from all sides, replaced by yet another resurgence of individual-focused, bespoke intuitionalism: one that has culminated in the final Great Awakening in which we find ourselves today.

One of the main factors in this pendulum shift was the decline of the classical nuclear family, and with it a religious identity rooted heavily in community and ritual located in a geographically shared place. Sociologist Robert Wuthnow has traced the history of religious affiliation in America from what he calls "dwelling-oriented spirituality"—spirituality primarily associated with a given community or sacred space—to the "spirituality of seeking" that dominated the 1960s and beyond.[30] The religious structure of the 1950s was, he argues, a spirituality of "dwelling." Whether you were mainline or evangelical, white, black, or Jewish, your social and communal life likely revolved largely, if not primarily, around your religious community and the sacred spaces and rituals—church on Sundays, Shabbat dinners—that gave that community its shape. Families and communities alike were large and close-knit. In 1957, the average American was just twenty years old at the time of their first marriage, and the average American woman birthed 3.8 children. By the decade's close, more than half of American families had at least one child under eighteen in the home. Sixty-five percent of all new-built houses contained at least one purpose-built family room. And 85 percent of seniors lived near their adult children; over a third lived with them.

Religious identity, community identity, and physical space all fused together to create a shared hermeneutic for viewing the world and your place in it. As more and more families moved into suburbia—potentially isolating themselves from like-minded neighbors and shared city stoops—houses of worship in particular gained ground as central spaces: places with the capacity to both preserve and intensify ethnic, religious, and familial ties. Churches began offering activities and programs for young people and adults designed to encourage them to spend more time on sanctified turf: from socials and potluck dinners to Sunday school classes to men's prayer breakfasts and ladies' aid societies.[31]

"Clergy wanted their flocks to be at home with God when they came to their places of worship," Wuthnow writes. "Congregations became comfortable, familiar, domestic, offering an image of God that was basically congruent with the domestic tranquility of the ideal home."[32]

But in the 1960s, all that changed. Between 1960 and 1979, marriage rates among white families declined from 76 to 64 percent, and among black families from 60 to 43 percent.[33] Birth rates similarly plummeted: from 118 births for every 10,000 women in 1960 down to just 66 by 1976. Soon the church attendance rates followed, dropping 10 percent throughout the 1960s.[34]

Trust in institutions also plummeted. In 1966, *Time*—that same magazine that, almost two decades earlier, had put Reinhold Niebuhr on its cover—asked the question "Is God Dead?" prompting both national outrage and serious debate.[35] Meanwhile, new youthful countercultures were emerging, offering sources of meaning, purpose, and ritual outside the community-focused structure of institutions. There were the Beats, of course, but also practitioners of New Age or Eastern spiritual traditions and explorers of drug- and sex-fueled forms of alternative spirituality. In each new practice were elements of the same intuitional impulses found a century earlier at the pinnacle of New Thought: a sense that society—its strictures and its structures alike—was at the heart of the soul's ills, that only an authentic, unrepressed self, making public its private wants and needs and fears and loves, could foment authentic meaning.

Just consider the words of Allen Ginsberg, Beat poet and mystic and mouthpiece of this new wave of intuitionalism, in one 1966 speech: "There is a change of consciousness among the younger generation . . . towards the most complete public frankness possible. . . . Thus, new social standards more equivalent to private desire—as there is increased sexual illumination, new social codes may be found acceptable to rid ourselves of our fear of our own nakedness, rejection of our own bodies."[36] He called for a new world, a free world, in which the countercultural youth would take from the best of every religious tradition, in which "we find our teenagers dancing Nigerian Yoruba dances and entering trance states to the electric vibrations of the Beatles who have borrowed shamanism from African sources. We find communal religious use of ganja . . . the spread of mantra chanting in private and such public manifestations as peace marches. . . . All the available tradition[s] . . . are becoming available to the United States unconscious through the spiritual search of the young. . . . There is more prescription here for the individual: as always, the old command to free ourselves from social conditioning, laws and traditional mores."[37]

Psychologist and writer Timothy Leary—known for his midcentury experiments with psychedelics—put it even more bluntly in his memoirs. "Everything we did in the 1960s was designed to fission, to weaken faith in and conformity to the 1950s social order. Our precise surgical target was the Judeo-Christian power monolith, which has imposed a guilty, inhibited, grim, anti-body, anti-life repression on Western civilization. . . . And it worked! For the first time in 20 centuries, the good old basic paganism got everybody moving again. White people actually started to move their hips, let the Marine crewcuts grow long, adorn themselves erotically in Dionysian revels, tune into nature. . . . Millions of Americans writing their own Declarations of Independence: My life, my liberty, my pursuit of happiness."[38]

But the Beats and the bohemians weren't the *only* people disillusioned by the 1950s social order. While Ginsberg and Leary were experimenting with ganja, psychedelics, and "basic paganism," Christians, too—dissatisfied with the seeming staidness of the mainline Protestant monolith—were taking an intuitional turn. The Jesus movement, no less countercultural than its less Christian counterparts, challenged Christians to return to the simple but spiritually challenging lifestyles of early Christian communities. Emphasizing personal powers and spiritual gifts—speaking in tongues, prophecy, faith healing—the self-proclaimed "Jesus freaks" paved the way for generations of subsequent intuitional movements within Christianity. These included Charismatic Christianity—associated with Pentecostal churches, which had an even greater focus on faith healing, speaking in tongues, and other personal powers—and the wider rise of evangelical Christianity, a Christianity based, after all, in the idea of a personal relationship with Jesus Christ. These moments, too, gave rise to the prosperity gospel theology: a New Thought–inflected idea, still popular with about 40 percent of evangelicals today, that holds that believers who pray hard enough (or tithe with sufficient generosity) will be rewarded materially, including with wealth and physical health.[39] Within this mindset, personal faith functions like positive thinking in the New Thought model, a theistic version of *Just dream it and it will come true.*

If the left had Leary and Ginsberg, the right had people like Billy Graham, the highly emotive Southern Baptist preacher who brought Christian intuitionalism into the mainstream. While the mainline Protestantism of the 1950s had focused on creating an ecumenical, communal church, Graham's preaching centered on the individual: how a person could be saved through a direct, unmediated relationship with Christ. He frequently told interviewers that his work was not "mass evangelism" but rather "personal evangelism on a mass scale."[40] Graham's folksy, accessible style—combined with his ability to harness the power of new communication technologies like television—made him an international superstar. Starting with rallies that resembled the tent revivals of centuries past, Graham ultimately built an empire of radio programs and television specials that reached at least *two billion* people.[41]

Unlike intuitionalist religious traditions like New Thought, intuitional Christianity still had a clear metaphysic—and a much less optimistic sense of the self. Evangelical Christianity still saw the self as fundamentally broken, in need of salvific grace through Christ. But, compared to its mainline counterpart, evangelical Christianity was also willing to place the blame for the evils of the world on a toxic, broken, and secular society. Distrustful of institutions, of experts, and of a world hostile to Christianity, Graham's evangelical Christianity shared with New Thought a tendency toward inwardness: personal piety, rather than the communal society-building favored by midcentury mainline Protestantism. It's worth noting that Graham's magazine, the evangelical *Christianity Today*, was founded as direct competition to the mainline bastion the *Christian Century*.

Taken together, these two strains of intuitionalism—pluralist bohemia and (mostly white) evangelical Christianity—have defined the last few generations of our religious landscape. In very different ways, they've offered adherents an intense sense of both **meaning** and **purpose** through challenging and consciously countercultural visions of the world. They offer smaller, more fragmented, but often more intense communities, which see themselves not as part of a civic whole but as brave Davids, rattling their sabers at the Goliath of contemporary civilization.

Even the institutionalization of white evangelicalism in the past few decades—bolstered since the late 1970s by evangelicals' alliance with the Republican Party—is rooted in narratives not of ecumenism but of cultural resistance. Following the rise of the reactionary Moral Majority, which sought to combat increasingly liberal attitudes on abortion and segregation by injecting Christian values into political decision-making in the late 1970s and early 1980s, media titans like Jerry Falwell and Pat Robertson began to shape public policy. Television networks like Robertson's Christian Broadcasting Network, home of *The 700 Club*, advocated for Republican political and economic platforms, while academic institutions like Falwell's Liberty University, which formally teaches creationism, were founded to galvanize and train new generations of politically committed Christians. Powerful, multimillion-dollar advocacy groups—James Dobson's Focus on the Family, Tony Perkins's Family Research Council—sprang up in a socially conservative response to the similarly politicized midcentury project of mainline Protestantism. At the same time, the sense of meaning and purpose these evangelical organizations provide their adherents remains the narrative of the brave underdog, valiantly fighting against the encroaching forces of post-1960s secularism.

Meanwhile, the old institutional religions are in decline. The mainline churches that were, just a generation ago, the bulwark of American civil religion are largely emptying. In 2017, self-described mainline Protestants composed just 10 percent of the American public. Of these, barely a quarter actually attended church. The New York Interchurch Center—once vaunted as the shining light of midcentury ecumenism— has become little more than a glorified office building; most of its original inhabitants have migrated to cheaper premises. Author and scholar Ed Stetzer has theorized that, if mainline Protestantism continues to decline at its current rate, the whole community will be wiped out by 2040.[42] Almost 10 percent of Americans are "former mainline Protestants."

Almost one in five Americans was raised in a religion, only to leave it to join the ranks of the Nones. (For most of these Americans, religion means Christianity; retention rates among Hindus, Buddhists, Muslims, and Jews all remain much higher than among Christians.) Meanwhile, just 4 percent of Americans raised by Nones join an organized faith.[43]

The pendulum has swung, once more, wholesale toward the intuitional. But this time—as we'll see in the next chapter—it may be here to stay.

three

TODAY'S GREAT AWAKENING
(AND WHY IT'S NOT LIKE THE OTHERS)

AMERICAN RELIGIOUS HISTORY HAS ALWAYS BEEN A STORY OF tension between institutional and intuitional models. Why should today's godless world be any different from, say, the "stammering" nineteenth century, with its craze for New Thought and Spiritualism and Transcendentalism and free love?

The answer can be boiled down to three main factors that make this iteration of intuitionalism more likely to stick around: the absence of wider demographic pressure, the power of consumer capitalism, and the rise of the Internet. All three have contributed to a fragmented and decentralized, but retribalized, religious landscape: one in which cult fads, subcultures, and personal practices can all rearrange themselves, kaleidoscopically, as today's new religions.

Today's religious Nones, after all, didn't appear in a vacuum. Rather, they are the direct inheritors of midcentury Protestant ecumenism: by and large a demographic disillusioned by the anodyne faith practices of their institutionally minded parents, but who feel far more secure finding alternative communities and rituals.

News outlets bemoaning (or celebrating) the rise of the religious Nones often spin a narrative that young people today are put off by the repression and outmoded values of religion. But the data doesn't fully bear that out. In fact, it seems that the very un-repressive strains of midcentury Protestantism and ecumenism—the theologically unchallenging "come for Christmas and Easter only" variants—have, for the past few decades at least, been doing significantly worse than their more conservative counterparts.

Today's Nones have grown up seeing religion as a social or communal institution—a "nice to have" teaching "good values" or solidifying family bonds—but not necessarily as a core part of their meaning or purpose. They're the kids who saw their parents attend church, or who went to Sunday school, but were nevertheless acutely conscious that their parents didn't actually *believe* all that stuff. A 2016 Pew study found that, among those raised in Christian households (and particularly among Protestant households), those families that talked about religion at home and were more observant were more likely, not less, to have children retain their faith. Of born Protestants whose parents talked about religion "a lot," 89 percent continue to identify as Protestant, while just 8 percent call themselves unaffiliated. But among those whose parents just talked about religion "sometimes," 15 percent call themselves unaffiliated. That number jumps to 21 percent of those whose parents spoke about religion "rarely" or "never."[1] White evangelicals—stereotypically far more theologically conservative than their mainline counterparts—have significantly better retention rates than either mainline Protestants or Catholics.[2] Fifty-eight percent of white evangelicals still attend services weekly—higher than anyone except Jehovah's Witnesses and Mormons.[3]

Likewise, children of interfaith households—where, presumably, a single consistent metaphysical doctrine was not taught and shared by all parties—were more likely to leave organized religion behind. Children raised either by a single observant parent or by two parents observing the same religion were significantly more likely to remain in their childhood faith than children who were raised in either mixed-religion households (including Catholic-Protestant) or by one religious and one unaffiliated parent.[4] The rise of mixed-religious marriages since the 1960s (back in 1960, just 19 percent of marriages took place between Americans of different faiths; that number has now risen to almost 40 percent) has heralded the rise of the millennial Nones today.[5]

The "raised religious" who are leaving organized religion aren't, for the most part, those whose parents found purpose and meaning in regular observance. Rather, they're the children of people who, for whatever reason—social expectation, a sense of obligation, a sense that religion was "what one does"—felt the need to publicly identify with something they felt was privately insufficient. In other words, millennials have more options—both in terms of determining their social identity and in terms of building their own spiritual fabric—than their parents did, and they feel entitled to seek them out. This generation has been raised to stress the institutional benefits of religion over its meaning-making purpose *at the same time that those institutional advantages are increasingly commonplace outside of organized religion.*

A child born to unaffiliated parents in 1925, for example, was born with a significant social handicap, functionally rendered an outsider at a time when religious affiliation doubled as an identity marker. That child, when asked questions like "What church do you go to?" would have had few socially acceptable responses. But a child born unaffiliated in 1990 or 1995 has no similar limitations. They are part of the fastest-growing religious group in America. They will see themselves reflected in institutions large and small, from the 2018-founded Congressional Freethought Caucus, designed to champion secular humanism in government, to the growing number of death doulas working to provide end-of-life care to those outside traditional religious institutions.[6] While the label "atheist" still carries a whiff of stigma in the public sphere—there are still no openly atheistic members of Congress, and in 2018 the US Navy denied calls to institute a secular humanist chaplain—the social pressure to adopt a religious identity is a fraction of what it once was.

One way of tracking this is by looking at how few people raised unaffiliated join a faith later in life. While just 26 percent of members of the silent generation (born between 1925 and 1945) who were raised in unaffiliated households remained unaffiliated into adulthood, a full 42 percent of unaffiliated-raised baby boomers and a staggering 67 percent of unaffiliated-raised millennials have preserved their irreligion.[7] This suggests that those children raised outside of faith traditions are finding less incentive—be it personal spiritual hunger, social pressure, or the desire to attract a suitable mate—to rejoin the ranks of the religiously organized.

The mass-communal benefits of institutional religion are less apparent in our increasingly fractured age. Meanwhile, the inherent drawbacks—a demand for adherence, for personal self-denial, for obedience—are culturally stigmatized. As New York University sociology professor Michael Hout, coauthor of *Century of Difference: How America Changed in the Last One Hundred Years*, told one interviewer, a major element in this sense of freedom is millennials' learned willingness—garnered in part from their boomer parents—to prioritize individual expression and autonomy over group affiliation and authority. "Many Millennials have parents who are Baby Boomers and Boomers expressed to their children that it's important to think for themselves—that they find their own moral compass," Hout said. "Also, they rejected the idea that a good kid is an obedient kid. That's at odds with organizations, like churches, that have a long tradition of official teaching and obedience. And more than any other group, Millennials have been and are still being formed in this cultural context. As a result, they are more likely to have a 'do-it-yourself' attitude toward religion."[8]

This sense of questioning and the premium placed on independence overwhelmingly dominate the rationale of those who have left organized religion behind. When asked why they left their faith, 60 percent of religiously raised Nones said they "questioned religious teachings," 49 percent said they didn't like the positions churches took on social or political issues, and 41 percent said they just plain "didn't like religious organizations." (Thirty-seven percent said leaving their church had anything to do with belief or disbelief in God.)[9]

Today's Remixed millennials are, in many ways, caught between a rock and a hard place, at least when it comes to traditional religious observance. On the one hand, they're disillusioned with what is, in most cases, their parents' religious tradition, which has failed to provide them with a coherent account of meaning and purpose in the world. On the other hand, they're alienated from the political conservatism of more hardline denominations, with stances on LGBTQ issues or sexuality that an increasingly progressive generation sees as at odds with their core values. These values, as was the case for Emerson and Ginsberg, see the self as an autonomous being, the self's desires as fundamentally good, and societal and sexual repression as not just undesirable but actively evil. These Remixed millennials are at once attracted to moral and theological certainty—accounts of the human condition that claim totalizing truth or demand difficult adherence because the challenge is ultimately rewarding—and repulsed by traditions that require setting hard limits on personal, and particularly sexual or romantic, desire.

That, for better or for worse, is where corporations come in. Increasingly, big-budget companies have recognized that there is a gap in the needs of today's Remixed: institutions, activities, philosophies, and rituals that manage to be challenging and totalizing while also preserving millennials' need for individualization and personal, intuitional freedom. It's the dot-com bubble for spirituality, a free marketplace of innovation and religious disruption. (Literally. Columbia Business School is currently hosting an incubator designed for "spiritual entrepreneurs." Those who complete a twenty-week course get a special Columbia Business School certificate in spiritual entrepreneurship.)[10] It's all but impossible to tell today's fringe movements from their savvy corporate-sponsored counterparts. No sooner does something become a viral movement than an ingenious start-up finds a way to recreate it at a more profitable price point.

The sociologist Ronald Inglehart has called this phenomenon the central crisis of "postmaterialism." In a society where we no longer fear securing the basic necessities of life, we gradually adopt a different value system, one dedicated to seeking out self-expression and fulfilling personal experiences.[11] Consumer-capitalist culture offers us not merely necessities but identities. Meaning, purpose, community, and ritual can all—separately or together—be purchased on Amazon Prime.

As journalist Amanda Hess writes in the *New York Times*, "Shopping, decorating, grooming and sculpting are now jumping with meaning. And a purchase need not have any explicit social byproduct—the materials eco-friendly, or the proceeds donated to charity—to be weighted with significance. Pampering itself has taken on a spiritual urgency."[12] Self-care has become both a call to emotional authenticity and an ascetic challenge: to put in the labor to perfect the body in the service of a soul whose emotions, desires, needs, and wants are considered not just valid but authoritative.

Consumer capitalism, and the corporate takeover of the spiritual marketplace, has effected a kind of institutionalization of practices that, in previous decades, were primarily associated with the grassroots fringe. More and more brands, seeking to capitalize on the spiritual gap in the market, are packaging and marketing religious and spiritual products, finding ways to integrate them seamlessly into lives defined by the capitalist machine. In 2019, you can use your paycheck to buy witch-branded candles at Urban Outfitters, then download Headspace or another meditation app to practice mindfulness on your morning commute. You can pop in to SoulCycle, or CrossFit, or an Ashtanga yoga class on your lunch hour. A 2018 study by the aptly named Virtue—the branding-partnership arm of Vice Media—argued that spirituality was the "next big thing" in millennial-focused marketing. "We now think brands should take a step further," Vice's chief creative and commercial officer Tom Punch told attendees at a marketing festival, "thinking more broadly about what their role is in society and how they can truly be a force for good in people's lives."[13]

Meanwhile, even brands that don't offer specifically religious or spiritual products are increasingly looking to spiritual traditions to improve their bottom line. In the early stages of its development, for example, Facebook set up internal "compassion research days," during which they brought in academics from Harvard and Yale to teach employees the benefits of Buddhist compassion so that they could improve the site's harassment-reporting tools.[14] Meanwhile, Google offers its employees Search Inside Yourself courses, designed to optimize productivity by encouraging Eastern-tinged meditation. (The company also regularly holds "mindful lunches," in which employees sit in total silence, save for the sound of Zen Buddhist prayer bells.)[15]

This pseudo-spiritual ethos also reaches consumers directly. Companies are increasingly using political advocacy to sell themselves as moral arbitrators. Whether it's Nike's advertisements celebrating Colin Kaepernick's decision to "take a knee" in support of the Black Lives Matter movement (garnering the wrath of more than a few white evangelical pastors) or Chick-fil-A's donations to anti-LGBT-marriage groups (a practice the company ceased in 2019 after backlash from progressives), a growing number of brands are selling not just products but values. In so doing, they are creating moral universes, selling meaning as an implicit product and reframing capitalist consumption as a religious ritual—a repeated and intentional activity that connects the individual to divine purpose in a values-driven framework. The rise of "woke capitalism" and its reactionary converse is endemic of the way today's new religions interface with the brands that so powerfully promote, reify, and profit off them.

Take, for example, Gillette. Gillette sells razors. Traditionally, a razor brand would sell its product by advertising its usefulness or emphasizing its sex appeal (buy this razor because it'll make you look more rugged). Back in 1989, for example, Gillette sold razors through its "Best a Man Can Get" campaign. Advertisements during the Super Bowl—traditionally the apex of the advertising season—featured handsome, macho American men playing sports, cavorting with beautiful women, and otherwise appearing generally like someone you'd want to imitate.

In 2019, Gillette's advertising campaign was a bit different. A direct response to the #MeToo movement, its Super Bowl commercial, titled "The Best Men Can Be," encouraged men to step in when women were being mistreated and to evaluate whether their own behavior was inadvertently misogynistic. While the commercial was largely pilloried—by the right as being misandrist and by the left as having pandered too obviously to "wokeness" culture—its goal was one increasingly shared by brands across the political spectrum. By liking or sharing the ad, or by buying the razors themselves, consumers were joining a different kind of unified tribe: Gillette customers. They were publicly allying themselves with Gillette's woke values and with other people who shared those values. In buying from Gillette, they weren't just purchasing a razor, or even a personal or experiential fantasy. They were buying a social and ethical fantasy: the fantasy of belonging to a moral community. You might even say that they were joining a Durkheimian church.

Of course, the rise of spiritual branding would be impossible without the third phenomenon that sets this Great Awakening apart from its predecessors: the dizzying transformations effected by today's new Internet culture. For one thing, it has made geography irrelevant—allowing communities to develop outside the traditional bonds of organized community and the dwelling places of traditional institutions. It's telling that among the most culturally significant new holidays in America is "Friendsgiving"—having Thanksgiving with your friends instead of making the potentially expensive trek back home to see family—which went from virtually unknown pre-2013 to a viral marketing term with more than a million tagged posts on Instagram in 2018. A holiday dedicated to chosen family among largely millennial, largely single and childless city dwellers, Friendsgiving represents the degree to which millennials in particular have been forced to explore and invent an alternative, less-rooted societal model than that of their forebears.

But the Internet hasn't just made us location-independent. It has also encouraged us, as consumers with a cornucopia of options, to seek out, even *demand*, a creative role in designing our own experiences, including spiritual ones. For a whole generation of millennials—many of whom, in marrying and having children later, are foregoing traditional markers of rootedness—the Internet provides highly specialized alternative communities, allowing people to find friends or partners who aren't merely like-minded, but almost identically minded. It disincentivizes compromise and conformity, even as it promises the bespoke ideal: people who think and feel and act *just like you.*

In 1969, long before the advent of the World Wide Web, Canadian academic Marshall McLuhan, often considered the father of media studies, envisioned a technological future characterized by what he called "retribalization." For McLuhan, the dawn of new forms of electronic media—television, for example—would usher in the "global village": a world in which disparate peoples from all over the world would be united by the ideas and images newly available to them. This technological change, McLuhan predicted, would not make us into one big, unified, happy family. Rather, we'd splinter into new, technology-driven "tribes." As McLuhan rather bombastically (and somewhat offensively) told a *Playboy* interviewer in 1969, "The compressional, implosive nature of the new electric technology is retrogressing Western man back from the open plateaus of literate values and into the heart of tribal darkness."[16]

McLuhan may not have predicted the Internet itself. But he was prophetic when it came to his vision of the way in which the Internet has retribalized us all. From *Harry Potter* fans to Wiccans, skin care fanatics to political activists, we're increasingly able to use the power of both personal social media (Facebook) and more public forums (Twitter, Reddit, 4chan) to find people like us, with similar interests, philosophies, and even sexual kinks. The Internet has made it possible to transcend old identity markers—institutionalized religions; national, ethnic, or parochial identities—in favor of the new.

But that's just one side of the coin. The Internet has also made us hungrier for individualization: for products, information, and groups that reflect more exactly our personal sense of self. Just look at how we consume our news. A political conservative might only ever see articles designed to reinforce their worldview; a die-hard liberal might likewise never come across an opposing source. A 2017 study by the Kellogg School of Management found that as many as 93.6 percent of Facebook users and 87.8 percent of YouTube users were "polarized"—

concentrating at least 95 percent of their online reading on controversial issues around one politicized narrative.[17]

Our systems of meaning, likewise, have become similarly constituted: purpose-made for our own intuitions and experiences. Bespoke products of all types have been gaining cultural traction. According to *Harper's Bazaar*, bespoke beauty—in which products are custom-made for the consumer—"is set to be the biggest beauty trend of 2018."[18] The *Financial Times* declared that bespoke skin care, too, is coming of age. ("It's All About Me!" proclaims the headline.)[19] Indeed, the term has reached such cultural saturation (you might say we've reached *peak bespoke*) that not only did a 2015 satirical video featuring a pair of stereotypical Brooklyn hipsters hawking "bespoke" water go viral, but apparently plenty of people actually tried to buy it.[20]

There is a natural irony to all this, of course. The very qualities that most characterize modern technology—speed and ease of reproducibility—have also kindled a cultural backlash. Our spiritual profiles, like our Facebook profiles, need to be individualized.

Just look at the Ritual Design Lab, founded by designers Kursat Ozenc and Margaret Hagan: equal parts tech start-up and latter-day religion. Callers into the "ritual design hotline" (past clients have included big brands like Microsoft) tell the lab a bit about their community and needs, and the lab in turn designs a custom, nontheistic ritual. (If you want even more independence, their custom app, IdeaPop, can help you brainstorm on your own.) "The new generation," Ozenc told the *Atlantic*'s Sigal Samuel, "want[s] bite-size spirituality instead of a whole menu of courses."[21] In Ozenc's view, this is a good thing. "Design thinking can offer this," he continued on, "because the whole premise of design is human-centeredness. It can help people shape their spirituality based on their needs. Institutionalized religions somehow forget this—that at the center of any religion should be the person."

What could be more intuitional than that?

four

HARRY POTTER AND THE BIRTH OF REMIX CULTURE

Masters voice I can heard loud and clear. I know when I do
wrong, I know when he is pleased.[. . .]

The way I see things is that we tend to limit ourselves,
our believes, our understanding, our willingness . . . due
to what? Society? Because people tend to be afraid of what
they don't understand!?! Oh well, your all's loss, my gain!
Does that make me sick? No more so then others! . . . MY
MASTER!!!! [. . .] I stand where I stand, and ever
so proudly![. . .]

"[My love is] beyond reason, understanding or
comprehension. I am completely and insanely obsessed."[1]

THE WOMAN WHO WROTE THESE WORDS IN THE MID-2000S, a user of the once-ubiquitous diary website LiveJournal, identified only as Rose, was not referring to a human being. The several years' worth of online blog posts, comments, and messages with other LiveJournal users, the rich body of love letters, spiritual memoirs, and fictional stories Rose wrote and posted, were dedicated to an incorporeal spirit, a mythic figure who, she frequently recounted, would visit her in dreams or on the astral plane. Along with a small coterie of like-minded worshippers who helped her "channel" her lover into writings in his voice and helped compose "marriage vows" by which she would consecrate herself to her beloved, Rose knelt at a very specific altar.

The object of her devotion?

Severus Snape.

The grumpy, antiheroic potions teacher of J. K. Rowling's wildly successful *Harry Potter* series, who became something of an unlikely sex symbol for a generation of young adult readers (no doubt helped by Alan Rickman's brooding portrayal of the character on-screen), Severus Snape might not be an obvious choice for spiritual veneration. But, for more than a few of the women who called themselves "Snapewives" or "Snapefen," Severus Snape was the closest thing they had to a god.

"I can say with very good reason that Severus IS indeed my Master, Lord, God, Savior," wrote Rose in one post.[2] In another, she boasted of a room in her house dedicated to memorabilia associated with the character—a room in which, she claimed, she experienced psychic visitations from him. "Also yesterday, after we rehung some of Masters pics in their room, I felt a harsh shove, push against my back and fell forward on the floor my hands catching. I was kneeling on hands and knees before my Master!! Later on he revealed to me what he had done, he had stood behind me, and with his knee shoved me forwards. THUD THUD!!!"[3] Sometimes, Rose reported, she even slept with Snape after he took over the body of her husband. "Master would 'take over' for my Hubby and have fun ;o) Basically my Hubby would do things in ways that only Master can and could!"

One of Rose's most frequent collaborators, a self-proclaimed Snape-wife who called herself Tonya, expressed similar sentiments: "I BELIEVE THAT SEVERUS SNAPE EXISTS INDEPENDENTLY OF JKR! HE IS A LIVING, FEELING SPIRIT," she wrote. "I BELIEVE ANYTHING IS POSSIBLE AND THAT SEVERUS DOES VISIT THOSE HE CHOOSES TO."

Another collaborator, Conchita, wrote frequently that she has taken a vow of celibacy: foregoing not just personal sexual relationships with other human beings but even masturbation. She criticized Tonya and

Rose for posting elaborate, graphic accounts of their sexual unions with Snape online, insisting that "I don't need to post dirty stuff in here to show the freaking world he was with me (No I am not jealous of that. If that would ever happen to me, I'd keep it *private*, like he wanted) My love is pure and unconditional, and also very patient. One day he will notice the difference, I am sure."[4]

These three women are extreme—even by the admittedly fervent standards of the *Harry Potter* fan base. But the story of the Snapewives is inseparable from the story of the rise of Internet fan culture as a whole: the story of how we as a broader culture have transformed the way we insert ourselves—our loves, our wants, our desires, our chosen narratives—into the stories we consume.

It's impossible to understand the rise of today's Remixed, or the resurgence of contemporary intuitional religious culture more broadly, without understanding, well, *Harry Potter* fandom. Its emergence was inextricably intertwined with the development of an Internet that fomented not merely consumers but content creators, and with a generation whose foundational "texts"—shared media that shaped our discourse around good, evil, and meaning itself—existed in online symbiosis with grassroots fandoms. Sure, Snape-driven erotic fan fiction isn't exactly, well, a lost Gnostic gospel. But the roots of contemporary millennial culture—its tendency toward Internet-driven communities, its obsession with individuation, its propensity toward rewriting scripts and recreating worldviews—all came out of 2000s fan culture. Dostoyevsky famously said that all Russian writers "come out from Gogol's overcoat." When it comes to Remixed religion, at least, we all come out from under Severus Snape's robes.

Today's witches, alt-right shitposters, social justice warriors, and poly utopians are all, in their ways, inheritors of the legacy of late '90s and 2000s Internet-driven fan culture. Some of these legacies are more obvious than others.

Just look, for example, at a Silicon Valley–based movement known as Rationalism: an umbrella term for followers of influential blogs like *LessWrong* and *Slate Star Codex*, which promote a kind of self-hacking through improvement of metacognitive skills. Today, the Rationalist movement is enormously influential in tech circles. Controversial tech titan Peter Thiel, founder of PayPal, donates hundreds of thousands of dollars to several of the Rationalist community's utopian projects, including the Machine Intelligence Research Institute: a think tank founded by Rationalist leader (and *LessWrong* scribe) Eliezer Yudkowsky to combat the existential threat of supersophisticated artificial intelligence. The far-right Neo-Reactionary movement sprang up as an offshoot of the Rationalist community, with its own leader Curtis Yarvin (better known by his nom de plume Mencius Moldbug) getting his start as a regular commentator on *LessWrong* and its predecessor blog, *Overcoming Bias*.

But it all started in the *Harry Potter* fandom. Back when *Overcoming Bias* was still a relatively unknown blog, read only by a few devotees particularly interested in, well, overcoming bias, Eliezer Yudkowsky was going viral with another writing project: *Harry Potter and the Methods of Rationality*. HPMOR, as it continues to be known among fans (and Rationalists), was a sprawling epic. Between 2010 and 2015, Yudkowsky posted 122 chapters, comprising 661,619 words (for contrast, *War and Peace* comes in at a bit under 600,000), on popular fan fiction sharing site Fanfiction.net. The novel, in which an alternate-universe Harry solves all the mysteries of both Hogwarts and wizarding life using clever metacognitive tools and Rationalist thinking, became something of a gateway drug to the Rationalist community. (A significant proportion of the Rationalists I spoke to cited *HPMOR* as their entrée into the movement.) It has garnered over thirteen thousand reviews on Fanfiction.net, making it among the most-reviewed pieces on the site.[5]

Yudkowsky's parallel-universe Harry became so popular among fans that, by 2018, a Planeta.ru campaign for Russian translation of the epic became the largest-ever crowdfunding project in that country, raising at least $70,000.[6]

Or look at *Harry Potter*'s influence on another group of politically engaged millennials: the participants in the contemporary social justice movement. In March 2018, for example, among the most striking signs at the March for Our Lives rally—a protest calling for more stringent gun control measures after the shooting at Marjory Stoneman Douglas High School in Parkland, Florida—were the ubiquitous *Harry Potter*-themed ones. "IF HOGWARTS STUDENTS CAN DEFEAT THE DEATHEATERS, THEN U.S. STUDENTS CAN DEFEAT THE NRA," one placard read. "DUMBLEDORE'S ARMY STILL RECRUITING," read another, referring to the teenage guerilla group that, in one installment of the series, bands together to fight the dark lord Voldemort. Another, celebrating the books' brainy female lead, exclaimed, "HERMIONE USES KNOWLEDGE NOT GUNS." Others simply read "EXPELLIARMUS," the Hogwarts disarmament spell.

As one breathless CNN headline read at the time, "Harry Potter Inspired the Parkland Generation."[7] *Teen Vogue*, a magazine that in the Trump age has increasingly made its reputation as a mouthpiece for the social justice movement, celebrated the signs with a listicle hawking the "Best 'Harry Potter' Signs at the March for Our Lives."[8]

"The wizardly motif was prevalent for a good reason," *Teen Vogue*'s De Elizabeth wrote. "The *Harry Potter* series conveys a theme of resistance, one that's similar to the fight for change today. Armed with stories of resilience, determination, and the triumph of good over evil, it's no wonder that this generation is ready to push back—and *hard*."[9]

These two examples speak to the degree to which the language, rhetoric, imagery, and structure of fan culture have seeped into our contemporary Remixed religions: on the progressive left and far right alike.

THE STORIES WE TELL

Fandom may not be a "religion" in the narrowest sense of the word. It does not require its adherents to subscribe to any formal beliefs about either the metaphysical realm or the world we live in now. But it is absolutely a mechanism for collective identity-making and reinforcement, the very definition of a Durkheimian religion. It may not by itself offer a sense of meaning and purpose, but it definitely provides plenty of scope for community and ritual.

It's impossible to look at, say, video footage of the Beatles landing in America in 1964 (or even a Justin Bieber concert now) and not see evidence of Durkheim's "collective effervescence": a group coalescing and affirming its identity around a beloved totem.

For decades, sports scholars have connected the intense rituals of sports fans—with their obsession with the "right" and "wrong" teams, their annual quasi-liturgical calendar of "seasons," their often highly stylized apparel at games—to religious practice.[10] (The word *fan* comes from *fanatic* for a reason.) Fandom, both as a practice and as a marker of identity, is at its core a kind of self-making: it's not just about *what we like* but *who we are*. Identifying oneself publicly as a fan—of a football team, of a pop star—is a public commitment to a tribe and a tribal identity. As sociologist Christopher Partridge puts it, "We are all fans of something or someone. To be a fan is to identify with that which 'matters' to us and has contributed in some sense to the construction of our identities."[11] That said, however, the stories that have the most traction as fan totems tend to be those that deal explicitly with metaphysical themes or good-versus-evil battles.

Often, the intensity of interpretation that thrives around fan culture—to look for clues in a cult television show like *Lost*, for example, or to parse the songs of a beloved singer for hidden meanings, or to wander the McKittrick Hotel in order to unlock *Sleep No More*'s secrets—becomes a kind of re-enchanting of the world. The outside world—the "real" world—may seem meaningless or inauthentic. But the world of Hogwarts, or of *Buffy the Vampire Slayer*'s Sunnydale, or of Leonard Cohen's songs, is seen as infinitely complex and drenched with meaning. As one sociologist of Bruce Springsteen fandom writes, "Christianity and fandom involve a particular kind of moral orientation in which people derive meaning and value . . . [from] signs and representations; as Christians' ongoing, daily life of devotion to God involves interpretation of the bible and thinking about how God's will is revealed in their lives, so fans' ongoing, daily life of devotion to music involves interpretation of Springsteen's songs and puzzling over how the music addresses their experiences."[12]

But the most widespread and resonant symbols of fandom aren't just pop culture memes. They're also means by which we understand the world around us. Just think of how, for example, the idea of Hogwarts houses—brave Gryffindor, loyal Hufflepuff, clever Ravenclaw, and ruthless Slytherin—have framed contemporary discourse about personality types. So, too, has the popularity of the Dungeons and Dragons classification system—whether you're chaotic good or lawful evil or something in between—spread far beyond any actual players of the games. The most successful fandom properties have been those that offer not just unity among their admirers but a coherent language for talking about the world. In an interview with *Wired* magazine in 2012, Joss Whedon—the creator of cult TV series *Buffy the Vampire Slayer* and *Angel*—called fandom the "closest thing to religion there is that isn't actually religion."[13]

And stories like *Harry Potter* and *Buffy* and *Angel* are taking on a canonical cast. Bible stories no longer have the cultural staying power that they once did. Only 39 percent of Americans, for example, know the story of the biblical Job, according to a 2010 Pew study.[14] This isn't just a phenomenon affecting Nones, either; the same poll found that just 50 percent of American Christians could identify the four Gospels by name.[15] Given that 61 percent of Americans have seen at least one *Harry Potter* film, it is very likely that more Americans can name the four Hogwarts houses than can name the Gospels.[16]

Culturally resonant stories that feature battles between good and evil—be they *Star Wars* or *Buffy* or the chronicles of that infamous boy wizard—are more likely to hold us together as a nation than the increasingly forgotten story of the suffering of Job. They're more likely, too, to inform our internal sense of meaning, our personal relationship with the concepts of good and evil, light and darkness. Snape may not be our collective savior, as he was for Rose and Tonya, but we're nevertheless more likely, demographically speaking, to think of the battle of good and evil in terms of Dumbledore versus Voldemort, rather than the biblical God against Satan.

You could, of course, say the same of slightly older fan cultures as well, such as the ones that sprang up around *Star Trek* and *Star Wars* in the 1970s—a decade that followed the emergence of pluralism in the Fourth Great Awakening of the 1960s. The most fervent early fan cultures of that time, like those of today, arose around mythic stories: stories that may not have had a developed theology as such, but which nevertheless provided their adherents with a sense of meaning and order they could apply to their own lives and communities.

Among the hundreds of thousands of *Star Trek* fans worldwide, you often find, according to sociologist Michael Jindra, a culturally resonant, coherent, and consistent theological strain: the "mythical resonance of a future universe-wide utopia."[17] *Star Trek*'s creator, Gene Roddenberry, spoke frequently in interviews about the utopian vision of technological progress and human potential that underscored *Star Trek*'s plotlines and grounded its moral systems.[18] Another of the show's writer-directors reflected on how the show had "evolved into a sort of secular parallel to the Catholic Mass. The words of the Mass remain constant, but heaven knows, the music keeps changing."[19]

Likewise, the rhetoric and implicit good-versus-evil value system of *Star Wars* have saturated our contemporary cultural symbolic network. The discourse of "the Force" versus "the dark side" and sage mentor Yoda's famous maxim ("Do. Or do not. There is no try.") are as culturally indelible as the Ten Commandments.

For some, Jediism—the belief system of the movies' "good" characters—is even a formal religion. While the number of people who say they consider themselves Jedi is relatively small—about 250,000 worldwide—it's worth noting that this still makes Jediism among the most practiced "alternative" religions in the world, beating out longer-standing traditions like Wicca and Scientology.[20]

Of course, the implicit content of Jediism—its vague but cosmically meaningful light-versus-dark dichotomy—is likely shared by far more people than those who formally self-identify as Jedis. The Jedi creed (actually adapted from the Christian prayer of Saint Francis of Assisi) is a similarly anodyne document. Adherents pledge their faith "in the Force, and in the inherent worth of all life within it . . . in the positive influence of spiritual growth and awareness on society," and "in the importance of freedom of conscience and self-determination within religious, political and other structures."[21] In other words, in the relatively open-ended moral and spiritual system suggested by the films.

In 2001, an early Internet email campaign encouraging religious Nones to put their religion down on census forms as Jedi went viral. Participants didn't have to assent to the Jedi creed—the email encouraged people to do it "because you love Star Wars . . . or just to annoy people"—but enough of them went through with it to make international headlines.[22] Almost four hundred thousand people in England and Wales decided to call themselves Jedis (outnumbering Buddhists and Jews), as did seventy thousand people in Australia—enough for the government to issue a befuddled press release warning respondents that "this may impact on social services provision if enough people do the same."[23] (The United States had conducted its decennial census the previous year, and thus never became part of the phenomenon.)

Sure, many of the religious Nones who put down "Jedi" weren't "really" Jedis, to the extent that their answers may have been flippant or ironic rather than belief driven (although a similar case could be made about cultural Catholics or Protestants who tick the "correct" box of their heritage rather than one that reflects their personal theological beliefs). But to the extent that we're talking about the cultural theology of Jediism—the degree to which the ideas about good and evil portrayed in *Star Wars* inform our perspective on the world—plenty of these people *were*, well, Jedis. The techno-futurism of *Star Trek* and the amorphous Force of *Star Wars* are unifying cultural myths that, replicated across pop culture, transcend their fictional origins and provide us with a handy vocabulary for envisioning a meaningful world.

Harry Potter, too, has had an indelible impact not just on our cultural touchstones but on our moral framework. A 2014 study at the

University of Greenwich found that just reading *Harry Potter* passages made children more likely to feel positively about immigrants.[24] Multiple studies have found that *Harry Potter* readers, overall, are more likely to favor progressive politicians and disfavor anti-immigrant ones, even when factors like race, religion, and class are controlled for.[25]

Harry Potter, in other words, isn't just a story we enjoy reading. Rather, it's had a measurable impact on a whole generation's moral universe. In an age when fewer and fewer people read the Bible, the media properties of fan culture are the closest thing the Remixed have to sacred texts.

THE CREATION OF THE DIGITAL TRIBE

But Internet fan culture wasn't just about sharing stories. It was also about creating emotionally fulfilling fan communities that were location-independent.

Early Internet pioneers had embraced the possibility of the Internet fostering new human relationships unbounded by physical space or existing social relations. In 1993, culture critic Howard Rheingold envisioned a utopian space of total, disembodied freedom for social exploration, a place, he prophesied, that would become just like "real life," only more liberated. "People in virtual communities," he wrote, "use words on screens to exchange pleasantries and argue, engage in intellectual discourse, conduct commerce, exchange knowledge, share emotional support, make plans, brainstorm, gossip, feud, fall in love, find friends and lose them, play games, flirt, create a little high art and a lot of idle talk. People in virtual communities do just about everything people do in real life, but we leave our bodies behind. You can't kiss anybody and nobody can punch you in the nose, but a lot can happen within those boundaries."[26]

Social networks, Rheingold predicted, would be transformed, defined not by happenstance but by intentional decision-making: "In a virtual community we can go directly to the place where our favorite subjects are being discussed, then get acquainted with people who share our passions." Whereas, in the offline world, "you can't simply pick up a phone and ask to be connected with someone who wants to talk about Islamic art or California wine, or someone with a three-year-old daughter or a forty-year-old Hudson," the Internet offered the possibility of doing precisely that.[27]

Rheingold, an early adopter of online culture, wasn't necessarily representative of Americans in 1993. But he was prophetic. More than anything else, it was the massive scale of fan culture that transformed Rheingold's vast vision of connectivity into a plausible social option for your average American.

Message boards like Reddit and the anonymous 4chan, narrowly targeted spaces like once-iconic pop culture website *Television Without Pity*, and popular blogging sites with community functions like Live-Journal, JournalFen, and, later, Tumblr transformed the possibility of fandom, making the benefits of fan community ever more accessible.

Early fan communities had revolved around older, slower, and more analog methods of community: annual or biannual conventions, postal mailing lists, local fan clubs. Fan magazines, privately printed and circulated, were the primary means of disseminating information and responding creatively to a property. (Between 1973 and 1980, for example, the number of *Star Trek*–related fanzines soared from eighty-eight to over four hundred.)[28] Fan campaigns required dedicated labor and materials—and necessitated gatekeepers.

One longtime, well-known *Star Trek* fan, Nancy Kippax, recalls in her memoirs the labor that went into creating just one issue of one *Star Trek* fanzine. Kippax details how she and her collaborators manually designed each page on typewriters, using a blue pencil and ruler to determine where to stop typing each line. They sought out places with suitable printers, usually local churches or fans' workplaces. But each step in the process, Kippax recalls, was an opportunity for socializing. "Did I mention the collating parties?" she writes.

> We sent out a call to everyone within driving distance to come on
> a specified date and help collate. . . . Bev and I would provide food
> and drink—buckets of fried chicken, or a crock pot of barbecue

beef, chips and other snacks, coleslaw, whatever we decided was
appropriate for the weather and the season. We would lay out the
pages all along Bev's extended dining room table, fanning them
as we'd been taught in the beginning, and we'd usually get about
15 pages (that would be 30 pages of the book) on one trip. . . . Bev
had green shag carpet in her dining room (well, it was the '70s,
after all!) and I tell you honestly that we eventually wore a path
in that carpet![29]

The Internet revolutionized these fan communities. Not only could information—and, more importantly, creative responses to media properties, such as fan fiction—be disseminated much more quickly, it could be shared in a totally location-independent, accessible way. You didn't need to start out as a sufficiently die-hard fan—someone willing to come to a collating party, for example—to access a community. All you needed was a search engine.

Early Internet fan culture was still segmented and at times relatively inaccessible. Throughout most of the 1990s, fan communities communicated through email listservs, or Yahoo groups, or on websites, some password protected, devoted to a particular property like *The X-Files* or *Xena: Warrior Princess*, to name two particularly influential emergent fandoms during that time. The broadening availability of site hosting engines like GeoCities (launched in 1994) and Angelfire (launched in 1996) allowed users to create simple websites without needing to know anything about computer programming.

In 1998, all that changed.

A new website, Fanfiction.net, collected diverse fandoms in one place, offering users the chance to post fan fiction geared toward their particular media property, fundamentally democratizing the process of both publishing fan fiction and finding a potential audience for it.

That same year, *Harry Potter and the Sorcerer's Stone* was published in the United States (the book had been published in the UK, as *Harry Potter and the Philosopher's Stone*, the previous year). Had *Harry Potter* come out at any other time, it might not have become the phenomenon it did. A reasonably straightforward good-and-evil-meets-boarding-school story, written in prose critics frequently derided as workmanlike, *Harry Potter* was hardly particularly original or particularly good. But what it was, was timely.

Harry Potter was the first media property to go viral in the Internet sense and the first to almost exclusively harness the Internet, rather than analog media, as the medium by which its fans converged. The growth of *Harry Potter* fandom and the development of what is often known as Web 2.0—the Internet characterized by a proliferation of user-generated content—were symbiotic. In the years between the publication of the first *Harry Potter* book and the fourth in the series (*Harry Potter and the Goblet of Fire*) the number of Americans who used the Internet increased by 500 percent: from nineteen million to a solid one hundred million.[30]

Harry Potter fandom modeled on a massive scale what was already becoming true, to smaller degrees, in other fandom cultures, as well as elsewhere on the Internet. Culture was becoming a moveable feast.

LiveJournal (and its imitators DeadJournal, JournalFen, and Dream-width) offered a hybrid community-diary function; users kept their own personal blogs, but could also choose to join often fandom-centric communities. The site was structured to foster not just dialogue but friendships. You might connect with someone in a community over, say, Harry-Hermione "shipping" (fandom parlance for supporting a romantic relationship between two characters), or Draco-Harry "slash" (queer shipping), only to click through to their personal page and find out about their unrequited crushes, their struggles with depression or an eating disorder, or their relationship with their parents.

If you loved something—whether you were living on a ranch in Texas, in a bungalow in the Cleveland suburbs, or in a penthouse in New York City—you could, with very little effort, find a whole group of people just like you. You were no longer limited by the culture or the ideology of the people you lived next to. You could find your people and, more importantly, you had the freedom to figure out who your people were. Whether you were posting stories or reviews on Fanfiction.net or exchanging off-site messages with a fellow member of a LiveJournal or JournalFen community, your online experience was an opportunity to engage in a form of sui generis self-creation.

At times, this self-creation could push or even barrel past ethical boundaries (the practice of "catfishing," or pretending to be a fictitious person online, is as old as the Internet itself). But, by and large, the new Internet provided a revolutionary basis for community-building. By its apex in 2007, LiveJournal boasted over ten million users, including high-profile fandom figures like George R. R. Martin, author of the *Song of Ice and Fire* series (better known as *Game of Thrones*, the title of the series' first book).[31]

Fan communities often cleaved along gendered lines. Certain spaces and fandoms—gaming, for example, or comic books—tended to be predominately male. Massively multiplayer online role-playing games (MMORPGs) like *World of Warcraft* and some games in the *Final Fantasy* series attracted tens of millions of subscribers (WoW peaked with twelve million in 2010), many of whom developed friendships—or, at least, long-standing virtual relationships—with their teammates.[32] Relationships developed through the game could even trump their real-life counterparts.

As one Kansas WoW veteran told an interviewer, "I remember my buddy had thrown this big party while we were in high school, and I found myself in a bed with my prom date. . . . At 3:30am, my cell phone started going nuts. . . . It was this random number from Los Angeles. I picked it up and it was one of the officers in the guild. He told me I needed to get home, get on my computer, and help kill one of the Emerald Dragons that had just spawned. He said 'welcome to the team' and just hung up. That was the expectation. I'm an 18-year-old dude with this girl, and I had to say 'I've gotta go kill this dragon.' We weren't hanging out for much longer."[33]

Media property fandoms like *Harry Potter*, however, tended to appeal to a female audience base. They, too, fostered close-knit community. As one lifelong fan, Kristina Busse, wrote in her book of essays on fan culture, "Many women describe fandom as the first place where they truly created friendship ties with other women and found levels of intimacy otherwise foreclosed to them."[34] Furthermore, Busse added, the veneer of anonymity that the Internet provided allowed such online friendships to foster more intensely than a comparable IRL (in real life) friendship.

Ethnographer Rhiannon Bury concurs. In her ethnographies of female fan culture across the mid-2000s Internet, she frequently reports the degree to which fan communities took on an outsize social role for their adherents, many of whom felt alienated from their dominant "home" culture.[35] "Geekdom was not valued in my peer group and I vividly remember being mocked and bullied for my reading interests," one of Bury's subjects recalls. "I don't know if I would have become part of fandom without [the Internet]. I suspect not. That reinforcement of a community that also values and wants to discuss these cultural artifacts has been really important to me over the years."

Another of Bury's subjects put it more succinctly: "Hey, we are fans! And fans are hard to find and we have found our tribe. Let's hang out!"[36]

Yet another recalls the importance of her fan community during the September 11 terrorist attacks:

> On at least 2 different Yahoo! Groups that I was on, somebody popped up and said, "Okay, folks. We are doing a roll call." Just check in; give us whatever information you are comfortable giving because there are some people don't want to reveal a real name or where they are. But just let us know you are still alive. We actually had some members who lived in New York City. And people were like, "Has anybody heard from? Has anybody heard from?" You know? There were people who were just displaced from their apartments because they couldn't get home. There was one gal who lived in lower Manhattan and she worked in the World Trade Center and her baby was in a daycare there. The child had got an earache. . . . She was at the hospital with her baby and couldn't get home; couldn't get to a computer. So when she finally got back home and she goes, "Thank you guys for worrying about me. Fortune favored us. We are okay."

Fan communities often developed the kind of formal qualities associated with their IRL counterparts. Forum moderators often served as the online equivalent of village elders, keeping the peace within communities and adjudicating disputes.

For gaming-based and fan-fiction-based communities alike, the Internet provided the mechanism for both finding tribes and defining what your tribe was. As Sherry Turkle writes of MMORPGs in particular, "Although the games most often took the form of quests, medieval and otherwise, the virtual environments were most compelling because they offered opportunities for a social life, for performing as the self you wanted to be."[37]

By 2007, nearly a quarter of teenagers reported using the Internet to make friends, with 12 percent saying they had online friends they'd never met in person.[38] Ten percent reported having friends that had no connection whatsoever to their existing localized social networks. Just nine years after *Harry Potter* had hit the shelves, forming geographically independent, tribally focused social networks through the Internet had become a viable strategy. It was an available option to anyone who felt, as Bury's subjects did, alienated or unseen by their home group. By 2015, a full 57 percent of teenagers aged thirteen to seventeen said they had made a new friend online, with almost a third saying they'd made at least five. Twenty percent of American teenagers have met at least one online friend in person.[39]

Today's adult millennials are, similarly, more likely than ever to use the Internet to seek out tribes, or, more broadly, to access a tribal identity. A *Harry Potter* fan, for example, may actively choose to join fan communities—make a Tumblr or post a story to Fanfiction.net. But they may also choose to "lurk," in Internet parlance, reading about elements of fan culture (and adopting the mantle of that identity) without necessarily actively participating in that culture. There are a seemingly infinite number of Internet subcultures, from goths to Gleeks to Beliebers to burners to several we'll be dealing with directly in this book: kinksters, poly folk, social justice warriors, devotees of particular wellness gurus or regimens, and men's rights activists. The list of websites on which they congregate is no less exhaustive. These tribes are even developing their own languages. A 2013 study published in the academic journal *EPJ Data Science* found that language usage patterns and slang phrases were so consistent across Twitter subcultures that it was possible to predict which tribe a user belonged to with up to 80 percent accuracy.[40] The idea of tribalization is so enmeshed in contemporary Internet culture that it has become the primary marketing strategy for brands. As marketing guru Seth Godin put it, "The Internet eliminates geography. This means that existing tribes are bigger but more important, it means that there are now more tribes, smaller tribes, influential tribes, horizontal and vertical tribes, and tribes that could have never existed before."[41]

That normalization has extended even to the most important relationships in our lives: romantic partners. Between 2005 and 2017, the percentage of the American population that said online dating was a good way to meet people grew from 44 percent to 59 percent.[42] As of 2015, the most recent year for which data is available, 27 percent of those aged eighteen to twenty-four, and 22 percent of those aged twenty-five to thirty-four, had used dating apps—and that number is projected to rise.[43] Around 40 percent of the couples that get together annually met online (that number jumps to 60 percent for queer couples), according to one study.[44] Meanwhile, the number of couples that report having met through friends has plummeted: from 33 percent in 1995 to just 20 percent today. The percentage of couples who say they met through family has also dropped from 15 to just 7 percent.

Here, too, we can see the extent to which the normalization of Internet tribalization has affected how we gather. The traditional bastions of social influence—personal friends and family—have been outsourced, even when it comes to our most intimate and socially significant moments.

Not all of the Internet's early fandom venues have survived. More and more, social media sites—Facebook and Instagram, for example—function as replications of users' day-to-day lives rather than as potentially anonymous sources of new community, and some of the old-guard sites have shuttered. After a series of fan-alienating business decisions, LiveJournal—since sold to a Russian company—has dwindled to a shadow of its former self, catering mostly to Russian speakers (the word for blogging, in Russian, means "to LJ"). JournalFen, a fandom-specific offshoot of LiveJournal, is no longer online. Fandom culture is primarily centered on the blogging platform Tumblr, which now boasts 456 million accounts and 168 *billion* original posts, although it has seen its user base decline precipitously in recent years.[45] With its lack of threading capabilities, Tumblr—which functions primarily as a "reblogging" tool, where users can repost existing memes and (less often) text, while optionally adding minimal commentary of their own—is less conducive to community-building than the gathering places of the previous decade.

But what has survived is the Internet's ever-growing culture of tribalization, and the ease with which a casual media consumer can become, with a few clicks, a full-fledged member of a tribe.

Today's tribes are less unconventional than the fan culture of yore. Marketing companies have long since grown savvy to the staying power of fans. Entire television shows—the high school musical *Glee*, the noir soap *Riverdale*—have made their reputations by actively courting their extreme online fan bases with plotlines that suggest the possibility for multiple "ships" (including, most popular among fans, queer ships) and actors who stoke their bases by referencing fan memes on social media. Fashion and wellness brands court hyper-specialized influencers—de facto leaders of tribes on Instagram—as advertising vehicles to increasingly narrow, but increasingly specific, bases. "Tribal marketing" (also known as "post-demographic marketing") has become a media buzzword. Consumers don't behave as they're expected to— which is to say, they don't behave along easily definable lines of class, gender, age, or income. Instead, they're defined by hobbies, activities, and practices—in other words, a chosen identity.

It's that sense of tribal individualization that engenders the most significant way in which fandom has affected the culture of the Remixed. A new willingness to reimagine and recreate foundational texts has transformed a generation of Internet users from content consumers to content creators.

WHAT ARE WE ENTITLED TO, ANYWAY?

Once upon a time, you read a book, or saw a movie, and that was it. After the invention of the printing press, reading was largely a unilateral phenomenon: somebody created something, somebody else printed and distributed it, you absorbed it. While the printing press enabled a largely democratic and personal approach to information, it nevertheless maintained a degree of top-down hierarchy. Oral traditions allowed for repetition, reimagining, and change (just think of the diverse and varying accounts of, say, the Greek myths, or the legends of King Arthur), but the printed word demanded the formal codification of information: *This* is the story. *This* is what happened.

The Internet has given rise to a different kind of media culture: one that privileges the reader and the watcher with the ability to reimagine a story, rewrite an ending, or reconfigure a romantic relationship. The privilege of authority is no longer exclusively with the makers of stories. While the "death of the author" as a critical phenomenon has been a subject of academic discourse since at least the 1960s, the rise of Internet creative culture has made that a real-world phenomenon.

We've transitioned from a strictly consumer culture into what media scholar Henry Jenkins has termed "participatory culture." Jenkins defines participatory culture as one:

1. With relatively low barriers to artistic expression and civic engagement
2. With strong support for creating and sharing one's creations with others
3. With some type of informal mentorship whereby what is known by the most experienced is passed along to novices
4. Where members believe that their contributions matter
5. Where members feel some degree of social connection with one another (at the least they care what other people think about what they have created).[46]

Today's freewheeling Internet is the fullest expression of that culture. Anyone, today, can create a story (or video, or meme, or joke tweet) and have it blow up to instant fame. But it was fandoms that first demonstrated the power of participatory culture in action. If you didn't like a romantic pairing between two characters, you could connect with other shippers who shared your disdain, finding a built-in audience for you to rewrite their romantic history to your exact specifications.

Today, Fanfiction.net hosts about 40,000 stories set in the *Star Wars* universe, 114,000 set in the television show *Supernatural*, and a full 743,000 *Harry Potter* stories.[47] Rival fan fiction site Archive of Our Own, which has fewer restrictions on sexual content, boasts nearly two million registered members, plus about seven hundred thousand individual visitors per day.[48] Particularly highly regarded fan fiction writers have launched stellar careers of their own. Author Cassandra Clare made a name for herself by writing the *Draco Trilogy*—among the best-known fan fictions, dedicated to rehabilitating Harry Potter's snobbish school rival—before transitioning her fandom fame to commercial properties with the *City of Bones* series. With only a few notable exceptions, mainstream authors and creators have embraced, or at least tolerated, fan fiction of their work, following the lead of J. K. Rowling herself, who in 2004 was one of the first to openly give fan fiction her blessing.[49]

Few fan fiction authors have made the transition to commercial success as completely as E. L. James, whose BDSM trilogy *Fifty Shades of Grey* sold 135 million copies worldwide and made her among the world's best-selling authors.[50] But *Fifty Shades* had its start as a fan fiction. "Master of the Universe"—a story reimagining the star-crossed lovers of Stephenie Meyer's young adult vampire series *Twilight* as kinky office dwellers—had been posted at Fanfiction.net under the pseudonym Snowqueens Icedragon between 2009 and 2011, garnering nearly sixty thousand reviews there before James got a mainstream publishing deal and deleted it.

Meanwhile, fan fiction and fandoms more broadly have transformed the way that media property creators conceive of and shape their creations. More and more shows—such as the new *Star Trek* series or *The Good Fight*, the spin-off of hit legal drama *The Good Wife*—are being made available exclusively on online platforms, the better to cater to fans accustomed to binge-watching, rewatching, and dissecting episodes. Television showrunners (often referred to, in fan parlance, rather unsubtly as "The Powers That Be" or the "Word of God") openly admit to reading fans' reactions on message boards and tailoring plot arcs to fans' preferred specifications.[51] A cult-hit character might be raised to prominence if they galvanize a sufficient fan base—for example, Summer Roberts from *The OC* was originally a glorified extra but ultimately became a series lead, and Jesse Pinkman from *Breaking Bad* was intended to die early on. A series lead or major romance, conversely, might be axed. A creative decision that proves unpopular or offensive to fans—such as the death of the lesbian character Lexa on *The 100* in 2016, which fans accused of playing into a queerphobic "dead lesbian" trope—might merit, as Lexa's death did, a public apology from showrunners and a pledge to do better.[52]

Meanwhile, video game companies offer users access to their development tools in order to encourage "playermods"—minor modifications to the game (such as character appearances) made by amateur designers.[53] And, for better or for worse, fan campaigns—often organized through Twitter hashtags—can alter designers' decisions. In 2018, to name just one example, a group of fans of the *Spider-Man* PS4 game convinced developer Insomniac Games to add a special suit based on the Sam Raimi version of the movie following a gigantic #RaimiSuit campaign.[54]

As consumers, in other words, we're increasingly used to demanding more from what we consume. Our ability to band together with like-minded would-be customers makes us more powerful—and we're more willing than ever to harness that power. At its most extreme, that power can look like entitlement: we demand products, and properties, that exactly resemble what we envision. The targeted individualization that has come to characterize nearly every aspect of our social life—the narrow quality of our digital tribes, the precisely calibrated nature of our suggested news content—has made us more certain than ever that we deserve precisely what we wish for. The more we become consumer-creators, the greater hand we want to take in that creation.

TWO RECENT POP CULTURE PHENOMENA OF THE PAST DECADE ENCAP-sulate this trend. The first is, once again, linked with the *Harry Potter* fandom, consistently the bellwether for technological and social shifts. Since the publication of the last *Harry Potter* book in 2007, J. K. Rowling has become increasingly irrelevant to—and despised by—her fan base. Not only was Rowling roundly criticized for "mishandling" the finale of her series (in 2016, she publicly apologized for killing off Severus Snape), but fans have called her out, publicly and often, for behavior they see as insufficiently woke.[55]

Rowling's habit of providing additional, often controversial, information about *Harry Potter*'s characters years later (such as the fact that kindly Hogwarts headmaster Albus Dumbledore was apparently gay) is, for many fans, an overreach of authorial prerogative. Rowling was castigated for having benefited from a seemingly pro-LGBTQ stance without having taken the risk of giving Dumbledore a concrete sexuality in the book itself. Rowling's remarks about wider social and political issues—her support for the state of Israel, and her refusal to condemn the casting of alleged spousal abuser Johnny Depp in a film adaptation of her book *Fantastic Beasts and Where to Find Them*—likewise earned her the ire of a fan base who felt she'd betrayed the Potterverse's progressive ideals. As *Kotaku*'s Gita Jackson put it in one 2018 article: "J. K. Rowling Needs to Stop Messing with *Harry Potter*."[56] That Potter owed his very existence to Rowling was immaterial. Rowling had, in fans' minds, betrayed them. If *Harry Potter* had in fact taught a generation of millennials liberal and progressive values then that generation, in turn, demanded a *Harry Potter* series that sufficiently reflected them.

Harry Potter may have started as J. K. Rowling's creation. But the story of *Harry Potter*, and of this millennium's raft of myths more broadly, no longer belongs to any one individual. As consumers, we demand the right to tell our own.

The second example is Gamergate. Among the most important cultural phenomena of the past few years, it was the first culture war between two very different camps of Remixed. While people at different ends of the political spectrum provide slightly different accounts of what, exactly, happened during the crisis, a few indisputable points capture the degree to which the phenomenon was emblematic of a growing sense of fan *ownership*.

Gamergate sprang largely from a wider debate within fan culture about the representation of women and minorities. A growing number of video game fans—mainly but not exclusively female fans, queer fans, and fans of color in a predominately straight, white, and male industry—were banding together publicly to advocate for video games that better addressed the concerns and reflected the interests of minority players. Among these was Anita Sarkeesian, who had published a series of YouTube videos introducing players to feminist theory in video games, as well as a reasonably well-known female developer, Zoë Quinn, who had created a game called *Depression Quest*, an adventure-style game designed to capture Quinn's experience of depression. The game proved relatively popular with indie critics.

Shortly after the game was released, Quinn's ex-boyfriend, Eron Gjoni, posted a 9,425-word blog post accusing Quinn of having garnered favorable reviews for the game due to her sexual relationship with video game critic Nathan Grayson, of popular fan website *Kotaku*, despite the fact that Grayson had never directly reviewed the game.[57] The post was shared widely on Reddit, 4chan, and other websites largely associated with a reactionary strain in gaming culture: men who feared the encroachment of social justice warriors (SJWs) on "their" turf. Soon, approximately ten thousand Twitter users congregating under #GamerGate were harassing Quinn and, subsequently, Sarkeesian and other women in the gaming world they saw as contributing to the rise of SJW culture.[58] Fans under the Gamergate banner called Quinn's parents, publicized her personal offline contact information (a process known as "doxxing"), and sent death threats to both Quinn and Sarkeesian, as well as other perceived SJWs, dismissing any male who came to their defense as a "cuck" (that is, cuckold) desperate for sexual attention.

Young, ambitious journalists and public figures, particularly on the right, amplified the media phenomenon. Mike Cernovich, Roosh V, and Milo Yiannopoulos—all of whom would go on to become alt-right or alt-lite celebrities—came to prominence sympathetically covering Gamergate's trolls. Among Gamergate's opponents, conversely, was Brianna Wu—an early target of Gamergate harassment now attempting a 2020 run for Congress in Massachusetts.

As journalist Charlie Warzel writes, "Gamergate's DNA is everywhere on the internet. . . . Everything Is Gamergate. It's evident in the way foreign actors use bot accounts to manipulate public sentiment. . . . One can draw a crooked line between Gamergate's online advertiser boycott, which caused Intel to pull ads from gaming sites like Gamasutra, and Sean Hannity's 2017 campaign against Keurig coffee, which led viewers to hurl coffee machines out of windows and post the destruction on Twitter; between anti-feminist YouTubers taking to Patreon to fund their screeds and the shady crowdfunding campaigns to 'fund the wall,' the pledge drives from Pizzagate or QAnon truthers."[59]

Gamergate wasn't the first widespread movement by Reddit or 4chan dwellers. As early as 2003, troll hacktivist group Anonymous, which successfully launched attacks on institutions as disparate as the Church of Scientology, the Westboro Baptist Church, and ISIS, had sprung up on 4chan's /b/ board, devoted to random and often offensive content. But Gamergate was, without a doubt, the first encroachment of Anonymous-style trolling on a sufficient scale to dominate the cultural conversation.

It was the first battle, too, between two distinct brands of religious Remixed who have come to dominate the wider cultural discourse: progressive social justice activists and their reactionary rivals. You might even call it the opening salvo in a new kind of culture war, not between Christians and secularists but between two different, utterly contemporary civil religions that have emerged in the new Remixed culture.

Without making excuses for the actions of the movement's trolls, it's easy to see the wider cultural root of the harassment that followed Gjoni's posts. Both camps of fandom—which is to say, the social-justice-minded would-be reformers and their reactionary, anti-SJW counterparts—took it for granted that video game culture was theirs. Both groups felt empowered, if not entitled, to demand change in media properties they felt represented women insufficiently well or had become too "cucked" in supporting the "feminist agenda." Whatever their methods, both groups never doubted that it was the right of a fan to have their property of veneration look like them and reflect their values.

Just two years later, the inheritors of Gamergate clashed once more over an all-female reboot of *Ghostbusters*, starring Melissa McCarthy and Leslie Jones. The film was designed quite nakedly to pander to self-identified feminist fans seeking to revel in the sheer fact of role reversal. Director Paul Feig cast notorious hunk and *Thor* actor Chris Hemsworth in the "secretary" role—a decision seemingly custom designed for crowingly empowered new media headlines like *BuzzFeed's* "Chris Hemsworth's Character in 'Ghostbusters' Is a Bimbo and It's Perfect."[60] Meanwhile, mostly male fans, outraged that SJWs had taken over "their" property, launched a viral campaign designed to sink the movie's performance, Tweeting racial abuse at Leslie Jones until she left the site and tanking the movie's rating on review aggregators like Rotten Tomatoes.[61] Three years later, Jason Reitman (son of original *Ghostbusters* director Ivan Reitman) announced he'd be making yet another *Ghostbusters* film starring the original (male) characters, due for release in 2020. Reitman told an interviewer he intended to "hand the movie back to the fans," a remark that was widely taken by both admirers and detractors of the 2016 film as an indictment of Feig's work.[62]

Whatever Reitman meant by the remark, he was tapping into a wider cultural zeitgeist. Our pop culture icons are indeed being *handed back to the fans*. And, with that, our understanding of authority—of what it means to tell a story, of who gets to shape it, of who is expected to conform—is undergoing a colossal shift. Stories now exist not to teach us or inform us, but to *serve* us. As we create new models of our own—

fan fiction, or memes, or any other aspects of our digital footprint—we learn to expect stories made specifically in our image.

It's impossible to understand Remixed spirituality—and the degree to which we seek out more precisely calibrated identities and tribes—without understanding the way that Internet culture, and fan culture in particular, primed us to expect, and even demand, narratives, practices, and communities that we found personally meaningful.

Seventy years ago—at the height of institutional, mainline Protestant America, our social options were relatively narrow. We could participate in the culture of our hometown and our family. Or, more rarely, we could participate in one of a few subcultures available to us. If these cultures, these communities, these foundational truths didn't satisfy us, we had little recourse: we'd either adapt or consign ourselves to a life on the margins. But now, we have access to people across the country and the world who think and feel and want the exact same things that we do. And we participate in a culture that incentivizes this individualism, which necessarily extends into our religious and spiritual lives. Why force our beliefs into a narrow category of organized religion, with its doctrines and creeds, when we can cobble together a metaphysical system that demands of us no moral, ethical, spiritual, or aesthetic compromises? Why not combine meditation with sage cleansing with the odd Christmas service and its aesthetically pleasing carols? Why not use the language of Hogwarts houses to talk about good and evil, alongside the rhetoric of social justice and metaphors garnered from *Star Wars*?

This, of course, silos us, for better and for worse. On the one hand, we're able to connect to people just like us, and to join with them in order to create a micro consumer-voter base: advocating as a group for policies, products, and cultural changes that we would like to see in the world. On the other hand, the social ease with which we can find people who share our views disincentivizes us from establishing common ground with those whose perspectives are different from (or simply insufficiently similar to) our own. Because we are no longer forced to base our primary social interactions on our physical and geographic neighbors, we have less reason to conform, or even to invest in them.

The strengthening of digital tribes inevitably weakens our commitment to less-targeted ones.

Marketers and would-be gurus have been swift to celebrate this change as a kind of revolutionary (and profitable) collapse of the mainstream. As Seth Godin crows in his aptly titled manifesto *We Are All Weird: The Rise of Tribes and the End of Normal,* "Do you want to create for and market to the fast-increasing population that isn't normal? . . . Which side are you on—fighting for the status quo or rooting for weird?"[63] Godin's implications are as unsubtle as they are unsettling. Weirdness—which is to say, a willful departure from any bedrock unifying culture—is the new black. Our highly specific opinions about *Star Wars,* or *Harry Potter,* or Justin Bieber, or the best romantic pairing on *Riverdale,* or the best character on *Glee,* unite us in narrower and narrower ways. We're used to getting exactly the stories and the communities we want, on demand, whether we're social justice warriors who want to discuss the inspirational political progressiveness of *Harry Potter* or erotically minded fan fiction aficionados who just share a fetish for stories where Harry, Severus Snape, and Draco Malfoy get it on in a three-way.

An old Internet adage associated with fandom culture, known colloquially as "Rule 34," states that if something exists, there is porn of it on the Internet. But the same is true more broadly online. Any concept, any ideology, any preference you can think of, you'll find a community of people willing to engage you on it. Or, to propose an evolution to Rule 34: if it exists, there is a tribe of it.

Seventy-odd years ago, the major cultural and spiritual project of America—funneled through midcentury mainline Protestantism—was liberal ecumenism: the utopian vision of varied, disparate traditions and denominations coming together to seek common ground and effect widespread change. Today, that project feels hopelessly obsolete. If once we sought common institutional ground, we now seek a kaleidoscope of kindred spirits. We are all our own individual religions. And the cultural myths and narratives we tell, customize, and individualize—a new kind of fan fiction—continue to shape the world around us.

In 1820, Thomas Jefferson, a committed Deist who preferred the teachings of Jesus Christ to the idea of him as a metaphysical savior, created a bespoke Bible. Cutting and pasting the lines from the Gospels that he thought best reflected his vision of Christ, excising those passages (like the miracles) that didn't quite fit, Jefferson created what might be considered the first American fan fiction: *The Life and Morals of Jesus of Nazareth*.[64] Now, we're all doing the same thing.

five

WELLNESS CULTURE AND
THE REBIRTH OF NEW THOUGHT

"IT'S ABOUT YOU," SAYS THE PRETERNATURALLY CHISELED woman with platinum blonde hair and tattoos. "Your perk. Your goals. Your drive."

"This is about you," several more equally lithe athletes echo. "What are you looking for? What are you going to come for? What do you need to be?"

"Everybody needs something different," one adds, before the litany starts up again. "What drives you? What motivates you? What inspires you? What lights you up?"

"Everybody gets something different" out of the experience—at least according to the advertisement, a 2017 two-minute commercial for meditative-cycling behemoth SoulCycle.[1] The "Find It" campaign, dreamed up by ad agency Laird and Partners, captures the essence of the fitness brand's sacralized promise. SoulCycle isn't just selling an exercise class or a weight loss aid. It's selling a double ideal of purification: one simultaneously characterized by material improvement (you'll look like Michelle Obama or Lady Gaga, two notable SoulCycle alums) and by spiritual transcendence. You're not just peddling on a bike to lose weight. You're peddling to become a better person: to become—in the words plastered on the cycling room's walls—a Renegade, a Hero, a Warrior.

SoulCycle's classes—which cost $34 before you add the (required) clip-in cycling shoes and (not required, but still recommended) bottled water—transform physical fitness into ethereal asceticism. The instructors—largely selected from a pool of actors and dancers for their Instagram followings and charisma rather than their fitness expertise—shout out motivational mantras ("Today is all about *you*"; "You were created *by* a purpose, for a purpose") from a raised platform, surrounded by lit candles. Participants gather in a semicircle, spinning furiously while following ever-more-complex (and, according to some exercise professionals, potentially dangerous) choreography, which largely includes push-ups on the bicycle that resemble genuflections.[2] The most dedicated and experienced members of the "pack" (signs posted within all SoulCycle studios also refer to it as a tribe, a crew, a posse, a cult, a gang, a community, and, somewhat confusingly, a soul) are encouraged to sit up front in order to lead the group in the choreography. Another sign, headlined Soul Etiquette, warns would-be cyclers that "there is a direct correlation between your energy and your neighbor's ride. If you want to do your own thing, please don't ride in the front row."

SoulCycle's Instagram, which boasts nearly four hundred thousand followers, posts regular mantras and memes lauding the virtues of SoulCycle as an emotional and spiritual outlet. According to an anonymous user quoted by the company's Instagram, a SoulCycle class is "an amazing place to cry uninterrupted for 45 minutes"; according to another, "God is a woman, and she's a SoulCycle instructor." The account celebrates motivational quotes by instructors: "Identify each of your limitations . . . and defy them"; "Focus on the things you can control"; "Don't shy from it. Reckon with it. Harness it."[3]

The company's official manifesto, likewise, doubles down on the class's spiritual and social underpinnings. ("Your Soul Matters," reads one subheading in the 2015 SEC filing.) At SoulCycle, the company promises, "our riders feed off the group's shared energy and motivation to push themselves to their greatest potential. In becoming part of our community, our riders are instilled with greater awareness of not only their bodies but also their emotions. We believe this awareness leads to healthier decisions, relationships and lives." Elsewhere in the document, the company is even more explicit: "SoulCycle is more than a business, it's a movement."

This may seem like little more than pseudo-utopian marketing pablum, designed to cloak a functional weight-loss business with a veneer of spiritual legitimacy. But the thing is, it's working. Between 2006 — when the company was founded by talent agent Julie Rice, real estate broker Elizabeth Cutler, and spin instructor Ruth Zukerman — and today, SoulCycle opened ninety locations across the United States, serving about three hundred thousand unique riders, and is now valued at about $900 million.[4] SoulCycle's users take about 10,378 rides per day. The company is expanding into additional fitness classes (it's currently piloting a program called SoulAnnex, dedicated to off-the-bike training) and at-home exercise media.[5] Cutler, Rice, and Zukerman have all since left the company — Rice and Cutler cashed out with an estimated $90 million each — after selling a 97 percent stake to luxury-gym behemoth Equinox.

Meanwhile, for its members, SoulCycle is becoming something akin to a cult, if not a full-fledged religion. Harvard Divinity School researchers Casper ter Kuile and Angie Thurston identified SoulCycle — alongside rugged fitness phenomenon CrossFit — as one of today's most notable secular religions.[6] Members are motivated to regularly attend, structure their schedules around access to classes, and feel a sense of tribal loyalty to one another. According to ter Kuile and Thurston's research, the ritual nature of SoulCycle attendance — the selection of a favored bike spot, say, or a preferred instructor and time — allows it to become a significant, if not the most significant, source of order in participants' lives. Often, ter Kuile and Thurston say, the very best instructors end up taking quasi-pastoral roles, fielding questions like "Should I divorce my husband?" alongside queries about calories or bicycle form.

SoulCycle has become a cultural phenomenon disproportionate to its (already very large) user base. But the mentality it has pioneered—marketing personal self-improvement and commodified self-care as quasi-religious experiences—has gone viral. The sense of meaning and purpose that contemporary wellness culture provides can be found in health and self-improvement discourse all over the United States. At its core, wellness isn't simply a marketing scheme, or even a self-help mantra. It's a cohesive philosophy of life: one rooted in both ethical notions about the self and metaphysical notions about energy. If fandom provided us with a structure for today's Remixed religious culture, wellness provides its implicit theology.

It's a theology, fundamentally, of division: the authentic, intuitional *self*—both body and soul—and the artificial, malevolent forces of *society*, *rules*, and *expectations*. We are born good, but we are tricked, by Big Pharma, by processed food, by civilization itself, into living something that falls short of our best life. Our sins, if they exist at all, lie in insufficient self-attention or self-care: false modesty, undeserved humilities, refusing to shine bright. We have not merely the inalienable right but the moral responsibility to take care of ourselves first before directing any attention to others. We have to listen to ourselves, to behave authentically, in tune with what our intuition dictates.

Others, after all, are potential enemies. The people in our lives, and the demands they make upon us, might well be sources of "toxic energy" if we're not careful to avoid them. The food we eat is full of "toxins," too.

Within this model, self-care—in the form of fitness classes, intense meditation apps, mindfulness courses, or ten-step skin-care routines—becomes at once a form of self-love and self-discipline. We are not challenged to love our neighbor as ourselves, or to overcome materialistic urges. Instead, our challenges come in the form of intense and often expensive rituals—that morning SoulCycle class, an evening thirty-minute beauty routine—that reaffirm our commitment to perfecting ourselves. If our bodies were once temples, to use a popular diet mantra, now they're miniature gods. Our ontological purpose, as human beings, is to live our best life: to shake off the demands of society and the meat industry and, well, other people.

This gospel of wellness has permeated the Western world. The wellness industry is a $4.2 trillion market—up from $3.7 trillion in 2015.[7] Across the globe, we spend half as much on wellness products as we do on medical health care. In America alone, the burgeoning "wellness real estate" industry—in which particularly wellness-minded customers can buy into purpose-built wellness communities—has reached $52.5 billion and is projected to grow. The American workplace wellness market—wherein employers seek to boost productivity by purchasing programs and opportunities for their workers—has reached $17.6 billion. There are twenty-one thousand spas in the United States, and Americans visit them 179 million times a year.[8]

Wellness and lifestyle brands are among the most profitable ways for mid-level or aging celebrities to build their social reach and outlast the vicissitudes of Hollywood-based fame. The most prominent of these is Goop, founded in 2008 as a relatively informal newsletter by *Shakespeare in Love* actress Gwyneth Paltrow before metastasizing into a $250 million aspirational brand that boasts 2.4 million unique viewers a month.[9]

Goop has promoted, among other things, a $66 jade "yoni egg" you're supposed to put in your vagina, a $185 Nepalese singing bowl, a $175 "Bel Ritual Candle" that makes noise as it melts, $40 tarot cards, and a $27 elixir that calls itself "Psychic Vampire Repellent," whose listed ingredients include "sonically tuned water, rosewater, grain alcohol, sea salt, colloidal silver, therapeutic grade oils of: rosemary, juniper and lavender; a unique and complex blend of gem elixirs, including but not limited to: black tourmaline, lapis lazuli, ruby, labradorite, bloodstone, aqua aura, black onyx, garnet, pyrite and nuummite; reiki, sound waves, moonlight, love, [and] reiki charged crystals."[10] (A 2017 collaboration between *Goop* magazine and *Vogue* publishers Condé Nast fell through, in part, because Paltrow would not allow any of Goop's scientific claims to be fact-checked.)

But Goop is far from the only notable celebrity-helmed lifestyle brand out there. Onetime action star Jessica Alba built the $1 billion

Honest Company, focusing on natural and eco-friendly products (including a $175 vegan-leather diaper bag) geared largely toward young mothers.[11] Former reality television star Kristin Cavallari published a *True Roots* cookbook focusing on gluten-free, healthy cooking.[12] Former *Catwoman* star Halle Berry partnered with wellness festival Beautycon to launch a website devoted to "building a deeper connection between health, wellness, and what we know as being beautiful."[13] In 2016, media titan Arianna Huffington launched wellness company Thrive Global, which focuses on partnering with corporations to ensure that their employees get enough sleep and cut back on their screen time. (An early Thrive blog post featured Amazon CEO Jeff Bezos boasting about getting eight hours of sleep per night.)[14]

That doesn't even include the people who have become celebrities through wellness culture, often harnessing the power of Instagram to mobilize thousands or even millions of young followers, like Amanda Chantal Bacon, whose smoothie and supplements company, Moon Juice, proffers items like Brain Dust ($55 for 2.2 ounces), an "adaptogenic potion" that "lights up your brain and increases mental flow . . . toning the brain waves . . . that connect to creativity."[15] Today, Moon Juice's products are widely available at mainstream retailers like Sephora. (Bacon initially rose to viral fame in spring 2015 after publishing her "food diary"—which was short on actual food and heavy on "vanilla mushroom protein . . . cordyceps, reishi, maca, and Shilajit resin . . . [with] ho shou wu and pearl . . . [and] three quinton shots for mineralization and two lipospheric vitamin B-complex packets for energy"—in *Elle*.)[16] So, too, Freelee the Banana Girl, an oft-nude Australian vegan blogger who in 2014 racked up an astonishing 425,000 Instagram followers and 785,000 YouTube followers by encouraging viewers to eat "monomeals" of a single ingredient, usually raw, usually bananas (Freelee boasted that she ate up to fifty-one bananas a day).[17]

Most of the products sold by these companies and influencers target a very particular demographic: affluent (or would-be affluent), young-to-middle-aged white women. At New York City's the Well, for example (not a gym, according to the advertising copy, but rather "a complete ecosystem for wellness . . . designed for urban professionals"), you can pay $375 per month for access to yoga studios, meditation studios, a juice bar, energy healing classes, and an on-site acupuncturist.[18] The Elizabeth Arden Red Door salons—once the expensive epitome of mid-century hauteur—have likewise rebranded as Mynd: a "self-care journey," whose advertising copy promises, with ungrammatical boldness, bespoke "self-care you can confidently say is my."

But among the most revelatory examples of contemporary wellness culture is the transformation of a once decidedly middle-class phenomenon. In September 2018, the stalwart, accessible, and affordable (the app costs $3 to $6 a week) weight-loss company Weight Watchers rebranded. WW, as the relaunched company called itself, was no longer focused on that grossly corporeal quality, *weight*. Instead, WW (which now stands, according to the company, for "wellness that works") announced that it would be promoting an "overall approach to health and wellbeing of inspiring powerful habits rooted in science."[19] It has since pioneered a partnership with $250 million meditation app Headspace, allowing WW users to cultivate mindfulness to develop both healthier eating habits and a healthier relationship with the wider world.

If SoulCycle, Goop, and Thrive represent the apex of early, aspirational wellness culture, then WW reveals its inevitable democratization. Wellness is no longer an exclusive, luxury good, but rather something we are all responsible for fostering within ourselves. It's not something you dream about doing (the same way you'd dream, for example, about owning a yacht or going on vacation to Tahiti). In fact, you no longer have any excuse for *not* doing it. It's not aspirational, but simply obligatory.

Today's wellness culture has trickled down to the middle class, inculcating a far broader demographic with the idea that your relationship to yourself sets the tone for your very worth. Whether it's a SoulCycle class or a week on WW, wellness culture thrives on the notion that self-care is at the foundation of our very purpose. Objectivism as asceticism: at once tempting consumers with the idea that their primary obligation is to themselves and punishing them with a seemingly endless list of requirements necessary for optimizing that selfishness.

As the instructor at one SoulCycle class I attended in New York put it, echoing sentiments I've heard more broadly, if less explicitly, in other fitness classes throughout the city: "This is *your time*. Don't focus on anybody else. Other people take away your energy. Just focus on *yourself*." The implicit mantra of wellness is equal parts Ayn Rand and John Calvin: you're not just allowed but in fact obligated to focus on yourself—but, no matter how much you do, it will never be good enough.

Scholars Carl Cederström and André Spicer put this particularly succinctly: "Wellness is not just something we choose," they write of our contemporary obsession with self-optimization. "It is a moral obligation. We must consider it at every turn of our lives. While we often see it spelled out in advertisements and life-style magazines, this command is also transmitted more insidiously, so that we don't know whether it is imparted from the outside or spontaneously arises within ourselves. This is what we call the wellness command."[20]

But the religious quality of wellness goes beyond mere moralism. While it's true that the imperative of self-care has an implicitly moral character to it, the religion of wellness is as much about enchanting the world as it is about judging it.

The language of energy, toxins, adaptogens, and neuron velocity— so much of it rooted in flawed or outright fallacious science—is also about providing us with a sense of meaning, of order. There is an implicit theology to wellness culture, even if it more closely resembles the Force of *Star Wars* than any more concretely developed system. Energy—something that is at once spiritual, metaphorical, and scientifically concrete—runs through us all. We can tap into its primal and mystical properties to achieve concrete, real-world results.

As clairvoyant, energy-healer, and "certified soul coach" Jakki Smith-Leonardini puts it in an article for Goop, "Everything is made of energy and has its own unique vibration, including you. Everything is in a constant state of receiving and radiating energy. The frequency of this energy falls on a spectrum from light to dark. Light energy is infinite, effortless, and rooted in love. Dark or shadow energy is dense and rooted in fear. As an electromagnetic being, you attract experiences and relationships that match your frequency."[21]

Or, as Australian self-help guru Rhonda Byrne puts it in *The Secret*, the best-selling 2006 book widely promoted by Oprah Winfrey, "If you're feeling good, then you're creating a future that's on track with your desires. If you're feeling bad, you're creating a future that's off track with your desires. As you go about your day, the law of attraction is working in every second. Everything we think and feel is creating our future. If you're worried or in fear, then you're bringing more of that into your life throughout the day."[22] Elsewhere, she doubles down on the metaphysical basis for this assertion: "You are the most powerful magnet in the Universe! You contain a magnetic power within you that is more powerful than anything in this world and this unfathomable magnetic power is emitted through your thoughts."[23]

Implicit in the wellness ideology of energy is that the world is inherently meaningful, even orderly. "Positive" feelings, like love or happiness, are concretely and measurably different from "negative" feelings like fear. When we tap into and improve our personal energy, we'll have a more fulfilling life; not just because we'll feel better, but because (by some metaphysical law) better things will happen to us.

Americans are increasingly taking this seriously. In 2018, a full 42 percent of Americans said they believed that "spiritual energy can be located in physical things." Those numbers were highest among the "unaffiliated" (47 percent) and, more specifically, the "nothing in particular" (61 percent). But Christians said they shared this ideology too. Thirty-seven percent of self-identified Christians also said they believed in "energy." This Remixed theology, in other words, isn't just found among people who consciously subscribe to it, such as the SBNRs. It's also found in hybrid form within ostensibly Christian culture.

It's important to understand that this intuitional gospel of wellness isn't new. In fact, it's an integral part of the American religious tradition, and has been since at least the nineteenth century.

THE REASONABLY OLD HISTORY OF NEW THOUGHT

"Anything is yours, if you only want it hard enough. Just think of it. ANY-THING. Try it. Try it in earnest and you will succeed. It is the operation of a mighty Law."[24]

Sound familiar? This maxim wouldn't sound out of place on Goop, or in Byrne's *The Secret*, or on SoulCycle's motivational Instagram. But these words come from a 1901 book, *Thought-Force in Business and Everyday Life*, by one William Walker Atkinson. Atkinson was a practitioner of New Thought, a cult self-help movement that took nineteenth-century America by storm.

Also known as the "mind-cure," New Thought was among the first Remixed mainstream spiritual traditions in the country. It blended extremely liberal Christianity with (heavily whitewashed versions of) Eastern meditative practices and the philosophical underpinnings of Transcendentalism—a smaller movement popular with members of the New England intelligentsia like Ralph Waldo Emerson (the "Sage of Concord"), Henry David Thoreau, and Bronson Alcott (father of Louisa May). For Transcendentalists—who were influenced by German Idealism and European Romanticism—the self was a person's only source for knowledge, or experience, of any higher power. Organized religion, or any mainstream institution for that matter, only got in the way of man's fundamental intuition and trust in himself. As Emerson put it in 1842, "The height, the deity of man is to be self-sustained, to need no gift, no foreign force. Society is good when it does not violate me; but best when it is likest to solitude. Everything real is self-existent. . . . All that you call the world is the shadow of that substance which you are, the perpetual creation of the powers of thought, of those that are dependent and of those that are independent of your will."[25]

The cultural influence of the Transcendentalist movement was largely confined to literature and the arts. But its successor, New Thought, became a mainstream phenomenon.

The movement proper began with a New Hampshire clockmaker named Phineas Parkhurst Quimby. In the 1830s, Quimby developed an interest in a popular craze of the time, "animal magnetism" or "mesmerism," a movement that had begun to gain traction in both Europe and the United States. Pioneered by German doctor Franz Mesmer (from whom we get the name), mesmerism had become something of a cult fad in the United States. Mesmer taught that all living things had a *Lebensmagnetismus* (living magnetism) that could be manipulated through psychic means, including hypnosis. Like today's vision of energy, the animal magnetism of mesmerism was characterized as at once scientific and spiritual—something at the heart of every part of the human condition.

Mesmer taught that there was "only one illness—and only one healing." All forms of ill-health and bad luck could be traced to flaws with one's *Lebensmagnetismus*, flaws only Mesmer and his followers could heal.[26] In theatrical displays—often open to the public—Mesmer would relax his patients, then run either his hands or magnets over their body, realigning their *Lebensmagnetismus*. By the 1840s, the craze for animal magnetism was so popular that there were over two hundred Mesmer-style faith healers in the city of Boston alone.[27]

Quimby soon became fascinated with mesmerism, attending multiple demonstrations by notable mesmeric practitioners Charles Poyen and Robert Collyer. Within a few years, Quimby began practicing and demonstrating mesmerism publicly across the Northeast, curing supplicants of their various ailments and diseases.

Over time, however, Quimby became suspicious of his own methods. Why did one form of hypnotism work on some people and a different form on others? He ultimately came to the conclusion that it was the patients' own attitudes, and not hypnosis itself, that allowed them to be cured. The patients who were best able to harness their own *Lebensmagnetismus*, thinking positively about their symptoms, were the ones who were best able to cure themselves.

And so, New Thought—with its emphasis on the power of personal responsibility and energy—was born. Quimby dismissed the modern medical establishment as causing, rather than curing, diseases with negativity. "I never try to convince a patient that his trouble arises from calomel or any other poison," he was known to say, "but the poison of the doctor's opinion in admitting a disease."[28] Instead, Quimby pioneered what he called the "science of health," equal parts proto-psychotherapy and positive thinking, with a little bit of Christianity thrown in. Jesus Christ himself didn't perform miracles, Quimby argued. Rather, Jesus—who was, Quimby thought, just a little bit more enlightened than the average man—had figured out how to harness the power of this science to create apparent miracles, which anyone who learned this form of wisdom could themselves replicate, helping them discover what Quimby called "the Christ within."[29]

By the 1860s, Quimby was seeing up to five hundred patients a year (scholar John Haller estimates that he saw at least twelve thousand in the course of his teaching), circulating his own published philosophical works, and leading a new generation of disciple-healers.[30]

At the core of Quimby's thought was an emphasis on both personal responsibility and individual energy. Human beings caused their own illness or misfortune and could only get better by changing their inner psychological state. "It may seem strange to those in health," Quimby wrote in 1865, "that our beliefs affect us. The fact is, there is nothing of us but belief. It is the whole capital and stock in trade of man. It is all that can be changed, and embraces everything man has made or ever will make."[31]

Quimby's successors only intensified this sense of personal responsibility, extending it not merely to physical health but to material success and good fortune, as well as to a wider spiritual question of connecting with the divine. God—or at least a nebulously defined higher power— was *in you*, and you had both the right and the responsibility to channel that spiritual relationship in order to gain personally fulfilling results.

As one of the most influential New Thought practitioners and teachers of the second half of the nineteenth century, Ralph Waldo Trine, put it in his 1897 self-help manifesto, *In Tune with the Infinite*: "In just the degree that we come into a conscious realization of our oneness with the Infinite Life, and open ourselves to the Divine inflow, do we actualize in ourselves the qualities and powers of the Infinite Life, do we make ourselves channels through which the Infinite Intelligence and Power can work. In just the degree in which you realize your oneness with the Infinite Spirit, you will exchange dis-ease for ease, inharmony for harmony, suffering and pain for abounding health and strength."[32]

Among Quimby's most devoted patients turned disciples was Mary Baker Eddy, who subsequently founded the Church of Christ, Scientist (aka Christian Science) in 1879, blending orthodox Christian theology with a belief in the power of faith healing, animal magnetism, and other quasi-occult elements. Eddy's most famous self-help book, *Science and Health with Key to the Scriptures*, also became a pop-culture phenomenon, selling over four hundred thousand copies by 1900.[33] At its peak in the 1930s, Christian Science boasted about 270,000 members; today, that number has dwindled to less than 100,000.[34]

By the twentieth century, though, New Thought had fused with the unbridled capitalism of the Gilded Age to focus as much on wealth as on a relationship with the divine. New Thought pioneers like James Allen (whose books included *From Poverty to Power* in 1901, *The Eight Pillars of Prosperity* in 1911, and *Foundation Stones to Happiness and Success* posthumously in 1913) celebrated what they saw as the survival of the fittest. People who correctly applied their energy toward self-betterment got rich. Those who chose to pity themselves or their situations would simply remain poor or get poorer. "A man does not come to the almshouse or the jail by the tyranny of fate or circumstance but by the pathway of groveling thoughts and base desires," Allen wrote in 1903's *As a Man Thinketh*.[35] His advice to those who were dealing with unethical employers or corrupt landlords was to, well, suck it up and think positively: "By so ennobling your present surroundings, you will rise above them and above the need of them and at the right time you will pass into the better house and surroundings that have all along been waiting for you and that you have now fitted yourself to occupy."[36]

Another New Thought business guru, Charles Benjamin Newcomb, echoed similar sentiments in 1897's *All's Right With the World*.

Celebrating what he called "the banquet of life," Newcomb warned the sick, the poor, and the infirm that "none is really shut out of the feast except the self-exiled."[37] Critiquing social justice movements of the day, Newcomb argued that sympathy for the poor was a surefire way of stymieing their growth. Instead, Newcomb propagated a mantra that seems straight out of SoulCycle's Instagram feed: "I am well. I am opulent. I have everything. I do right. I know."[38]

In many ways, this held heady potential for human liberty: we are all responsible for our own lives and successes. But it also held within it a terrifying kernel of responsibility—one that has pervaded many of the wellness and New Age movements we see in America today. *If something bad happens to you, it's your fault.* Positivity, within this paradigm, becomes both a blessing and a curse.

One of the movement's most famous practitioners, scholar and writer William James (brother of novelist Henry), captured this tension, writing of the movement in 1907:

> *The blind have been made to see, the halt to walk; lifelong invalids have had their health restored. . . . Cheerfulness has been restored to countless homes. The mind-cure principles are beginning so to pervade the air that one catches their spirit at second-hand. One hears of the "Gospel of Relaxation" of the "Don't Worry Movement," of people who repeat to themselves, "Youth, health, vigor!" when dressing in the morning, as their motto for the day. Complaints of the weather are getting to be forbidden in many households; and more and more people are recognizing it to be bad form to speak of disagreeable sensations, or to make much of the ordinary inconveniences and ailments of life.*[39]

Like its contemporary wellness iteration, New Thought spilled over into plenty of explicitly Christian spaces, creating new (you might even say remixed) ideologies that divinized positivity and treated the outward signs of success—health and wealth—as proof of a person's internal and spiritual worth.

Among the most influential books in American religious history is 1952's *The Power of Positive Thinking*. Written by Norman Vincent Peale, then a pastor at Marble Collegiate Church in New York City, the book blended orthodox Christianity with a distinctively New Thought obsession with positivity. Exhorting his readers to "picturize, prayerize, and actualize,"[40] among his most famous slogans, Peale assured them that "When you expect the best, you release a magnetic force in your mind which by a law of attraction tends to bring the best to you."[41] Peale may formally have been a Christian, but the exercises he promulgated were pure New Thought: "Formulate and stamp indelibly on your mind a mental picture of yourself as succeeding," he wrote. "Hold this picture tenaciously. Never permit it to fade. Your mind will seek to develop the picture. . . . Do not build up obstacles in your imagination."[42] Peale's legacy extends beyond his wide readership. At Marble Collegiate, he was the personal pastor to the Trump family and officiated Donald Trump's 1977 wedding to Ivana. (For his part, Trump has frequently extolled Peale's virtues and cited him as an influence.)

But the most New Thought–inspired Christian movement of all may be the prosperity gospel, which holds that divine favor yields material, financial results. The prosperity gospel grew out of something called the Word of Faith movement, essentially a Christianized version of New Thought that took hold in the Charismatic and Pentecostal churches that flourished in the 1960s and '70s as an antiestablishment reaction to the more sedate institutional church culture of the time. Televangelists like Kenneth Hagin, Kenneth Copeland, Joel Osteen, and Jim and Tammy Faye Bakker (whose Christian theme park, Heritage USA, was at one time the third-most-visited site in America) preached that prosperity and good health were part and parcel of the Christian promise. Jesus hadn't just died on the cross to save your souls, the narrative went, but your bodies and your bank accounts too. True believers—those who held and expressed sufficient faith (and who, more often than not, demonstrated that faith by donating to churches)—would inevitably be rewarded.

A little under 20 percent of Americans officially subscribe to the prosperity gospel. But a higher proportion, 31 percent, say that they agree with what is essentially the gospel's main tenet: "If you give your money to God, God will bless you with more money." And a staggering 61 percent of American Christians agree with the New Thought–tinged fundamental premise of the prosperity gospel: "God wants you to be rich."[43]

Contemporary wellness culture, in other words, wasn't formed in a vacuum. Its implicit ideology—that the universe is conspiring to keep the success you deserve from you until you reach out and take it—has been part of the American religious landscape for centuries, and has already spilled over into both explicitly religious and SBNR spaces. But where contemporary wellness culture departs from its New Thought forebears is in the degree to which it *doesn't* rely on a single clear conception, scientific or spiritual, of how it works. Few SoulCycle instructors quote Quimby (or, in all likelihood, even know who he is). Ideas about energy, wellness, and spiritual journeys are ubiquitous, but they're rarely coherent or wedded to a clearly structured metaphysical system involving, for example, animal magnetism.

While Quimby's and Trine's early writings, Peale's *Power of Positive Thinking*, and the prosperity gospel all at least paid nominal lip service to the idea that there was some kind of divine or objectively moral system out there, contemporary wellness culture implicitly collapses the distinction between the divine self and its purely corporeal counterpart. The energy you tap into in a yoga class and the energy you get from drinking a Moon Juice concoction and the energy you get from positive thinking are at once unifying spiritual constructs—the world is an inherently meaningful place with energy running through it—and gauges of your personal material contentedness. The world revolves around you. The existence of a higher power and the dewiness of your skin (or balance of your bank account, or circumference of your waist) are inextricably intertwined. It's the best of both worlds. It combines moral relativism with a comforting veneer of metaphysical universalism: an inherently meaningful world where you can still, ethically, do whatever you want.

Wellness begins—and ends—with the self.

THE SELF WE'RE SELF-CARING FOR

"People mistakenly assume that a meditation rooted in compassion begins with a deliberate focus on other people. Not so. We must first cultivate a sense of loving-kindness toward ourselves with the intention of being kinder and more forgiving toward others. For many people, it can feel strange and perhaps even indulgent to spend a meditation directing kindness inward. But the more we notice how it feels to take time out for ourselves and the more we enjoy how good that feels, the more easily we are able to share it outward. Compassion for others begins with self-compassion."

This paragraph of advertising copy introduces a would-be buyer to Headspace, a meditation app worth $250 million as of 2017.[44] Founded by an advertising guru for Axe deodorant, Richard Pierson, and a British Buddhist monk, Andy Puddicombe, Headspace is meditation for the mindfulness generation. Intentionally stripped of religious or spiritually loaded language, Headspace caters to beginners to meditation. Targeted "packs"—for anxiety, or fear of flying, or patience, or generosity, or cancer—allow users to specify their area of greatest need. (A built-in SOS button—designed for use when a customer is having a full-on mental breakdown—apparently had a 44 percent jump in usage the week after Donald Trump's election.)[45] Today, Headspace has been downloaded at least eleven million times. Its user base grows by approximately 15 percent per month. Jessica Alba is an investor. Gwyneth Paltrow and Richard Branson are fans. Big corporations—Goldman Sachs and the Dana-Farber Cancer Institute among them—have bought bulk subscriptions for their employees.[46] (Meanwhile, General Motors, General Mills, and Target have all pioneered additional mindfulness programs for their employees. Google even developed its own, Search Inside Yourself, created by in-company engineer Chade-Meng Tan in 2007.)

But it's Headspace's blithely capitalistic ads—"I meditate to crush it," one subway-plastered client testimony reads; "I meditate to have the edge," says another—that have made it a particular target of media coverage and, at times, suspicion. Meditation, in Headspace's rhetoric, is a kind of self-optimization: encouraging users to focus on themselves — their thoughts, their needs, their desires — in order to, as in New Thought, improve their surroundings.

The "loving-kindness" Headspace refers to derives from what is known in Tibetan Pali as *mettā bhāvanā*. It was historically practiced as an outwardly focused meditation of love. Monks would, for example, chant and meditate on their good wishes for the laity. Its genesis was focused on the other. But in Headspace's paradigm, other-focus — outwardly directed love — comes secondary to self-care.

Ironically, the term "self-care" began as a political one. Black feminist activist Audre Lorde coined the term in 1988.[47] For Lorde, self-care was about valuing traditionally marginalized bodies, those that society as a whole had abdicated responsibility for. "Caring for myself is not self-indulgence," she wrote then. "It is self-preservation, and that is an act of political warfare." But self-care has long since been commodified.

There are currently almost fourteen million posts on Instagram with the hashtag #selfcare. A representative sample: A weight-loss coach and Herbalife sales rep in Chicago exhorting followers to "fall in love with taking care of yourself. Mind. Body. Spirit."[48] A New Hampshire yoga practitioner showing off a pose (additional hashtags include #raiseyourvibration, #journeyjunkie and #namaslay).[49] A woman in a bathing suit in an outdoor bathtub in Peru (#solotravel).[50] Self-care has become a marketing slogan, one designed to lend legitimacy to behavior that might, in other moral systems, be considered merely selfish.

A 2018 article on popular women's website *Bustle*, for example, offers a primer on "How to Tell Someone You're Flaking on Your Plans for Self-Care": "Cancelling, and therefore instantly signing yourself up for a night with Netflix instead of a night out at a restaurant or a party, can be a huge #blessing when you're not having a good mental health day, or when you're just not feeling quite up to it."[51] Likewise, a 2017 blog post by a contributor to Arianna Huffington's Thrive initiative, "Self-Care Is Not Selfish," does little to demarcate the line between the two, instead advising readers, "Routine self care will cause those around you to adjust naturally, the same way if you have a dog it will adjust to your schedule once you get in a routine." This, the writer notes, will allow you to practice self-care "without feeling selfish"—no word on *being* selfish.[52] "If it requires asking your partner or a friend to help," she continues, "do it and allow them to have the oppotunity [*sic*] to feel good supporting you as we all want to be of service to one another and we all need to learn to allow for that."

People who don't serve your needs, or optimize your experience, are more often than not labeled "toxic," language that is at once medicalized and spiritual. One representative 2017 article from *PopSugar*, "How Being Selective About the People You Keep Around Is an Important Form of Self-Care," endorses a strategy the author presents as that of her friend. "Every now and then, she creates a list with two columns: 'People Who Invigorate Me' (left) and 'People Who Deplete Me' (right). She categorises friends, coworkers, acquaintances, and those she's newly met into one of the two sides and cuts ties with anyone on the right. That might sound a bit harsh to some of you, but think about it—why waste your energy and time on people who don't add any value to your life?"[53] In the implicit cosmic battleground of self-care culture, there isn't so much *good* and *evil*, in the universalist sense, as there is *good for me* and *bad for me*.

An article on Goop by Habib Sadeghi theorizes that excessive selflessness might in fact cause breast cancer. In language that seems cottoned straight from the New Thought playbook, Sadeghi insists that "after seeing thousands of patients over my career, and going through cancer myself, I can tell you that UNRESOLVED EMOTIONAL PAIN and UNEXPRESSED DESIRES are at the core of what I call 'DIS-EASE' or a body-mind that's not at ease," ultimately concluding that "women who live only to serve and nourish the lives of others develop subconscious resentment because no nourishment is coming back to them—without replenishment they become emotionally depleted." He wonders aloud, "Is it just a coincidence that these women often develop cancer in the most nourishing organ of the female body, the breast? I don't think so."[54] For Sadeghi, there can be no greater good than what he calls "selfless selfishness," because, in his words, "giving to yourself first is one of the greatest gifts you could ever give to those you love."

You can trace the origin of this particular ethos all the way back to Oprah Winfrey, who in 2002 pioneered her "oxygen mask theory": as on an airplane, put on your own oxygen mask before attending to the people around you.[55] But in the past half decade or so, the idea has gained new currency. A study of New Year's resolutions in 2015—which largely dealt with self-care essentials like eating healthier and exercising more—found that millennials spent, on average, a little under $300 a month on achieving their self-care goals, almost twice what their boomer elders were spending.[56] In 2014, about 1,800 apps devoted to self-care were added to either Android or iPhone stores. In 2016, about 3,000 were added. In 2018, 3,400 more.[57] That same year, Apple named self-care their "App Trend of the Year."[58]

The top ten wellness apps—including Headspace and competitor Calm—made 170 percent more in revenue in the first quarter of 2018 than they did one year prior.[59] You can currently buy almost 4,200 different bespoke self-care kits on Etsy.[60]

As with many elements of today's Remixed, wellness culture saw a turning point with the election of Donald Trump in 2016. Self-care—like modern fandom, contemporary occultism, and the modern sexual revolution—is more often than not linked to progressive politics.

Between November 13 and 19, 2016—the first full week after the presidential election—online searches for "self-care" reached a five-year high. Left-leaning websites like *Mic* and *Quartz* published pieces with headlines like "The Rise of Donald Trump Demands We Embrace a Harder Kind of Self-Care" and "A Self-Care Guide of TV to Watch to Forget About Donald Trump's Rise" (they suggested *Project Runway*). "Self-care" first hit the *New York Times*' style section—the canary in the coal mine of trend pieces—on December 6, 2016.[61]

Since then, there's been *Dame* magazine's "How to Practice Self-Care in Trump's America":

> *Those people you are fighting against every day, the ones who hate immigrants, and don't want women to be able to make their own health-care choices. . . . They want you, and people like you, and the people you are fighting for, to be miserable. If you forget how to enjoy your life, you are helping them win. Self-care is a revolutionary act, particularly for marginalized people. Get that pedicure because you deserve feet that don't snag your sheets! The bad guys want you to have nasty feet! If you're going to be out there marching against their bullshit all damn day, AT LEAST HAVE NICE FEET, DAMN IT. And then post those pretty ass toes on Instagram, because you are a human being and you deserve to be able to share your full humanity with people.*[62]

There was Girlboss's 2018-midterm-pegged "10 Self-Care Ideas to Help You Get Through These Rough Political Times": "Find ways to focus on *your* needs for an uninterrupted period of time."[63] There was MTV News's "Self-Care in the Time of Trump": "Survivors and activists alike ultimately don't owe anybody anything except the care of themselves."[64]

One reason for this resurgence of wellness culture—and intuitional religion more broadly—may well be in its power to contend with institutional failure. For voters dismayed by the outcome of the 2016 election (and the Remixed tend to lean progressive), Trump's unexpected election marked not merely a disappointment but a shock. It was a failure on the part of traditional bastions of certainty: political polls, pundits, and the institutions of Washington, DC. That failure, in turn, encouraged anti-institutional feeling to flourish. If our trusted sources of authority couldn't predict Trump's election, why shouldn't we fall back on more immediate sources of authority: our feelings, our wants, our physical needs?

The fatalism of the Hebrew Bible—the book of Ecclesiastes laments aloud that "what happens to the fool will happen to me also; why then have I been so very wise?"—has always been anathema to the American religious tradition. But, for our Remixed, wellness culture represents a new apex of spiritual individualism. It provides a framework of meaning, divinizing and reifying the significance of individual experience in a seemingly chaotic and senseless world. You're tapping into your primal energy at SoulCycle, you're clearing your body of toxins with a juice cleanse, creating meaning on demand, but only in arenas that yield materially beneficial results. You're becoming purer and more fulfilled by becoming skinnier or having better skin.

The more seemingly absurd the outside world gets—the more politicians and professors and journalists and doctors and other representatives of the establishment fail in their perceived duties—the more traction these myths and rituals get. Getting your toes done (as *Dame* suggested) may not be the most practical avenue of #resistance. But it's an acknowledgment that our physical and emotional selves may be all we feel we can rely on. For all its claims to positivity, wellness culture is, at its core, nihilistic.

In Claude Lévi-Strauss's 1958 handbook, *Structural Anthropology*, he gives the example of a South American shaman who sits at the bedside of a pregnant woman.[65] While she struggles with labor pains, the shaman recites an old myth, known to the woman, of warring gods in her belly, shadow and light fighting for dominance. Once the woman's pain is put in terms that she can understand, he argues, she suffers less.

Meanwhile, on Goop, one more Paltrow-approved specialist, Dr. Alejandro Junger, provides us with a modern myth. "There is another 'inconvenient truth' still hidden from popular awareness," he writes. "Global warming is just a symptom. At the root of it is global toxicity, the build-up of chemicals that is threatening all life on earth. The air we breathe, the water we drink and shower with, the buildings we live and work in, and most of all, the foods we eat, are loaded with chemicals that alone or in combination cause irritation, inflammation, sickness and, ultimately, death."[66] (It goes without saying that there's no such thing as "toxins," at least not in the manner that Junger is describing.

Real toxins are automatically flushed out by organs like the liver and kidney, whose job it is to do precisely that.)

The cure for modern life (if not quite death itself), Junger tells us, is his several-day detox plan—a standard liquid diet—combined with "skin brushing," meditation, saunas, and sunshine. It's a cure any one of us can buy into. And it's a story that just might take away some of our pain.

six

THE MAGIC RESISTANCE

I n October 2018, a Brooklyn store called Catland held an unconventional protest. Its target? The imminent apointment to the Supreme Court of Brett Kavanaugh, who had just been publicly accused of sexual assault by Christine Blasey Ford. Its tools? Magic. Over ten thousand people had registered interest for the "Hex Kavanaugh" event—an astounding number for a shop whose back room could accommodate sixty at most.

Catland is an occult supply and magic shop that's made frequent headlines for its marriage of witchcraft and social justice, and its owners were undeterred by the largely Christian protesters outside. Antifa volunteers provided security.

Inside, the protesters—led by shop cofounder Dakota Bracciale, a self-described "queer, trans, disabled person who goes by they/them"— assembled before a series of effigies: Kavanaugh, Mitch McConnell, Donald Trump. They wrote down the names of their own abusers on pieces of paper and left these, too, alongside the effigies, which were flanked by phallus-shaped candles into which the organizers had affixed several needles. Above the altar was a chalkboard, on which Catland's owners had inscribed *lavetur in nobis sanguis tyrannis*: to bathe in the blood of tyrants.

First, everybody started with an om, a meditation and ritual centering of the self.

"You don't have to believe it or have a spiritual path," Bracciale told listeners, according to the *Daily Beast's* Alaina Demopoulos. "Say it as a rallying cry."

They read Psalm 109: "Appoint someone evil to oppose my enemy / let an accuser stand at his right hand / When he is tried, let him be found guilty."

Then, everybody began to stamp and scream.

"Yes, there's a nuts and bolts magical spell that happens in the room," Bracciale told Demopoulos later. "But it's just as potent of a ritual as it is an act of catharsis where people can recognize trauma and process through it."

One by one, attendees shared their own stories of abuse, of assault, of the shame of being disbelieved. Participants were encouraged, but not required, to close their eyes.

"If you don't feel comfortable closing your eyes," Bracciale explained, "you probably have a good reason for thinking that." Some attendees sat in silence. Others wept.

The media reaction to Catland's mass hexing was outsize—bolstered, in part, by the event's timely proximity to Halloween. The BBC, *Time* magazine, UK newspaper the *Independent*, and Reuters all covered the hex, as did *Fox News* anchor Tucker Carlson, who described Catland's plan to donate part of the proceeds from the event to Planned Parenthood as an effort to "help [witches] continue to fund their human sacrifice rituals."[1] Meanwhile, on MSNBC, Amy Kremer, cofounder of the Women Vote Trump super PAC, said the event was a harbinger.[2] "It is a scary time right now," she said. A time when even God-fearing Christians had to worry about the wrath of witches.

She's not wrong. For a growing generation of progressive Remixed, contemporary occultism—and modern witchcraft in particular—offers a powerful spiritual counterpoint to organized religion, one that's not merely orthogonal to traditional Christianity but actively opposed to it. From the streets of Brooklyn's Bushwick neighborhood to the shelves at international chain stores like Sephora to the presidential campaign of New Age spiritualist Marianne Williamson, modern occultism has proliferated as an identity marker, a religious practice, and a mechanism for community formation.

Or, as Jaya Saxena and Jess Zimmerman put it in their 2017 how-to guide, *Basic Witches: How to Summon Success, Banish Drama, and Raise Hell with Your Coven*, "Witches are everywhere this days."[3]

As a spiritual practice, witchcraft may be the biggest thing since yoga. According to 2014 data collected by the Pew Research Center, around one million Americans actively identify their primary religious affiliation as New Age, Neo-Pagan, or Wiccan (a contemporary reconstructionist pagan religion founded by mystic Gerald Gardner in the 1950s).[4] Using slightly different methodology, Alex Mar, author of the 2015 book *Witches of America*, puts the number of pagans in the country at approximately one million.[5] In other words, there are more witches in the United States than Jehovah's Witnesses.

And those numbers are on the low side. The Pew data doesn't take into account the thousands, if not hundreds of thousands, of religiously hybrid Americans who don't think of themselves as pagans or witches but who practice New Age rituals, from crystals to tarot cards to cleansing sage. Social media platforms, particularly Instagram, have transformed the visual witch aesthetic into a culturally resonant identity marker.

Monthly "witchy" subscription boxes have gone mainstream. One such business, Goddess Provisions, went from having three hundred subscribers in early 2016 to six thousand in the middle of 2017.[6] That same year, *BuzzFeed*'s Corin Faife wrote that searches on the Instagram hashtag #witchesofinstagram yielded almost 700,000 posts, with 3.7 million on the hashtag #witch. As of 2020, there are 3.9 million #witchesofinstagram posts, and a staggering 10.5 million under #witch. Astrology, too, is undergoing a resurgence: about 40 percent of American adults aged eighteen to twenty-nine say they believe in astrology at least a little.[7]

The reasons for this season of the witch are many. The rise of the witch tracks almost exactly with the rise of the religiously Remixed overall. Witchcraft, as a diffuse and decentered practice and spiritual system, lends itself easily to contemporary intuitional eclecticism. It's easy to incorporate small acts of folk magic, like burning sage, into a day that also includes meditation, or yoga, or other forms of individualism. It often stresses progressive, queer-friendly, and feminist values and symbol systems, which makes it particularly appealing to this demographic. And, of course, there's the influence of fandom. Many of today's millennial witches grew up on media properties like *Harry Potter*, *Buffy the Vampire Slayer*, and *Charmed*, which largely portrayed magic sympathetically as a tool of personal empowerment. While the worries of religious leaders that *Harry Potter* would inspire a generation of children to practice witchcraft were, certainly, overblown, it's nonetheless true that many contemporary practitioners of magic trace their interest in it to their childhood reading. In an article for *Vice*'s now-defunct women's site *Broadly*, for example, witch and activist Sarah Lyons profiles numerous witches who credit *Harry Potter*, Philip Pullman, or *Sabrina the Teenage Witch* with introducing them to the idea of magic as an alluring and viable practice.

"Harry Potter was definitely my gateway drug to the world of witchcraft," Lyons writes of her own experience. "Reading stories focused on witchcraft made me so excited and curious that I went out to seek the real thing; I can still remember finding a copy of *The Witches' Almanac* in a tiny bookstore when I was 13 and feeling like I had finally gotten my own letter inviting me to a magical world."[8]

But witches aren't just to be found in fringe millennial outlets like *Vice*. They're part of the new normal. In spring 2019, The *Los Angeles Times* profiled the city's "working witches": a group of women and non-binary people who offered "spiritual counseling" alongside spells. One of the article's subjects, Amanda Yates Garcia, also known as the "oracle of Los Angeles," teaches "intuitive empowerment sessions" and sends out a regular newsletter; another, Bri Luna (better known as "the Hood-witch") has 420,000 followers on Instagram. That same week, the *New York Times*—hardly a bastion of fringe spirituality—featured a personal essay by self-proclaimed witch Pam Grossman, who blended reflections on her teenage tarot usage with an activist manifesto. For Grossman, the term "witch" signifies "that I am a feminist; someone who celebrates freedom for all and who will fight against injustice; a person who values intuition and self-expression; or a kindred spirit with other people who favor the unconventional, the underground and the uncanny."[9]

For Grossman, personal and political spirituality are intertwined: "I'm a witch when I'm celebrating the change of the seasons with my coven sisters," she writes, "as well as when I stand against the destruction of the environment. I'm a witch when I'm giving thanks to the sun, moon and stars, and when I'm working to subvert the corrosive narrative of sexism, racism, queer-phobia and xenophobia."

WITCHCRAFT, LIKE WELLNESS, HAS BECOME AN INDELIBLE PART OF millennial cultural discourse—and consumption—with profoundly ambivalent results.

In autumn 2018, for example, international makeup chain Sephora announced it would be selling a "Starter Witch Kit" manufactured by fragrance company Pinrose.[10] The kit—featuring a tarot deck, several fragrances, a rose quartz crystal, and "cleansing sage"—would have been sold for $42.[11] A few weeks later, Sephora abruptly pulled the product, citing widespread social media opposition and charges of cultural appropriation from practicing witches, many of whom saw the product as a shameless attempt to capitalize off witch (counter)culture.

Critics focused their objections on the starter kit's use of white sage, a plant often used by Native Americans during religious purification rituals. Witch and author Gabriela Herstick, one of many to condemn the collaboration, told feminist website *HelloGiggles* that it "felt like capitalism at its worst, selling something because it's trendy instead of working with actual stores owned by witches."[12]

Days later, Pinrose issued a public apology, telling customers, "Our intention for the product was to create something that celebrates wellness, personal ceremony, and intention setting with a focus on using fragrance as a beauty ritual."[13]

The debacle illustrates the tension at the heart of witch culture—and in Remixed culture more broadly. On the one hand, the renaissance in modern occultism is fueled in large part by the degree to which it fulfills a palpable American need for explicitly spiritual practices and language that don't conform to the dominant model of institutional Christianity. Witchcraft is increasingly appealing to its Remixed practitioners because it's both flexible and intuitional, the mirror image of American political Christianity.

On the other hand, the more popular witchcraft gets, the less alternative it becomes. Witches have become numerous enough to be a viable consumer base, a marketing tribe. In so doing, witchcraft risks losing the oppositional rough edges at the heart of its appeal. It's one thing to learn to cast folk spells from a favorite aunt, or learn from a grandmother or friend how to use a divination rod for fortune-telling. It's another thing entirely to be able to head straight to the home page of *Vice* and find an easy, accessible ritual to "get over your ex" or cast a Venus retrograde spell.[14] Or to head to popular hipster chain store Urban Outfitters to pick up a copy of Semra Haksever's 2018 spell book *Everyday Magic: Rituals, Spells & Potions to Live Your Best Life*, or to Amazon to buy an iPhone case emblazed with A WITCH BOWS TO NO MAN for $8.99.[15]

Wellness culture, confronted with consumer capitalism, proliferates. Why *shouldn't* we spend our hard-earned dollars (and precious free time) investing in the project of ourselves? But witch culture is a trickier phenomenon to reconcile with one's personal brand. At its core, contemporary occultism is profoundly antiestablishment, blending the intuitional quality of wellness culture with a far more concrete set of political and interpersonal goals.

While wellness culture is firmly apolitical—obsessively focused on self-care and self-optimization—witch culture turns its attention outward, toward the System it aims to bring down. It is anti-institutional not merely in practice—modern witches cobble together a personal pantheon spanning several cultures and symbolic systems—but in its theology. Combining progressive feminist politics with a fervent opposition to institutional Christianity—which is dismissed and derided as a bastion of toxic patriarchy, repression, and white supremacy—modern witchcraft embraces its power to transgress. It doesn't just celebrate the individual and the intuitive, but actively seeks to combat the institutional and burn down the patriarchy.

In this, modern witch culture is distinct from both wellness culture and the New Age culture that preceded it. While New Age spirituality from the American midcentury onward has long been associated with progressive feminism, its ethos has tended toward feel-good ideas of "love and light" or "positive energy." Contemporary witchcraft, by contrast, embraces darkness—including imagery of the downright diabolical—as a necessary political corrective to what they see as unjust Christian supremacy. These witches are, implicitly or explicitly, champions of the Miltonian Satan, striving against a seemingly oppressive God.

It's that sense of opposition that defines witch culture more than any actual metaphysic. As Jaya Saxena and Jess Zimmerman write in *Basic Witches*, envisioning their novice reader, "You're not necessarily a practicing witch. You might not believe in magic or mysticism or spirituality at all. But you're intrigued by the power, or the sisterhood, or the devil-may-literally-care attitude of the witches you've seen in pop culture and history. You don't think women should be considered frightening or ridiculous just because they don't toe the line."[16]

Ultimately, they conclude, witchcraft is a form of personal, anti-establishment empowerment. It "is your birthright. . . . [The] mainstream wants you to fit into a predefined role. Witchcraft enables you to find personal purpose, truth, and intention. It allows you to discover the crafts, talents, and interests that make you you. . . . You already have the potential to be a strong, self-actualized, powerful, ass-kicking witch. All you have to do is recognize your abilities . . . and channel them into making some magic."[17]

To identify as a witch isn't just to cast a personal love spell or bind an opponent. Rather, it's to adopt a series of symbols—visual, verbal, and magical—that express violent opposition to patriarchy, white supremacy, the gender binary, and the System conceived more broadly. As Kristen J. Sollee, author of the zeitgeist-capturing 2017 *Witches, Sluts, Feminists: Conjuring the Sex Positive*, writes, "Who, exactly, is the witch? . . . She's Hecate, the ancient Greek goddess of the crossroads. She's Lilith, the blood-drinking demoness of Jewish mythology who refused to submit sexually to her husband. . . . She's Joan of Arc, the French military hero in white armor burned by her brethren for cross dressing and heresy. . . . She's Malala Yousafzai. . . . She's every woman . . . at once female divinity, female ferocity, and female transgression."[18] The witch, for Sollee, is every woman who violates the rules of repressive institutions, regardless of what they personally believe or practice. Contemporary Remixed witchcraft is less about the specifics of belief than it is about the creation of a sense of existential purpose revolving around cultural resistance.

Modern witchcraft's rituals may be eclectic, but the cosmic narrative it crafts and the purpose it demands of its adherents is consistent. Christianity—particularly white, male, evangelical Christianity—is outmoded and morally abhorrent. Its symbols are vehicles of oppression. Its theology valorizes not just hierarchy but tyranny. Witches, conversely, are intrepid modern-day Davids, underdogs bravely fighting against the Goliath of institutionalism. By valorizing and promoting symbols, ideas, and cultural markers associated with the traditionally marginalized—women, people of color, and queer people—witches can create an alternative, oppositional theology of resistance.

They're wedding the intuitionalism of the New Age to the solidarity of the social justice movement. And, in so doing, they're creating an utterly contemporary new religion.

FROM THE AGE OF AQUARIUS TO THE AGE OF TRUMP

The New Age, as it later came to be known, was among the most explicit of America's waves of intuitional religions. Born in the countercultural milieu of the 1960s, New Age culture emphasized the power of personal spiritual sensibility over the outmoded regulations of organized religions. The first self-proclaimed New Agers saw themselves as pioneers in a transformative and unprecedented era of human existence—a "new age" of personal fulfillment, in which religion as traditionally understood would become obsolete, and the long-awaited "age of Aquarius." By the 1970s, however, the scope of New Age discourse had expanded, and the phrase became an umbrella term for interest in a variety of esoteric, reconstructionist, or non-Western spiritual traditions. Transcendental meditation belonged to the New Age. So, at one time, did yoga. So, too, did interest in channeling, UFOs, Reiki, acupuncture, crystal healing, and the kind of creative visualization ubiquitous in the New Thought movement. Self-identifying New Age stores would carry a range of books and products dealing with many, if not all, of these movements and practices.

It's difficult to talk about any unifying principles within the New Age movement because, for the most part, there weren't any. A largely decentralized phenomenon, the New Age had few practitioners who could be considered spokespeople. But a few central ideas ran through the majority of New Age thought.

Like wellness culture, New Age philosophy promoted radical self-reliance and a doctrine of emotional authenticity. As in Transcendentalism and New Thought, this manifested as a deep suspicion of any form of institutional expertise—be it spiritual, psychological, political, or pharmaceutical. At best, the thinking went, these institutions were misguided: dotards blinded by their own habits and traditions. At worst, they were downright evil: part of a conspiracy designed to stymie the self's personal and spiritual growth. One of the most influential scholars of the movement, Paul Heelas, characterizes the predominant trait of the New Age as "self-spirituality."[19]

As in Transcendentalism and New Thought, too, the self was treated as the ultimate source of authority and divinity. Outside pressures—social norms, expectations, and institutions—only got in the way of experiencing one's true self. By focusing on that "true" and intuitive sense, and ignoring or repudiating institutions, a person could achieve not just self-actualization but also material and physical improvement. In New Age culture, as in its nineteenth-century antecedents, knowledge and intellect took a back seat to emotion and feeling, which represented the uncontaminated knowledge of the true self.

The Swedish religion scholar Olav Hammer has written on the New Age distrust of disembodied expertise. While giving a university lecture on science and the New Age, Hammer recounts in an essay, he made reference to a number of seemingly magical or mystical practices that, he told his listeners, could be conclusively explained with science, including walking on fire. An angry audience member immediately interrupted him, insisting that he was wrong.

"My interlocutor," Hammer writes, "triumphantly responded that she wasn't interested in hearing me summarize what other people had written or said. Only two things mattered: did I have my own opinion, and was it based on my personal experience? . . . [I] soon realized that I had lost the discussion. Since I didn't speak from first hand experience, but was quoting authorities that the New Agers did not recognize as such and felt no particular respect for, I had alienated my audience."[20]

Another common feature of the New Age was its faith in interconnectedness. A single source of divine energy ran through all people. While individual religions, ideas, and traditions might appear to differ from one another at a surface level, at their metaphysical core all faiths were really the same. Gods from, say, the Greek pantheon could coexist alongside gods from the Norse one (and might in fact be the same deities under different names). A person's magical practice, too, might well blend Native American smudging, the *brujería* witchcraft of the Latinx tradition, Zen Buddhist meditation, and elements of the ceremonial magical tradition common to late-Victorian Europe.

In *Witches of America*, Alex Mar captures this multiplicity by looking at the offerings at a single weekend pagan convention:

> *Workshops, meet-and-greets and rituals for nearly every variation*
> *on today's American Pagan: Gardnerians and Alexandrians and*
> *eclectic Wiccans and Druids and Heathens and Asatru and Feri*

and Golden Dawn initiates and Thelemites and nouveau voodoo and Hoodoo folk and Feraferia practitioners and Hellenic Reconstructionists and Celtric Reconstructionists and white-skinned shamans . . . lessons in Heathen ancestor rituals, Scottish folk curses, Elder Futhark runes, "otherworld travel through BDSM," prison ministry for Pagan prisoners, healing from "our conditioning in Patriarchy," Pagan twelve-step recovery, how "magical tools" can be used in the Occupy Wall Street movement, how to reclaim the slur "warlock," and psychic and magical development for kids . . . a guided meditation, a talk about Hermetic Qabalah, a workshop on poisonous herbs.[21]

A practicing New Ager might attend any or all of these workshops. The actual external, propositional content of most religious or magical systems—the names and histories of deities, the source of their power, their specific demands on adherents—is, within the New Age tradition, largely immaterial. By and large, New Agers cast these as the results of limited human understanding, futile attempts on the part of flawed societies to understand a transcendent energy that exists both *outside* the believer and, even more importantly, *within*.

As author Starhawk, one of the early New Age movement's most influential voices, wrote in 1979, "Witchcraft has always been a religion of poetry, not theology. The myths, legends, and teachings are recognized as metaphors for 'That-Which-Cannot-Be-Told,' the absolute reality our limited minds can never completely know."[22] This truth, Starhawk and others implied, could in theory be found in any faith, but organized religions were more likely to have polluted it. To speak of God, Starhawk wrote in 1982, was to speak of "the God of patriarchal religions . . . the ultimate source and repository of power-over." Rather, to speak of a feminized Goddess, while perhaps no more technically accurate, was to evoke "ancient images, symbols and myths of the Goddess as birthgiver, weaver, earth and growing plant, wind and ocean, flame, web, moon and milk," symbols that evoked "the powers of connectedness, sustenance, and healing."[23]

THE PROLIFERATION AND TRANSFORMATION OF WICCA—AMONG THE most common New Age faiths—from a formal religion into a more loosely defined "witch" identity, is an illustrative example of both the New Age's self-focused spirituality and its theological flexibility.

Technically, Wicca is a reconstructionist religion that was created in England in the 1950s, after amateur anthropologist Gerald Gardner published a book called *Witchcraft Today*, claiming to reveal the secrets of a lost "witch cult" (to which he now belonged) in the country.

While virtually all contemporary scholars believe that the cult was, in fact, invented by Gardner—albeit drawing on a few surface elements of pre-Christian Celtic spiritual traditions—Wicca became increasingly popular in both England and the United States. Wiccans worshipped two deities: the Horned God and Mother Goddess, who were often identified interchangeably with fertility and seasonal gods in other more established pagan pantheons (and, sometimes, even the Judeo-Christian Yahweh and the Virgin Mary).

While early Wicca ran (and, according to purists, still runs) on a "coven" system—to join, you have to be initiated into a coven that traces its lineage directly to Gardner's coven—the Internet in particular has transformed Wiccan identity into a much more diffuse phenomenon. From the 1980s onward, the trend of the solitary witch—who identifies with Wiccan practices but buys materials and books from New Age shops rather than learning from a coven—began to proliferate, and the Internet only made the trend more pronounced. As Mar describes, "Suddenly solitary practitioners, or witches still 'in the broom closet,' could seek each other out, swap spells, arrange to meet way up on the hillside behind the local Walmart. Entire virtual networks of tens of thousands of witches multiplied, connected, and fused into covens in cities and suburbs across the country."[24]

Back in 1990, there were only about 8,000 Wiccans in America. By 2001, that number had leaped to 134,000, making Wicca technically the country's fastest-growing religion.[25] And although the Pew data from 2014 lumps Wiccans and other Neo-Pagans together, it nevertheless puts Wicca and Wicca-adjacent religions at close to a million practitioners.

Despite the relative formality of early Gardnerian Wicca, with its focus on codified rituals and lineages, the fundamental elasticity of its structure—the way in which, for example, the Horned God and Mother Goddess could be interpreted through a variety of disparate and even contradictory religious traditions—made it ripe for constant reinvention. Anyone with an Internet connection and access to the hundreds, if not thousands, of Wicca and magic-centric sites and message boards online could download or post a spell, ritual, or prayer.

The intense individuality of New Age thought (and Wicca in particular) didn't necessarily make it apolitical. From the 1970s onward, the presence of a vital Mother Goddess in Wicca (as opposed to the male-dominated structure of Christianity) made it a powerful and appealing option for feminists in search of what came to be known as "Goddess spirituality" or the "Goddess movement." Offshoots of Wicca, such as Dianic Wicca, developed to cater exclusively to female practitioners and honor exclusively female deities.

For practitioners, Goddess spirituality was an intensely political act, designed not merely to provide personal fulfillment but to correct for what adherents saw as centuries, if not millennia, of systematic devaluation of women in Abrahamic traditions. One of the most influential figures in the movement, author and scholar Carol P. Christ, attracted widespread attention in 1978 when she gave a paper entitled "Why Women Need the Goddess" at a California religion conference. Christ argued that "religions centered on the worship of a male God . . . keep women in a state of psychological dependence on men and male authority, while at the same legitimating the political and social authority of fathers and sons in the institutions of society."[26] Meanwhile, Christ insisted, "as women struggle to create a new culture in which women's power, bodies, will, and bonds are celebrated, it is natural that the Goddess would reemerge as symbol of the newfound beauty, strength, and power of women."[27]

In Christ's essay, as in the decades of Goddess worship that followed, the political and the personal were fundamentally intertwined. Both rested, after all, on conceptions of and divinization of the *self*—in particular, the idea that a worshipper was reclaiming a marginalized self. Quoting the playwright and activist Ntozake Shange, author of *For Colored Girls Who Have Considered Suicide / When the Rainbow Is Enuf*, Christ tells her listeners, "A woman who echoes . . . Shange's dramatic statement, 'I found God in myself and I loved her fiercely,' is saying, 'Female power is strong and creative.' She is saying that the divine principle, the saving and sustaining power, is in herself, that she will no longer look to men or male figures as saviors. The strength and independence of female power can be intuited by contemplating ancient and modern images of the Goddess. This meaning of the symbol of Goddess is simple and obvious, and yet it is difficult for many to comprehend."[28]

Personal reclamation and self-divinization of a marginalized identity became a conduit for collective growth. As in Audre Lorde's paradigm of self-care, only by loving and venerating yourself—your intuitions, your instincts, your embodied experiences—over and against seemingly authoritative or outside structures, will you be able to advocate collectively for those like you.

For much of the 1980s, 1990s, and early 2000s, New Age political spirituality was defined by the specific demands and value systems of Goddess feminism. Essentialized femininity—including the visceral experiences of the female body, like menstruation and childbirth—was valorized; women were encouraged to get in touch with their primal, life-giving strength. This emphasis on femininity, in turn, led to an increased focus on Mother Nature (the earth as a life-giving force) and ecological and ecofeminist activism. Within the ecofeminist paradigm, the patriarchy—which values intellect and authority over intuition and personal knowledge—had sought to "civilize" the earth, transforming (and destroying) "feminine" natural beauty and chaos into "masculine" order. To be a witch was to honor, value, and reclaim that feminine natural world.

In her 1982 book, *Dreaming the Dark: Magic, Sex and Politics*, Starhawk encapsulates this utopian vision: "A society that could heal the dismembered world would recognize the inherent value of each person and of the plant, animal and elemental life that makes up the earth's living body; it would offer real protection, encourage free expression, and reestablish an ecological balance to be biologically and economically sustainable. Its underlying metaphor would be mystery, the sense of wonder at all that is beyond us and around us, at the forces that sustain our lives and the intricate complexity and beauty of their dance."[29]

Witchcraft did, at times, take a more explicitly subversive political form. As early as 1968, the radical leftist feminist group Women's International Terrorist Conspiracy from Hell (W.I.T.C.H.) was making headlines by, for example, publicly cursing the New York Stock Exchange. (It seemed to work. The stock exchange fell thirteen points the next day.)[30] But W.I.T.C.H.'s interest in, well, witches, was more symbolic and political than it was spiritual, and W.I.T.C.H. itself was an anomaly alongside the more accommodationist Goddess movement, which tended to avoid the worldly concerns of leftist politics.

But if Starhawk's and Christ's approaches to activism, and feminism, reflected the individualism and gender essentialism of the '70s and '80s, so, too, do today's witches reflect their current political and social climate.

Wicca, and New Age spirituality more broadly, have gotten less white and less heterosexual than they were in their heyday. Queer adults are six times more likely than the average population to be members of New Age faiths.[31] More and more practitioners of color are joining the ranks of the New Age, raising questions about the ways in which "ethnic" or seemingly exotic spiritual traditions—like the Native American practice of smudging, or traditional Latinx folk magics like *brujería*—have been denatured in order to make them more commercially accessible to a (primarily) white New Age audience.

And so the political aims of Wicca and witchcraft are widening. Concerned with racial, economic, and social injustice, as well as with expanding and subverting expectations of gender, today's witches are seeking a newer and more intense version of Christ's imagined "new culture": one that doesn't just destabilize the patriarchy but dismantles all the systems of power and privilege—systems that they see as having given us, well, Donald Trump.

DEFINING THE #MAGICRESISTANCE

Twenty-first-century witches, and particularly post-2016 witches, are warier of what they see as the anodyne "love and light" culture of their predecessors in the New Age movement. Language associated with the first wave of popularized Neo-Pagan practice—such as the "rule of three" (the karmic idea that any spell craft, positive or negative, will come back at you threefold, which was absent from Gardnerian Wicca but became common in later Wiccan culture), or the celebration of Wicca as being exclusively about "white magic"—is often rejected as being rooted in a practitioner's unchecked privilege.

A series of zines, written by Catland co-owner Dakota Bracciale (writing as Dakota Stalkfleet), encapsulates this new, social-justice-focused approach to witchcraft. In a zine devoted to the art and magic of cursing, Stalkfleet cautions readers against a revulsion to black magic. The desire of a witch to practice nothing but white magic, Stalkfleet writes, is "deeply and inextricably rooted in white supremacy, colonialism." For Stalkfleet, what is traditionally called black magic "refers to those practices rooted in African spirituality, made manifest in the diaspora and the dozens of syncretic traditions born therein . . . magical practices 'white magic' would never touch." These practices aren't evil, Stalkfleet stresses, but they are dangerous—and proudly so. They are the practices of a marginalized people seeking to use whatever tools they have at their disposal.

Stalkfleet condemns the ways in which witchcraft has lost sight of its fundamentally countercultural roots. "Witchcraft has largely, if not exclusively, been a tool of resilience and resistance to oppressive power structures, not a plaything for bored, affluent fools." That resistance may well take the form of imagery that invokes Christian specters of evil. "If one must ride into battle under the banner of the Devil himself to do so then I say so be it. The reality is that you can be a witch and worship the devil and have sex with demons and cavort through the night stealing children and burning churches. One should really have goals."

For Stalkfleet, the language and rhetoric of full-on Satanism—sex with demons, devil worshipping, baby kidnapping—can and should be politically reappropriated, transformed into an act of resistance. Cursing, black magic, and diabolism alike are forms of symbolically reclaiming power.

Nowhere is this clearer than when Stalkfleet provides a series of spells for cursing evildoers, characterizing them as the only avenue for justice available to the downtrodden. "If you practice witchcraft and you have never considered cursing someone," Stalkfleet writes,

> I have to assume you haven't been through much in the way of violence, trauma, or abuse. . . . Folk magik is what arms the poor, the downtrodden, and the outcast. How could anyone fault me for cursing my rapist? Even if I was to subject myself to the terrifying police, the exhaustion of telling and re-telling and re-telling the story of how I was attacked and robbed and violated to people who will blame me or not believe me at all, and the trauma of having my body violated again for a rape kit, which won't be tested, there is an almost surefire guarantee that he will not be caught or brought to justice or made to answer for what he has done. How could anyone blame me, let alone shame me for seeking to be the arbiter of my own justice by cursing that evil made?

In the wake of the 2016 election, the aesthetic and practice of witchcraft have become inseparable from the rhetoric of #resistance. Throughout 2017, around thirteen thousand self-proclaimed witches gathered together monthly on platforms like Facebook (one group explicitly termed itself the "Magic Resistance") to cast spells to "bind" Donald Trump, using spiritual energy to limit his power to effect, in their minds, socially regressive and oppressive policies. Even pop star Lana Del Rey, known for her countercultural aesthetic, got in on the action, posting photographs of herself alongside information about one such binding spell.[32]

Witchcraft as a politically progressive act has become a whole cottage industry. Since 2016, scores of books on magic as activism have appeared on New Age stores' shelves: from the anthology *The New Arcadia: A Witch's Handbook to Magical Resistance* to Michael M. Hughes's *Magic for the Resistance: Rituals and Spells for Change* to David Salisbury's *Witchcraft Activism: A Toolkit for Magical Resistance (Includes Spells for Social Justice, Civil Rights, the Environment, and More)* to Sarah Lyons's *Revolutionary Witchcraft: A Guide to Magical Activism.*

While not all of these books mention Donald Trump explicitly, they all frame the rituals of witchcraft as connected to a wider social and spiritual purpose: to dismantle toxic and oppressive structures associated with patriarchy, white supremacy, and other unjust hierarchies.

Readers of Salisbury's book can learn, for example, how to petition the Greco-Roman god Hermes to ensure that delivery of a letter to an elected official is both read and taken seriously, or to cast a spell to ensure resilience after a long day of protesting (set flower heads or petals in a bowl of spring water and light a candle before chanting, "The world's at times a frenzied fire / and I the calm in tempest dire / still the waters, calm the fire").[33] "Witchcraft is the unconquerable shout at midnight," Salisbury writes. "It screams to be heard because it is the lighthouse for the voiceless."[34]

Witchcraft, and modern occultism, is at its core a religion of revolution. Its spirituality, structure, and social codes all revolve around subverting the symbolic hierarchy of Christianity. It valorizes intuition over institution, female energy over male power, sexual freedom and agency over repressive chastity. Mythical figures associated with evil—such as Lilith, whom a satirical Jewish text characterizes as the original first wife of Adam and a demonic being who refused to have missionary sex with him—have been reclaimed as symbols of feminine power. In one essay for *Vice,* Sarah Lyons, the website's onetime "witch in residence," writes a paean to Lilith, the ultimate "chill demon," concluding that "by reclaiming Lilith's story, women can push against this unrelenting and oppressive status quo."[35]

That sense of revolution extends to today's political climate. While the New Age witch culture of the 1960s and '70s tended toward gender essentialism—the founder of the Dianic Wiccan tradition explicitly excluded transgender women from her covens, demanding that "if you claim to be one of us, you have to have sometimes in your life a womb, and ovaries and MOON bleed and not die"—contemporary witch culture rejects any easy association of biology and identity.[36] Its sense of subversive power extends to smashing not merely the patriarchy but also the gender binary. Its feminism isn't rooted in notions of a singular Goddess or a divine feminine, but rather in resistance to the limitations of gender itself.

Today, any self-respecting witch can pick up a tarot deck like the one designed by queer illustrator Cristy C. Road, which primarily depicts characters of color, sex workers, and nonbinary characters and bills itself as "about smashing systematic oppression, owning their truths, being accountable to the people and places that support them, and taking back a connection to their body that may have been lost through trauma or societal brainwashing."[37] There are so many queer-friendly tarot decks out there that lesbian website *Autostraddle* made a full listicle of them in 2015.[38] Progressive occult spaces tend to be increasingly open to gender nonconforming and transgender witches, preferring to reject the rhetoric of masculine-feminine binaries common to early Wicca in favor of the language of freedom and subversion—a subversion that both magic and genderqueer presentation can provide. As one gender nonconforming witch told *Vice*, both magic and playing with gender allow him "to express myself without this constant ego filter," he says. "When I picture myself [as a witch], without judgment, everything just fits."[39]

Likewise, contemporary witch spaces are increasingly calling for cultural authenticity and returning folk practices to their historic roots. For witches of color in particular, magical traditions connected to specific ancestral folk practices—as opposed to the more anodyne remixing of New Age movements—have become more popular. The annual Black Witch Convention, for example, has been running since 2016, linking young black women with Afro-Caribbean traditions like Haitian Vodou,

Yoruba spirituality, and hoodoo. *Brujería*, too, has been making a come-back among Latinx millennials.[40]

Other groups blend magic with anti-racist or pro-LGBTQ activism even more explicitly. The Instagram account of the Portland chapter of "W.I.T.C.H."—an "intersectional feminist coven" that brands itself as the inheritor of the 1960s' W.I.T.C.H. movement—is devoted to social-justice-focused memes. One photograph depicts a group of protestors holding a THANK GODDESS I'M GAY sign; another depicts more protestors advocating ABORT PATRIARCHY; REPRODUCE FEMINISM.[41] Another post, themed for May Day, depicts a woman in a skull mask surrounded by a "garland for May Day" emblazoned with banners saying SMASH HIERAR-CHIES and END CAPITALISM.[42] For these witches, the boundaries between spirituality, politics, and performance art blur.

Sometimes, the rituals of modern-day occultism don't require any spirituality at all. Just consider the Satanic Temple (TST), a nonthe-istic religion founded in 2012 by Malcolm Jarry and Lucien Greaves (both pseudonyms). The group began as high-level absurdist political performance—the closest thing to real-life trolling—using the rheto-ric of devil worship in order to call attention to potential loopholes in religious-freedom laws designed to benefit the Christian right. Greaves and Jarry made clear that they did not believe in a literal Satan (nor in a literal Christian God), but rather in what Satan represents: oppo-sition and subversion to a hierarchal institutional order. Greaves told goth magazine *Haute Macabre* in 2017, "The Satanic Temple espouses a non-supernatural anti-authoritarian philosophy that views the meta-phorical literary construct of Satan as a liberator from oppression of the mind and body," citing as influences John Milton's *Paradise Lost*, William Blake, and French novelist Anatole France.[43]

In 2013, for the group's first high-profile outing, members donned suitably gothic flowing black robes in order to pay homage to then Florida governor Rick Scott, who had recently passed a law that would allow schoolchildren to read "inspirational" (which meant, in practice, Christian) messages at school functions. TST made headlines by prais-ing Scott for opening the door to Satanic evangelization in schools,

safeguarding "our American freedom to practice our faith openly."
Three years later, TST attracted even more attention by demanding
that they were entitled to religious liberty exemptions from Florida's
new "fetal burial rule," which required official burial for aborted fetuses. According to TST's official doctrine, fetuses are not considered
people. And so, TST argued, Satanists shouldn't be subject to the rules.
The group has also lobbied for "after-school Satan clubs" and started
a troll campaign demanding that bakers who refuse to make LGBTQ
couples wedding cakes make pro-Satan cakes instead (religious freedom, unlike sexual orientation, is a protected class).

Lucien Greaves, now TST's de facto spokesperson, has spearheaded
numerous additional lawsuits, often going after corporations he sees as
having taken the group less seriously than they would more formal, organized religions. (TST is, for example, currently suing Twitter for sus-
pending Greaves's account after he called upon TST followers to report
the tweets of former child star Corey Feldman, a right-wing activist who
publicly advocated for the burning of TST's headquarters.)

The Satanic Temple was explicit in separating itself from the
Church of Satan, a more established movement founded by Hungarian
author Anton LaVey in the late 1960s. The Church of Satan, like the
Satanic Temple, treated Satan as a symbolic rather than literal figure.
But unlike the founders of TST, LaVey saw Satan as representing—and
advocating for—pure, primal selfishness. Heavily influenced by the
Objectivism of Ayn Rand, as well as by the Übermensch obsession of
Friedrich Nietzsche, LaVeyan Satanism preached, in the words of *The
Satanic Bible*, "indulgence, instead of abstinence! . . . Vital existence
instead of spiritual pipe dreams . . . kindness to those who deserve it,
instead of love wasted on ingrates . . . responsibility to the responsible
instead of concern for psychic vampires . . . all of the so-called sins,
as they all lead to physical, mental, or emotional gratification."[44] In
many ways, LaVeyan Satanism, which reached its peak in the 1970s,
was very much of its time: rejecting the conformity and institutionalization of the 1950s in favor of a vision of total personal freedom. But
while the contemporary Satanist movement shares with its predecessor

a willingness to embrace Satan's symbolic countercultural appeal, it combines Satanism's focus on the self with clearer, more outward-looking political goals.

Since its early days as performance art, the Satanic Temple has grown into equal parts national activist group and nontheistic religion. Although it doesn't release a public membership tally, its Facebook members' group numbers seven thousand, while its public Facebook has a full eighty-five thousand likes. TST members regularly protest—often in full Satanic regalia—at anti-Trump rallies such as the 2017 Women's March, and in 2019 were profiled extensively in the Penny Lane documentary *Hail Satan?* The Temple's headquarters—located (where else?) in Salem, Massachusetts—double as an experimental art gallery, complete with a giant statue of the demon Baphomet and a variety of local artwork depicting the demonic.

As former national TST spokesperson Jex Blackmore, a self-proclaimed "Satanic feminist," put it in an essay on a TST-affiliated website, "[I am] a Satanist, an individual who embraces her pariah status and actively challenges arbitrary authority in defense of personal sovereignty. To The Satanic Temple, Satan is a symbol of defiance, independence, wisdom and self-empowerment, and serves as an affirmation of natural existence."[45] Blackmore later appeared in the documentary *Hail Satan?* performing a Satanic ritual involving half-naked worshippers and pigs' heads on spikes, and announcing, "We are going to disrupt, distort, destroy. . . . We are going to storm press conferences, kidnap an executive, release snakes in the governor's mansion, execute the president."

The group has dwindled since 2018—in part due to Lucien Greaves's choice to engage the services of Marc Randazza, a free-speech lawyer known for his representation of alt-right icon Alex Jones, in the Twitter lawsuit. Several prominent members of TST, including Blackmore, ultimately disaffiliated from the organization while maintaining their wider Satanist principles. Nevertheless, during its heyday, the Satanic Temple represented the extreme form of contemporary witchcraft as a new religion: the transformation of symbols traditionally associated with evil into a holistic countercultural system.

Language like that of Bracciale, Blackmore, and the Satanic Temple may be extreme. But the rhetoric and symbol set of resistance witchcraft has permeated activist culture more broadly. In spring 2019, for example, when pro-choice advocates marched on the South Carolina state house to protest the Alabama abortion ban, protesters held signs identifying themselves as "the grandchildren of the witches you could not burn." (This phrase has also been spotted on placards at the annual Women's March.) Meanwhile, millennial-focused women's websites often use the language of witchcraft, dark magic, and diabolism interchangeably with the language of empowerment. One *Vice* profile of a Los Angeles–based Satanic doo-wop band, for example, praised them as "feminist as fuck."[46] A *Marie Claire* article celebrates "How Real-Life Resistance Witches Say They're Taking Down the Patriarchy," and a *Bustle* how-to activist guide encourages us to learn "What Witches Can Teach Us About Fighting Back against Trump."[47]

What all of these outlets have in common is a celebration of witchcraft as an oppositional and anti-institutional spiritual tradition: one that rejects established rules, regulations, and hierarchies in favor of transgression, subversion, and emotional authenticity. It is a religion of both personal empowerment and social change. Like the theology of wellness, the theology of witchcraft is rooted in the rejection of the System, and the reaffirmation of the individual self against it. Its worldview rests on the promise of personal and political empowerment through untraditional and literally unorthodox avenues.

"A witch is someone who recognizes and owns their power," one witch quoted in the *Bustle* piece says. "From witches we can learn that magic is available for the empowerment of everyone, no matter what their circumstances."

Granted, most self-proclaimed witches of Instagram are more interested in, say, cleansing sage or private meditation than they are in outright hexing the patriarchy. But for those religiously Remixed who want a wider sense of cosmic purpose to accompany their rituals of self-care, progressive occultism offers a framework both accessible and compelling. It offers a clear vision of meaning: a cosmic battle between the repressive forces of institutional Christianity and the liberating guerrillas of the marginalized. It offers a sense of concrete purpose, as each witch is called to participate in the dismantling of toxic social structures. It offers a wealth of rituals—from elaborate spell craft to more contained meditations to the kind of magical activism espoused in resistance handbooks—that witches can use to tap into that purpose. By hexing Donald Trump, they're able to tap into their spiritual identity as beings both marginalized and newly empowered—heroes for a new world order. And, no less importantly, modern witchcraft provides a community, one able to ascertain its members through a clear and effective visual shorthand. The gothic witch aesthetic is easily recognizable (and highly Instagrammable).

In recent months, progressive occultism—and the witch aesthetic—has become a visible part of the contemporary cultural mainstream. In spring 2019, for example, New York representative Alexandria Ocasio-Cortez's staff shared her birth time with a self-described psychic and astrologer, Arthur Lipp-Bonewits. While political candidates have often been intentionally cagey about the details of their birth—Hillary Clinton famously refused to give out her birth time to avoid precisely this kind of speculation—Ocasio-Cortez had no such compunctions.

It was a canny move. The mainstream media, predictably, went wild. Outlets from Vox to the Cut to Allure all speculated about what Ocasio-Cortez's astrological chart might tell us about her fitness for political office. The Cut quoted an expert astrologer's prediction that America was entering "Pluto return"—something that only happens every 250 years—which "means we're about to go through a major revolution in the country."[48] Meanwhile, Allure's Jeanna Kadlec concluded that "AOC's Aries Moon indicates that she's emotionally fed by a certain amount of independence, self-determination, and spontaneity," before determining that "independence always finds a way home."

Followers of Ocasio-Cortez's star chart, contemporary witch feminists, serious proponents of Satanic feminism, and dabblers in Sephora-accessible tarot cards alike all share both a hunger for the grounding effects of spiritual presence and a fervent conviction that personal spirituality should resist, rather than renew, the newly waning power of institutional religion. Our personal brands and our personal faiths are about creating a newer, freer version of ourselves.

Perhaps Saxena and Zimmerman put it best in *Basic Witches*, where they encourage would-be witches to place a "hex" on expectations of standard femininity by shaving their heads in what they call a "banishing spell."

"We witches cackle in the face of perfect femininity," they write. "We aren't interested in conforming to standards so much as triumphantly watching people squirm when the standards are destroyed. Your witchy hairdo can be an engine for confidence and power—power that comes from you alone."

seven

THE NEW PERFECTIONISM:
OUR SEXUAL UTOPIAS

N 1848, AN AMERICAN PREACHER NAMED JOHN HUMPHREY Noyes founded a new religion for a new world. Gathering his followers on a tract of farmland in Oneida, New York—the heart of the "burned-over" district known for generations' worth of religious revivals—Noyes, a well-to-do graduate of Dartmouth and Yale, preached a gospel of what he called Perfectionism. Human beings, he claimed, could make themselves sinless, not just in the hereafter, through the grace of Jesus Christ, but right here, right now, on this earth. The second coming of Jesus Christ, he told his followers, had already occurred sometime around 70 AD. Believers had nothing to wait for. They could be made perfect already. All they had to do was embrace the spirit of Christ within themselves.

Noyes's critics found this optimism suspicious. "Perfectionism . . . is the abrogation of all law," one naysayer wrote. After all, if you were already perfect, what did you need rules for? Didn't Perfectionism lead inexorably to moral relativism? "Mental impressions supposed to be from the Spirit of God are deemed perfect, truth, and law," another doubter worried, "paramount even to the Bible itself."[1]

Undeterred, eighty-seven original believers joined Noyes at Oneida — all lit by the fire of the same conviction — a number that would climb to about three hundred in the subsequent decades. They formed a commune, living off the proceeds of manufacturing silverware. They raised children together. They shared property in common.

And, perhaps most importantly, they shared wives.

The Oneida commune practiced something that Noyes had termed "free love." Human perfection and human sexual freedom, Noyes argued, went hand in hand. Once human beings were fundamentally good, the societal pettiness associated with sexual exclusivity — envy, possessiveness, lust, shame — could be done away with entirely. Human beings could transcend the trappings of a broken biology.

"The marriage supper of the Lamb," Noyes wrote, "is a feast at which every dish is free to every guest. Exclusiveness, jealousy, quarreling, have no place there, for the same reason as that which forbids the guests at a thanksgiving dinner to claim each his separate dish, and quarrel with the rest for his rights. In a holy community there is no more reason why sexual intercourse should be restrained by law than why eating and drinking should be, and there is as little occasion for shame in the one case as in the other."[2]

It's impossible to separate Noyes's vision of Perfectionism — of human transcendence and human potential — from his view of sex. Sexual liberation was part and parcel of his intuitional strain. If human beings were fundamentally pure, if their mostly deeply felt desires — even their erotic ones — were sanctified, then they should be free to act upon them. Food, drink, sex: all of these were normal, healthy, and even desirable appetites. Civilized society and its unjust and inefficacious institutions, including the institution of marriage, only separated human beings from their authentic selves. Why, Noyes asked, did human beings not breed as livestock did, allowing evolutionarily desirable men to impregnate the most women possible?

"We are too selfish and sensual and ignorant to do for ourselves what we have done for animals," he lamented. "We have surrounded ourselves with institutions corresponding to and required by our selfishness and sensuality and ignorance. But . . . we need not give up the hope of better things." He argued that there was nothing "natural" or "physiological" about jealousy or monogamy. Rather, Noyes said, these tendencies were "only passional and institutional." They had been learned. And so, in communities like Oneida, they could be *un*learned. "We may set the very highest standard of thorough-breeding before us as our goal," Noyes concluded, "[and] believe that every advance of civilization and science is carrying us toward it."[3]

Noyes may have been the first to coin the term "free love," but he wasn't the only one interested in it. As popular movements like New Thought and Spiritualism swarmed what seemed like every drawing room in Boston and New York, Americans became as obsessed with sexual liberation as they were with spiritual fulfillment. And, more often than not, the two were deeply intertwined. Practitioners of America's intuitional religions were likely to extend their suspicion of institutionalism to the institution of monogamous, heterosexual marriage.

There was, for example, a remarkably strong overlap between free love and the occult, with many of the nation's most prominent Spiritualists—such as the feminist and medium Victoria Woodhull, who was incidentally the first American woman to run for president—doubling as proponents of this new and radical sexual ethic. "I am a free lover," Woodhull wrote. "I have an inalienable, constitutional and natural right to love whom I may, to love as long or short a period as I can; to change that love every day if I please, and with that right neither you nor any law you can frame have any right to interfere. And I have the further right to demand a free and unrestricted exercise of that right, and it is your duty not only to accord it but as a community to see that I am protected in it."[4] Free love, too, was a not-uncommon doctrine among abolitionists, feminists, and other would-be nineteenth-century reformers, including utopian socialists.

While free-love proponents tended to couch their relationships in the language of spiritual connection or socialist radicalism, rather than sexual desire proper, they nevertheless treated the rejection of traditional sex paradigms as the first step toward throwing off the shackles of an unjust and obstinate society. "I only spoke against the injustice of all laws," one famous trance speaker, Achsa Sprague, insisted in a newspaper article, "the Laws of marriage among them."[5] Journals like the anarchist *Lucifer: The Light-Bearer* preached free love as a form of political resistance against an outmoded social order, while also casting doubt on the religious and medical establishment. In one 1893 issue, for example, the editor accuses local doctors of conspiring to pass laws against their New Thought–led brethren, before concluding, irritably, that "the American people seem about ready to meekly close their eyes and humbly say 'thy will be done' to the law-and-majority God."[6]

Both anti-institutional, intuitional spiritual practices and sexual freedom rested on the same fundamental principle: that humans were, at the deepest level of their being, not simply good but *perfectible*. Human frailty was, if not altogether an illusion, then at least a by-product of a society that failed to demand the best of its members. The newly perfected self was not subject to the same strictures as an ordinary, unenlightened person. It did not require societal rules or stringent sexual mores to limit its dizzying self-expression. Its desires, social and erotic alike, were sanctified by virtue of their authenticity: they were true, so they were good.

We see that same optimism at work in the romantic culture of the Remixed, a culture that doubles as communal expression. The Remixed, after all, are forming not just new brands of romantic attachments but also new forms of family units (including, through increasingly tribal friendship networks, chosen as well as biological family). The shape of the community that underpins the Remixed—and, in particular, the younger, progressive, urban Remixed—cannot be divorced from its implicit metaphysics. Intuitional religion yields practical results. Today's Remixed spiritual culture cannot be divorced from the way it shapes not just the Remixed's sense of meaning and purpose, but also their way of living in the world and with one another.

Or, to put it more bluntly, it's impossible to talk about the Remixed without talking about sex and the way in which our changing attitudes about sex are linked to our changing attitudes about the self and its cosmic purpose in the world.

Remixed culture, with its focus on individualism, personal choice, and the authenticity of the self, is inseparable from changes in American sexual and romantic mores. Remixed culture's valorization of sexual agency, its rejection of traditional proscriptive gender roles, and its willingness to rewrite the script of social and sexual interaction have all come to shape how the Remixed define their community and, implicitly, their church: the society and tribe with which they identify.

The idea that your spiritual and personal identity should be unique, bespoke, and authentic lends itself to an ethos of autonomy when it comes to defining ties with friends and family. Today's Remixed don't just want to choose how and what they worship, building a bricolage spiritual identity out of the narratives and elements that evoke meaning for them. They also want to apply that ethos in their most intimate spaces, envisioning nontraditional sexual, romantic, and familial bonds outside the script of heterosexual marriage (and, naturally) the parish church that solemnized it.

The implicit Noyesian Perfectionism of Remixed culture—we are good as we are; our jealousy and pettiness is the fault of our societies and not our souls—lends itself to a robust erotic optimism. We've hacked and optimized our diets, bodies, and spiritual practices. Why shouldn't we hack and optimize our sexual relationships too? Why should our relationships in community not reflect the "best selves" that intuitional culture has told us we are not merely allowed, but indeed called, to be?

Our faith in ourselves as perfected human beings demands a rethinking of our faith in heterosexual monogamy. Or, as one self-proclaimed Silicon Valley polyamorist told *Wired*'s Julian Sancton, "If life extension is possible, we might have to think about relationships differently. It's pretty hard to have an exclusive relationship with someone for 300 years."[7]

It's important to stress that today's intuitional model of sex, like Noyes's, isn't purely appetitive. It doesn't mandate orgies on demand or affirm that sexual fidelity is totally impossible. It does, however, make a fundamental metaphysical assumption that puts it at odds with the majority of organized religious traditions. Within Remixed culture, sexual desire, at its core, is fundamentally good and pure. Furthermore, its un-fettered consensual expression—within a marriage, outside a marriage, in a one-night stand, within a polyamorous triad, or with multiple unfamil-iar partners—is inherently empowering, an act of emotional and physical honesty, allowing your external actions to reflect your internal desires.

To act on your sexual attraction isn't just acceptable within this theo-logical system, it's a de facto act of bravery, a willful defiance of a society that mandates repression and enforces heterosexual monogamy. Fur-thermore, even if you and your partner do choose lifelong monogamy, it should be done not as a passive acquiescence to cultural or institu-tional norms (the height, Remixed culture suggests, of moral laziness), but rather as a carefully negotiated discussion, at times even a formal contract—a relationship that fits the precise and particular emotional, intellectual, and sexual needs of its specific participants, valid only inso-far as those needs are met.

It's important to stress, too, that what we're seeing in the Remixed sexual revolution isn't necessarily a renegotiation of *private* sexual ex-pression. Certain kinds of discreet polyamory, kink, or other nontradi-tional sexuality—the married man who quietly keeps a mistress, the established couple that swings with neighbors on the weekends, the married pair that keeps handcuffs in the nightstand—have never been wholly absent from the landscape of American sex. Rather, we're see-ing renegotiations of sex as a *social* phenomenon: how we choose not our private but our public partners and how we establish communal ties. The establishment of these new sexual-social relationships—and, with them, the wider community bonds fostered in their respective scenes—is as political as it is personal. A Remixed millennial in an open polyamorous triad, say, or a couple that practices a 24-7 master-slave relationship (attending "play parties" and other kink events where their relationship is taken for granted) are implicitly and often explic-itly redefining what relationships and families should look like. They're making statements not merely about the panoply of sexual options available to them, but also, more often than not, about what they see as the moral and ideological insufficiency of the institution of heterosexual, monogamous marriage, with its millennia of gender-specific baggage.

These social-sexual identities are, like witch culture, both personal and ideological—rooted in a conscious dissatisfaction with existing social institutions and a fully spiritual faith in the innate human ability to transcend them.

As kinky and polyamorous author Tristan Taormino puts it in her book *The Ultimate Guide to Kink*, "Where many people are content to just sit back and let life happen, we're not. We constantly engage our identities . . . and relationships." The monogamous, the vanilla, she implies, are simply content with the status quo, following tired and outmoded gender norms. But, among the kinky and polyamorous, "there are those who strive to go farther, faster, deeper." Kink in particular, she writes, is "a sacred space where we feel safe enough to try new things, push our boundaries, flirt with edges, and conquer fears . . . [with] the potential to heal old wounds and generate spiritual renewal."[8]

AMONG THE MOST PROMINENT OF THE NEW SEXUAL-SOCIAL IDENTITIES is the practice known as polyamory. Also known as ethical nonmonogamy, polyamory—the practice of having multiple romantic or sexual partners, with the full knowledge and consent of all involved—has, over the past decade, expanded from a seemingly fringe curiosity to one socially acceptable romantic model among many. Open relationships, "monogamish" relationships, "relationship anarchy," and "throuples" all fall well within the Overton window of culturally discussed dating options.

In 2009, *Newsweek*'s Jessica Bennett kicked off polyamory's entrée into mainstream culture by asking if the practice was—to quote the piece's headline—the "new sexual revolution." At that time, Bennett estimated that there were about half a million polyamorous families in America.

A decade later, that sexual revolution seems to have come to pass. Nearly every mainstream media outlet has published one, if not several, pieces on polyamory as the next frontier for sexual freedom.

In 2012, the cable TV network Showtime premiered a reality show, *Polyamory: Married and Dating*, which ran for two seasons. In 2013, it was *Scientific American*, echoing Bennett's phrasing and calling polyamory a "sexual revolution." In 2014, the *Atlantic* concluded that "poly and mono relationships are more alike than they are different." In 2017, the *Guardian's* Sunday paper, the *Observer*, praised polyamory as "a new way to love."[9] In 2017, the *New York Times* asked, "Is an Open Marriage a Happier Marriage?"[10] Two years later, the paper's style section ran an extensive photo feature called "It Works for Them," profiling members of a Brooklyn-based sex-positive "intentional community" called Hacienda.

By 2017, "polyamory" was one of the top-searched terms on Google.[11] As many as 5 percent of Americans now identify as polyamorous, with around 20 percent saying they've tried ethical nonmonogamy at some point in their lives.[12]

And even among those who don't practice it, public attitudes toward polyamory are ever more favorable. A 2015 YouGov poll found that about 25 percent of American adults find polyamory acceptable. That number skyrockets to 58 percent, however, among adults who consider religion "not at all" important, suggesting that attitudes about polyamory are directly correlated with traditional, institutional religiosity.[13] For our Remixed, at least, polyamory is a perfectly acceptable and available option.

THE POLYAMOROUS AREN'T THE ONLY NEW SEXUAL UTOPIANS OUT THERE. Kink culture, too, has gone mainstream. It has done so not merely as a private sexual practice, although the popularity of books like the risqué *Fifty Shades of Grey* series (another example of fandom going mainstream, as the series started as an alternate-universe erotic retelling of the popular Stephenie Meyer *Twilight* vampire novels) has done much to normalize nontraditional sexual practices as an acceptable middle-class way of spicing up a dead bedroom. Rather, kink—as an identifiable transgressive aesthetic, an identity marker, and a form of community-building—has reached cultural saturation. To be publicly and socially kinky isn't just to participate in a little light boudoir spanking, something plenty of Americans have been doing since long before the Kinsey report. (Contemporary North Americans are a pretty privately kinky bunch: one 2005 Durex survey suggests that 36 percent of Americans like being tied up, or doing the tying, during sex, while a 1999 study of university students in Canada found that 65 percent reported fantasizing about bondage.)[14] Rather, it's to embrace an identity, a community, and a utopian narrative of sexual reformulation no less visionary than Noyes's ethos of free love. Adults interested in BDSM (bondage, discipline, sadism, and masochism) or other nontraditional sexual practices don't just have newly unfettered Internet-based access to interested partners or instruction manuals about, for example, how to paddle someone safely. They also have access to a ready-made tribe: fellow attendees of "munches" (casual social gatherings of BDSM enthusiasts), play parties, fetish nights, or educational events who share the conviction that sexual liberation is at the heart of both personal perfection and political transformation.

These identity kinksters may not be as numerous as their privately kinky counterparts, but their numbers too are growing. The kinky social networking website FetLife has almost eight million users—primarily, but not exclusively, in the United States—and is the six-hundredth most popular website in the country.[15] Back in 2015, the website Kink.com publicized that Portland was the "kinkiest city" in America, with 4 percent of its population on FetLife. Two years later, five cities (including Boston and San Francisco) outstripped Portland, while in Atlanta— America's per capita kinkiest city—a full 7.5 percent of the population has signed up to the website.[16]

Nearly every major city in America, and most minor ones as well, has an established, if small, BDSM or kink community, complete with regular social gatherings, play parties, and workshops.

TODAY'S POLYAMOROUS AND KINKSTERS—LET'S CALL THEM "SEXUAL utopians"—are following in a centuries-old American tradition. From the days of Noyesian free love onward, American anti-institutionalism and American sexual liberation have been closely associated. For queer Americans, in particular, the creation of a sexual-social identity and the development of a robust subcultural community have long been intertwined.

It would be impossible to overestimate the significance of queer culture, not just as a model for sexual utopianism, but for the development of today's Remixed tribes more broadly. For much of the nineteenth and twentieth centuries, queer Americans, alienated from the predominant cultural institutions and traditional family structures, by necessity turned to creating their own. The queer chosen family is structured not around blood or birth or neighborhood or parish (it's worth remembering here that almost half of queer Americans are religiously unaffiliated), but rather around affinity and identity. It develops its own parallel institutions, vocabulary, and rituals. It rewrites the script of living in the world. (For much of the late nineteenth and early twentieth centuries, queer communities even had their own language: Polari, derived from Romani and fairground slang, which was primarily used among queer English people.) Even today, almost two-thirds of queer baby boomers report that they consider their friends chosen family—a testament to the degree to which queer culture has modeled the kind of affinity-based tribalization that now dominates Remixed approaches to community.[17]

Queer culture may well have been the first American subculture. Throughout the Prohibition era in particular, drag performances and masquerades and other queer-friendly spaces were ubiquitous in illicit urban nightlife. In New York City, drag venues like Rockland Palace's Hamilton Lodge, with a capacity of six thousand people, were regularly full of high-society gawkers like the Astor and Vanderbilt families.[18] And whole neighborhoods—Manhattan's Greenwich Village, the Castro district of San Francisco—came to double as de facto institutional homes for queer people unable to live freely elsewhere.

The end of the Second World War saw the birth of a specifically kinky queer culture, one in which the transgressive quality of kink and the transgressive nature of queer sexuality converged. Far from being intuitional, however, early kink culture was highly ritualistic and formalized: a conscious creation of a parallel institution to the heteronormative culture of the American military.

What came to be known as the "Old Guard" of BDSM culture arose among queer servicemen dealing with the aftershocks of coming home. For many of these men, the military had provided both a safe space for homosocial behavior (you could get both physically and emotionally close to other men) and a sense of meaning through ritualistic discipline. "War was (and is) serious business," writes Guy Baldwin, a historian of the Old Guard. "People died, buddies depended on each other for their lives, and the chips were down. Discipline was the order of the day, and the nation believed that only discipline and dedication would win the war and champion freedom."[19]

In the absence of the structure the military provided, ex-servicemen sought out communities that could replicate its hierarchical order and camaraderie. Just as many heterosexual veterans sought solace in motorcycle clubs, their queer counterparts developed leather clubs—echoing both the leather bomber jackets many servicemembers had worn and the motorcycle club aesthetic, albeit with a far more sexual component. "Club members would exchange their insignia with members of other clubs in friendship," Baldwin writes. "Christening rituals were transferred from tanks, ships and airplanes to motorcycles. . . . Piss was substituted for champagne; the military dress uniform hats became the leather bike caps. . . . All these elements were just as they had been during military service."[20]

Hierarchy, not affinity, governed sexual roles. Typically, a man would be expected to serve as a submissive—the erotic counterpart of a junior officer—before earning his way into dominance. Protocols tended to be standardized across a club or the community at large: never interact with or touch the collar of another man's designated "bottom" or submissive; ensure that bottoms always walk at least half a step behind their dominants. Early gay male kink identity was much less about self-expression than it was about subsuming the self into a wider institution—a parallel military that provided not just immediate pleasure but a sense of place in the world, a vision of both purpose and community. This community, in turn, offered its members something akin to a church: a shared identity cloistered from the prejudices and dangers of the outside world.

As one longtime BDSM practitioner, Patrick Califia, reflects: "Once upon a time . . . a bottom was expected to do some research on a master before approaching him . . . .If you made a bid for his attention and he took you home, you were supposed to make yourself available for whatever he liked to do. He was God and you were dirt. Whining later was seen as sissy bullshit. If you whine, no top would touch you—you were an unreliable coward who might make secret and sacred things public to the authority."[21]

While early leather culture wasn't a monolith—there was no single central authority or headquarters, and different clubs and groups did things differently—leather culture almost always involved clearly defined familial roles. Individual leather clubs offered a hub for interested participants and, eventually, wholesale leather families.

"These clans supplied many of the things we couldn't get from our own families of origin," recalls Baldwin, "including advice for love life and sex life; a home-life with our own kind; information about how leathersex worked; a place to barbecue on weekends; information on who were the responsible players in the community and who was best avoided; the very important Protocols, of course; and general mentoring."[22]

Throughout the 1960s and '70s, these leather clubs expanded—in part because of the proliferation of ex-servicemen from Korea and Vietnam, and in part because the leather scene had widened to include nonveterans (including women, with lesbian leather clubs becoming relatively common by the late 1970s) and, by the 1990s, straight BDSM practitioners as well.

MEANWHILE, POLYAMORY WAS UNDERGOING A SIMILAR FLOURISHING. While the swinging subculture of married recreational "wife swappers" had been around since the 1940s or '50s—like early kink, a result of military culture and, in particular, the close-knit communities that had grown up on military bases—it didn't go mainstream until the 1960s. It gained popularity largely among an otherwise traditionally staid demographic: white, heterosexual, upper-middle- and middle-class married couples. By 1969, swinging was a sufficiently recognized phenomenon that swingers Robert and Geri McGinley were able to found the Lifestyles Organization, America's oldest swinging group. In 1973, the organization pioneered its annual convention, which by the 1980s had attendees numbering in the two thousands. Nena and George O'Neill's book *Open Marriage: A New Life Style for Couples,* became a cult best seller.[23] But, by and large, neither swinging nor open marriage was particularly political or utopian at this time, focusing instead on the recreational elements of sexual pleasure (and its benefit for shoring up an otherwise conventional marriage) than on rewriting the rules of engagement on a broader scale.

But the explicitly utopian forms of poly culture—which valorized multiple mutually engaging and loving relationships over maximizing sexual encounters—arose more narrowly out of the California counterculture. Throughout the 1960s and '70s, several Noyes-style free-love communities—queer and straight—sprang up in San Francisco. Among the most famous of these was the Kerista commune, founded in the midseventies by Bro Jud Presmont. Like Noyes's Oneidans over a century before, Keristas saw intentional shared sexuality as integral to their overall mission—a "polyfidelity" that would allow the group to flourish while discouraging or forbidding sexual contact outside of it. Political multi-partnered sexuality continued to slowly gain traction in subcultures across the country. Newsletters like *Loving More* (founded in 1984) and books like Deborah Taj Anapol's 1995 *Love Without Limits* and Dossie Easton and Janet Hardy's 1997 *The Ethical Slut* provided information and guidance to the curious. (The term "poly-amorous" only entered the public sphere in 1990, in an article by activist Morning Glory Zell-Ravenheart.)

It was the Internet, however, that transformed kink and poly culture from relatively fringe institutions into easily accessible, easily consumable relationship options for the uninitiated. Today's kinksters and poly-curious don't need to seek out physical communes, nor do they need to participate in Old Guard–style hierarchies. The ubiquity of pornography, both "vanilla" and kinky, has made it possible not just to learn how to put fisting or spanking into practice, but also to discover altogether new fetishes, following pornographic webpage hashtags down the rabbit hole from #bondage to #hucow (don't Google it). FetLife forums allow users to trade tips when it comes to, say, Japanese rope bondage or hypnosis kink. Kink and poly communities are both simultaneously subcultures—in the sense that they function as parallel social nodes for their adherents—and accessible to the mainstream. The burgeoning number of resources—social networking websites, local kink or poly groups, multiple regional munches, play parties, informational books and websites, and workshops at adult stores—provide a straightforward path for any interested novice to invest time, money, and energy into joining this tribe. Kink itself has gone more mainstream in no small part due to the popularity of *Fifty Shades of Grey*, ironically often decried by practicing kinksters as highly inaccurate (emergency doctors reported a doubling in sex-toy related injuries in the past decade, with a significant spike following the book's publication).[24] But also, kink *as a lifestyle* has become an increasingly viable, visible option for the interested initiate. The barriers to entry are lower. The intensity and comprehensiveness of the lifestyle are more flexible. You can join an online kink group, for example, without having to commit to a regular presence in a tight-knit social scene. And the rules are less strict than they once were.

Unlike the kink communities of the Old Guard, today's kink and poly communities tend to focus on personal identity, rather than structural hierarchy. A self-identifying top or dom is no longer expected to put in his hours as a submissive. Unifying protocols—the idea that all submissives must refer to their dom(mes) as "master" or "mistress" every time they interact—have largely been replaced by more private negotiations between individual partners. Indeed, today's sexual utopians tend to reject labels altogether—be they hierarchal, religious, or political.

As you might expect, sexual utopians are significantly more likely to reject organized religion than their vanilla-monogamous peers. According to a 2018 study conducted by Gallaudet University's Julie Fennell, kinksters are significantly more likely than the national average to identify as religiously unaffiliated or as members of alternative or non-traditional religions. About 42 percent of the kinksters Fennell interviewed—all of whom reported "medium to high involvement" in their local kink scene—identified as religious Nones, with 24 percent calling themselves pagan, 7.5 Buddhist or Taoist, and 6.5 percent "other." Just 16 percent of them identified as Christian.[25] The polyamorous were likewise significantly less likely than their monogamous peers to affiliate with an organized faith. According to another 2018 study conducted by researchers at Western University in Ontario, while nearly 30 percent of monogamous participants identified as Christian, just 11 percent of poly respondents did.[26]

That study also found that, while poly respondents tended to be more progressive than their monogamous counterparts, a more significant difference was that they were much more likely to abandon party and religious labels altogether, instead opting for write-in responses. When it came to religion, for example, a full 31 percent of poly respondents (versus just 12 percent of monogamous ones) chose the "other" religion option available in the study, with the majority writing in "pagan" or "Wiccan" or (less commonly) "spiritual." Likewise, when it came to politics, the polyamorous were significantly more likely than their monogamous counterparts to choose third party or far-left affiliations and labels (such as the Green Party, Democratic socialist, or anarchist), while the monogamous were much more likely to identify as Republicans or Democrats.[27]

Sexual utopians often point to sex itself as a conduit for spiritual release. Participants in the study described the kind of intimacy fostered in a polyamorous relationship or a BDSM scene as profound and transcendent—a ritual that connects members of the community to one another and to something bigger.

"For me, BDSM is a lot more spiritual than religion," one of Fennel's respondents reports. "Religion for me is like, 'Oh, that's cool. I can believe that.' . . . But in the BDSM community you find a lot more spiritual people dealing with things such as energy or auras. Energy play or even things like astrology. And while I cannot logically fully believe in those things, I have felt the energy."

Likewise, a contributor to Taormino's anthology on kink, writing about anal fisting, celebrates how "to open up one's body and offer it to another is the height of strength and trust. To be the person who is invited to enter should be embraced with humility, compassion, and joy. Fisting is transcendent sex. If done in a way that honors all participants, it can take us on a journey to the farthest reaches of our growth as sexual, kinky, beings."[28] For many participants, sexuality represents an immediate, intuitive connection to other people and to a higher self.

"It was one of those moments of clarity," said another longtime lesbian BDSM participant, describing her experience to a sociologist. She evokes a sense of transcendence, "in which I feel that I am exactly where I am supposed to be, full of purpose and with an internal stillness that exists only in absolute surrender. Submission is a gift of full surrender to another person. It's the removal of ego and self-indulgence. When I engage in a heavy D/s [domination/submission] scene, I picture myself as a hollow cane of bamboo; I allow energy to flow through me, keeping complete focus and attention to my surroundings on my Dominant, without drawing attention to myself."[29]

Another participant in a study highlighted what she saw as the authenticity of her sexual experience, compared to the illusory and artificial nature of the "real," non-kinky world. Day-to-day life, she says, "is a trite fantasy world where you conceal who you are, where you conceal your feelings, where you conceal the truth because you have to get along with people. And the fantasy world, that's the reality because that's where people come out, that's where you see who people are and people see who you are." Kink isn't just about pleasure, but about honoring a fundamental moral and internal truth, being an unadulterated and unencumbered self. "You live for that world," she says. "Everything else is paying the rent, getting by, but that's where you live. That's where the masks come off. That's where you become yourself."[30]

If wellness culture centers the perfectibility of the body as the locus of personal spiritual growth, then sexual utopianism takes that corporeality to its logical conclusion. If the divine is to be found not just within ourselves but in the specifically physical experience of our *embodied* selves, why shouldn't sexuality be the place for us to access not just pleasure but meaning and purpose?

REWRITING THE SCRIPT

But that purpose isn't just individualistic. As with witch culture, sexual utopianism is predicated on institutional opposition—in this case to the strictures of heterosexual marriage. Embedded within both poly and kink culture is a deep suspicion of the status quo as fundamentally unjust and immoral, rooted in toxic misunderstandings of the gender binary and the purpose of love itself.

When we let society (and, in particular, Judeo-Christian society) get in the way, the intuitionalist narrative goes, it perverts our natural, healthy, and loving desires. It makes us jealous, possessive, and insecure. It demands that we love fewer people, or love them in a way that does not accord with our libidinal nature. It places arbitrary rules on what we can and cannot do, both in and out of the bedroom. When we choose to rebel against these societal restrictions and forge our own path, however, we're able to get in touch with our true selves and engage in more authentic and meaningful human relationships.

In one of her posts, Page Turner, of well-known polyamory blog *Poly.Land*, excoriates "toxic monogamy culture," implying that most monogamously inclined people have been brainwashed by it. If a polyamorous person wishes to be in a relationship with a monogamous person, Turner writes, they must be cautious, because "the beliefs that accompany toxic monogamy will consistently torture a person in a polyamorous environment."[31] The solution, she writes, is to "challenge the underlying assumptions of toxic monogamy," including the idea that "affection is zero sum. When you care for someone, that leaves less caring to give to others." She also pushes back on the notion that "one person must meet every possible emotional and social need that we have" and that "we must do whatever is needed to protect The Relationship—a simultaneously fragile and all-important entity."

Likewise, author-activist Tristan Taormino details the failures of the institution of monogamy in her guide to polyamory, *Opening Up*: "Monogamy sets most people up to fail. . . . We've collectively been sold a fairy tale of finding that one person with whom you'll live happily ever after. . . . Your one-and-only is your soul mate, the person with whom you are 100 percent sexually and emotionally compatible. . . . He or she will fulfill all your needs."[32] Because this standard is unrealistic, she writes, so many people fall short—especially when it comes to cheating. "Cheaters do at least one honest thing," she writes. "They acknowledge that one partner can't meet all their needs."[33] Their problem, according to Taormino, is not that they cheat (a normal human expression of desire) but that they lie about it, showing that they're fundamentally unable to embrace, and express, who they authentically are.

The nonmonogamous, by contrast, are, in Taormino's schema, "daring revolutionaries." "They don't stifle their behavior based on how they're supposed to act. They open the lines of communication. They talk honestly about what they want, face their fears and the fears of others, and figure out a way to pursue what they desire without deception. They don't limit themselves to sharing affection, flirting, sex, connection, romance, and love with just one person."[34] Elsewhere, Taormino extends her optimism to kinksters, whom she brands "lifelong learners . . . self-motivated to continually seek out new knowledge and skills . . . to constantly develop and improve themselves . . . to create alternative utopian worlds."[35]

Sexual utopians, in other words, take the Remixed focus on emotional authenticity and individualization to argue that human beings should tailor-make their own relationship models. Authors Dossie Easton and Janet Hardy put it best in their 1997 handbook *The Ethical Slut*, the de facto urtext of polyamory: "We believe that the current set of 'oughta-be's,' and any other set, are cultural artifacts. . . . Nature is wondrously diverse, offering us infinite possibilities. . . . We are paving new roads across new territory. We have no culturally approved scripts for open sexual lifestyles; we need to write our own. To write your own script requires a lot of effort, and a lot of honesty, and is the kind of hard work that brings many rewards. You may find the right way for you, and three years from now decide you want to live a different way—and that's fine. You write the script, you get to make the choices, and you get to change your mind, too."[36]

While poly and kink relationships do have rules—and indeed, intense BDSM settings often have many *more* rules than the average monogamous vanilla couple—these rules are determined not by outside moral or ethical systems but by the particular proclivities, values, needs, and desires of the participants. As one longtime submissive involved in a 24-7 master-slave relationship told me, "If we had a god, that god would be consent."[37]

That divinization of consent is twofold, and telling. On the one hand, it rightly prioritizes the importance of explicit sexual consent—that all practices, however risky or outré, be enthusiastically agreed to by all parties. But the valorization of consent as the foundational basis for human action among the sexual utopians says something much bigger about the way the Remixed see the world. Our purpose, at a very real and deep level, is to express our authentic selves, and to pursue that self through freedom. We are totally free beings, beholden to nobody but ourselves. Exerting that freedom, furthermore, is at the core of what it means to pursue the good. Our choices, in this model, both define and liberate us. When we choose to reject existing outlines and predetermined scripts about what our life should be like—allowing personal and particular negotiation to take the place of extrinsic moral authority in our lives—we are achieving something close to our purpose.

When it comes to sexual utopianism, the idea that practitioners are actively choosing the precise contours of their relationship is paramount. Partners—whether in couples, throuples, or master-slave relationships—are expected to come up with rules and expectations specific to their situation. Rules for the polyamorous might include the commitment to "fluid bond"—having sex without a barrier method of protection—exclusively with a primary partner, or allowing a primary partner to vet or veto additional ones. They might involve terms of disclosure or negotiations about the number of nights spent at the home of one partner or another.

In the BDSM community, likewise, relationship contracts spelling out precisely which practices are acceptable and consensual, and which beyond the pale, are commonplace. A pair of practitioners might mandate, for example, that a master or mistress has control over their slaves' finances and their clothing choices, but not their professional life or family relationships. It might delineate the proper etiquette around wearing a collar—a common mark of ownership and control in the community. It might spell out circumstances in which a submissive has the right to veto a punishment or command if it crosses a boundary, or choose a "safe word," which, when used, calls an immediate stop to a sexual or kink scene. In each case, what matters most is that the structure of the relationship is negotiated, implicitly or explicitly, as a personal contract between its participants. Societal rules and expectations about what a relationship should look like, on the other hand, are easily discarded at best, actively harmful at worst.

Perhaps the most extreme form of designed relationship is "relationship anarchy," a term coined by Andie Nordgren in 2006. Equal parts radical libertarianism and radical free love, relationship anarchy runs on the principle that relationships should never be based on the "foundation of entitlement" that traditional monogamy culture demands. Obligations and hierarchy lead to relationships in which people are treated as their social roles rather than as unique individuals. Ordering relationships—having a primary and a secondary partner, or delineating sharply between partners and friends—is itself oppressive. "Don't rank and compare people and relationships," Nordgren exhorts, but "cherish the individual and your connection to them. . . . Each relationship is independent, and a relationship between autonomous individuals."

Nordgren goes on to explain, "Relationship anarchy is not about never committing to anything—it's about designing your own commitments with the people around you, and freeing them from norms dictating that certain types of commitments are a requirement for love to be real, or that some commitments like raising children or moving in together have to be driven by certain kinds of feelings. Start from scratch and be explicit about what kind of commitments you want to make with other people!"[38]

This intuitional approach to sexuality lends itself naturally to the language and rhetoric of self-care. Because our sexual desires are ingrained and inherent—needs that one person (or at least one person without a toolbox full of whips and dildos) cannot possibly fulfill—we have not just the right but the moral obligation to satiate them. Only by acting on what we want can we be our true, authentic selves. To fail to do so would be an act of violent repression. But if we mix and match our partners to sate our various emotional, sexual, and physical needs, then we are taking admirable ownership of our longings.

In her study on polyamory in America, sociologist Elisabeth Sheff quotes one practitioner, a magazine editor named Melanie Lupine. "[What] I've learned is polyamory helps me, especially as a woman, to keep my autonomy so that I don't lose myself," Lupine tells Sheff, "whether it be within a relationship, like a man or a woman, or my children. It helps me to define what I want and set my boundaries and take relationships at what I need." She adds, succinctly, "My number one relationship is with myself."[39]

THE CREATION OF CHOSEN TRIBES

Not all Remixed practice polyamory or kink, of course. But these practices represent a formalized extreme of the way that more and more of the Remixed, particularly millennials, think about not just sex but familial relationships and community more broadly.

Once, our churches and our synagogues doubled as our chosen family—the extended community we could trust to support us in times of major life upheaval, to see us through births, marriages, and deaths. There was a clear series of concentric circles of communal obligation: the heterosexual, monogamously married couple relied on its extended family; that extended family, in turn, relied on its neighborhood and religious institutions.

Today, however, heterosexual marriage—and the religious institutions that have traditionally solemnized it—seems to have failed. The boomer parents of most millennials, after all, were more likely than those of any other generation to get divorced. The 1970s and '80s were the peak time for divorce in America, spiking in 1979 at 5.3 annual divorces per one thousand Americans.[40] Even throughout the 1990s, divorce rates for that same boomer demographic continued to double, while divorce rates for all other age groups declined.[41] Meanwhile, those marginalized by mainstream institutional religious culture—particularly queer Americans, but also those suspicious of monogamy or heteronormative romantic expectations—now have viable and public alternative models of what sex, love, and family might look like.

The younger Remixed have grown up with clear examples of marriages and relationships—largely, but not exclusively, heterosexual—that don't work, and they have the technological tools and social freedom to seek out like-minded people with whom to forge relationships that do. They're marrying later—the median age of marriage is now 29.5 for men and 27.4 for women, up from 23 for men and 20.8 for women fifty years ago—and are three times as likely to never marry at all as their grandparents were.[42]

Meanwhile, they're exposed to alternate models of sexual relationships that offer their own parallel rituals and ceremonies, their own language, and their own communities to support them. The Remixed can get married, sure, but they can also participate in a "collaring" ceremony, in which a dominant puts a formal ownership collar around the neck of his or her chosen submissive. They can have a boyfriend, a girlfriend, a husband, a wife, or a "metamour" (the lover of one's lover). They can choose casual sex, or date multiple people at once, or date a married couple.

They can also use apps to search for partners precisely within their desired parameters, rather than relying on meeting people within the same community, social set, or neighborhood. They can also choose the metrics by which they judge those partners. There are dating sites that cater specifically to stoners, goths, and cat lovers, as well as mainstream sites like OkCupid, which has over fifty million members and encourages would-be matches to fill out hundreds of searchable questions about their values—including their kinks, sexual appetites, political leanings, and openness to vegetarianism. Millennials can also find people from similar tribes—fandoms or wellness or yoga or witchcraft—on the apps and allow that affinity to define their relationship parameters, if they so choose.

How effective these apps are at creating community beyond sexual pairings is, however, debatable. A 2019 study found that about 30 percent of millennials report experiencing loneliness, compared to 20 percent of Gen Xers and 15 percent of baby boomers.[43]

It may be tempting to ask what sex has to do with religion. But it's impossible to separate societal attitudes toward sex and family from the creation of a societal church—a wider moral and social community that solemnizes, affirms, and encourages the familial bonds of its members. Sexual utopianism is, at its core, the systemized creation of idealistic churches that preach a doctrine of human perfectibility and transcendence and that envision the fulfillment of the body and the soul as one and the same. Like Transcendentalism, New Thought, and Noyesian free love, contemporary Remixed culture links personal success and spiritual well-being, envisioning a world in which we become our best selves by embracing and celebrating, rather than repressing, our wants and needs.

The same intuitional strain that has come to define how today's Remixed approach their sense of meaning and purpose has also influenced how they build community and approach the rituals associated with life stages, including marriage. The Internet-driven individualization of the contemporary American Remixed religious landscape—with its focus on mixing and matching practices, valorizing emotional authenticity, and honoring care for the physical body as sacred—is inseparable from a consumer-capitalist model of sexuality, in which we are encouraged to choose the relationship model that best meets our specifications. The moral communities we create around ourselves increasingly share the same value on which we predicate our decision-making: the idea that self-fulfillment is the surest avenue to the ultimate good. Now, no less than in Noyes's Oneida, our attitudes toward sex and the body are based on a fundamental optimism about human potential and human goodness, a goodness that not only doesn't need society but indeed actively rebels against it.

Seventy-four percent of American millennials now say that they agree with the statement "whatever is right for your life or works best for you is the only truth you can know."[44] Just 39 percent of seniors feel the same way. (Likewise, among the religiously unaffiliated of all ages, 67 percent of respondents said they agreed, compared to just 41 percent of Christians.) Members of Generation Z (born between 1999 and 2005) are twice as likely as boomers (24 to 12 percent) to say that "what is morally right and wrong changes over time based on society." Twenty-one percent of millennials felt the same way.

Our sexual utopianism and spiritual self-care, ultimately, are two sides of the same coin. They replace the extrinsic bastions of morality and authority—the state, the church, the institution of marriage—with the self. We are the arbiters not just of our personal or sexual lives, but of our own individual moral universe. Our acts are sanctified and solemnized.

In 1856, the abolitionist and Spiritualist Francis Barry wrote an editorial in the antislavery paper the *Liberator*, arguing that "free lovers demand perfect freedom and unconditional freedom for love . . . and they are perfectly willing that the heart shall decide for itself."

Today's Remixed culture takes this freedom as gospel.

eight

TWO DOCTRINES FOR
A GODLESS WORLD

*I am the only truth I know. My emotions are God-given.
They tell me what to do and how to live. To be my truest
self I should follow my instincts. My body and my gut know
more than my mind. An unjust and repressive society has
held me back from becoming my best self. It has warped my
faith in my own abilities and my relationship with others. I
owe it to myself to practice self-care. I owe it to the world
to perfect myself: physically, spiritually, and morally.*

*There is no objective right or wrong. Different people and
different societies have different moral obligations.*

THESE ARE, AS WE HAVE ALREADY SEEN, THE FOUNDATIONAL tenets of contemporary American intuitional religion. While not all of the Remixed would explicitly affirm every aspect of this ideology, these tendencies nevertheless run through all of Remixed consumer culture. They permeate the wellness industry, and how we think about health more broadly. They permeate the oft-commodified spirituality of the spiritual but not religious—from the tarot cards briefly sold at Sephora to the New Thought–tinged mantras posted on SoulCycle's

Instagram feed. They permeate how we think about our relationship to foundational texts and established tradition, how we feel about our bodies and health, how we envision explicit spirituality, and how we think about sex, romance, and the families we choose to make our own.

But the question remains: How can these many and varied religions of the self come together? The kaleidoscopic nature of intuitionalism necessarily lends itself to fracture, to ever-smaller, ever-more-fragmented, and ever-more-ideologically-aligned tribes.

But if these ideologies are to survive, they will need to take on a more formal shape. They need to become not merely religious sentiments or implicit theologies, but, ironically, institutions — narratives and communities capable of both withstanding the weight of internal dissent and providing a unified front against more established spiritual rivals. Beyond offering a pleasing product for individuals to consume at will, they need to provide a wholesale ideology no less powerful than, say, American evangelical Christianity or the Catholic Church.

In other words, can the Remixed intuitional strain be reworked once more into a civil religion? And what would that even look like?

Are there ideologies, rooted in and derived from intuitional culture, that provide a sufficiently strong narrative, that offer a robust sense of not only meaning and purpose but also ritual and community, that could replace the benign optimism of midcentury Protestantism?

IN OUR CURRENT POLITICAL MOMENT, TWO OPTIONS ARE CURRENTLY contending for the role of Remixed culture's de facto civil religion.

The first and perhaps most likely claimant is social justice culture: a movement that already underpins much of the current raft of occult-tinged, explicitly SBNR practices. Utopian in scope, progressive in its vision of history, social justice culture transforms the personal and individualistic tenets of New Thought (a repressive society warps our sense of cognition and ability to be our truest self) and gives it a firmly political cast: the Goliaths of society that must be struck down are racism, sexism, and other forms of bigotry and injustice.

The solution to the problem of society comes not merely through self-care, though, but through struggle, tearing down the bastions of what has come before. All of society is the script that must be rewritten. The arc of history bends toward a new Eden. The intuitionalist focus on emotions and authenticity manifests itself in the primacy social justice culture puts on lived experience as perhaps the most authoritative force for moral determination.

The second claimant—one that is less visible in the American media landscape but perhaps more politically and financially potent— is the no-less-utopian culture of Silicon Valley: the Rationalists and Transhumanists and proponents of the Californian Ideology who envision an equally radical account of human potential. Their vision of history, too, is at once linear and progressive, wending toward a tipping point of human technological progress. Less likely than their social justice counterparts to put their faith in lived experience—these are, ostensibly, men and women of science after all—they're nevertheless all the more confident in the intellectual potential to hack, improve upon, and even optimize elements of human nature. They're confident, too, in the moral imperative to do so. The ultimate good, within this technoutopian framework, is an optimized self, a finely-tuned machine.

Politically and demographically, these two movements are very different. Social justice culture is, as you might imagine, extremely progressive. The techno-utopians tend toward a libertarianism so strong that it borders on Randian Objectivism. Social justice culture is disproportionately composed of women, people of color, and queer people. Techno-utopianism is largely, although not exclusively, male and white.

Although there are points of overlap—the annual Nevada-based Burning Man festival, for example, which celebrates "radical inclusion" and "radical self-expression," and where tents devoted to kink communities and witchcraft stand alongside the private tents of Peter Thiel, Mark Zuckerberg, and Google's Larry Page—social justice culture and techno-utopianism are largely distinct entities and identities.

When it comes to hot-button culture-war issues, furthermore, the two groups are more likely than not to be on wildly opposing sides.

The 2017 firing of Google engineer James Damore, for example, whose leaked memo "Google's Ideological Echo Chamber" claimed that gender differences in STEM fields were largely biological and innate, became a cri de coeur for techno-utopians and social justice activists alike. Social justice activists saw it as evidence of a Silicon Valley culture rooted in pseudoscientific sexism; techno-utopians, conversely, claimed that Damore was unfairly maligned for making public scientifically valid research and for resisting the would-be "social justice warriors" of Google in the first place.

Writer and blogger Scott Alexander, a prominent member of the techno-utopian subculture known as the Rationalist community, publicly defended Damore's scientific stance, lamenting that "everyone knows that disagreeing with social justice is a firing offense these days."[1] Meanwhile, popular feminist website *Jezebel* condemned Damore as "a white man who might as well be gunning for a position in the Trump administration . . . [who] argued what only a privileged white man could."[2]

But, despite their cosmetic and demographic differences, social justice culture and techno-utopianism are both inheritors of American Remixed intuitionalism as a whole.

Both groups treat society—its rules, maxims, and mores—with disdain and suspicion. In the social justice and techno-utopian ethos alike, expectations and institutions exist solely to be torn down. Disruption is, quite literally, a virtue. PayPal founder and techno-utopian titan Peter Thiel told the *New Yorker* in 2011 that "disrupt" and "risk" were his two favorite words.[3]

Traditional markers of expertise and authority, such as a PhD from an elite university or a fancy job title, are as likely as not to be seen as bugs, not features. Members of both subcultures are highly open to nontraditional romantic and sexual relationship models, particularly polyamory.

And, most importantly, both groups treat earthly self-actualization—whether of the self alone or of the self in the context of its varied ethnic and sexual identities—as the ultimate goal of their utopian vision. Both groups are fundamentally eschatological yet thoroughly materialist.

They seek not salvation *out there*, but a purification *down here*, a kingdom of heaven that can be realized fully on this earth, rather than in a world to come—whether in a Marxist-style cultural revolution or in a robot-fueled singularity. The seeming tyranny of biology—the apparent gender binary, or even death itself—can be overturned or else overwritten. Both groups valorize transcendence, not off the material plane but rather within it. To transcend biology or to transcend deep-rooted prejudices is to achieve a kind of earthly divinity.

Ultimately human beings, and only human beings, are the arbiters of goodness in these new faith systems. The techno-utopian faith in intellectual potential (to become cyborgs, say, or defeat death) and the social justice movement's faith in the priority of lived experience (to adjudicate disputes) both place the fundamental judgments of goodness, morality, and progress in the hands of human beings, not God.

Back in 1841, Transcendentalist philosopher Ralph Waldo Emerson—among the first of the American intuitionalists—envisioned the potential of human self-reliance to make ordinary mortals into miniature gods: "He who knows that power is inborn, that he is weak because he has looked for good out of him and elsewhere . . . [and who] throws himself unhesitatingly on his thought, instantly rights himself, stands in the erect position, commands his limbs, works miracles."[4]

More and more of us are miracle workers, now.

THE GOSPEL OF SOCIAL JUSTICE

Over the past half decade, the progressive vision known as the social justice movement has become an integral part of the American cultural landscape, morphing from a relatively small movement, largely confined to college campuses, to one that think tank More in Common identified as comprising a full 8 percent of the American population.[5]

According to that study, these "progressive activists"—to use More in Common's preferred terminology—are deeply suspicious of what they see as white and male privilege, and the role of both racism and sexism in shaping a society they see as fundamentally, and perhaps irremediably, unjust. They see government and wider civil institutions—the police, for example, or border control forces—not merely as ineffectual, but as actively malevolent agents of structural inequality and the cruelty and brutality such inequality manifests.

Compared to the national average, they are more than twice as likely to say that they "never pray," twice as likely to have finished college, and about three times more likely to say they're "ashamed to be an American." They overwhelmingly reject the idea that "men and women have different roles." They are dubious both of authority (only 13 percent say it's more important for children to be well-behaved than creative) and of the efficacy of traditional routes to adulthood (just 5 percent say they believe "hard work will always lead to success"). They're slightly whiter, and slightly younger, than the national average. And politics matters to them as an integral part of their identity and the way they spend their time. Seventy-four percent of them call politics one of their hobbies, compared to just 35 percent of Americans at large.

The movement has made its way into the corridors of power. The 2018 midterm elections saw the induction into Congress of what became known as "the Squad": four freshman representatives—Alexandria Ocasio-Cortez, Ilhan Omar, Rashida Tlaib, and Ayanna Pressley—who openly espoused social justice values, from wealth redistribution to reparations for black Americans to the abolishment of US Immigration and Customs Enforcement (ICE), and advocated for them on the House floor. Ocasio-Cortez's Green New Deal—a proposal to reach net-zero global carbon emissions by 2050, sponsored with Massachusetts senator Ed Markey—has become among the most hot-button issues in the country. Openly progressive candidates, such as Elizabeth Warren and Bernie Sanders, have become viable front-runners for the Democratic presidential nomination in 2020.

The ideals of social justice culture—with its distrust of unjust institutions, its fury at those deemed both perpetrators and benefactors of this unfairness, and its radical demand for a rewriting of the political script—have fueled movements like #MeToo, condemning the widespread nature of sexual harassment in America, and Black Lives

Matter, protesting police brutality and racism against African Americans. Fueled by social media and, in particular, by Twitter, which allows total strangers to find one another on thematically relevant hashtags, these movements have metamorphosed from social media cris de coeur to culturally transformative events with resonance far beyond the bounds of digital space.

The first use of the #BlackLivesMatter hashtag came in 2013, following the controversial acquittal of George Zimmerman in the shooting death of unarmed black teenager Trayvon Martin. The movement came to national prominence the following year after two more unarmed black men—Michael Brown of Ferguson, Missouri, and Eric Garner of Staten Island, New York—were killed by white police officers, sparking a wave of protests and riots across the country. The hashtag's originators—Alicia Garza, Patrisse Cullors, and Opal Tometi—later transformed the online movement into an advocacy network with thirty chapters across the country, overseeing protests like the one that took place in 2015 at the University of Missouri over accusations of normalized on-campus racism and that resulted in the resignation of university president Tim Wolfe. Between 2013 and 2018, as #BlackLivesMatter was tweeted thirty million times, police brutality—and racism more broadly—became an integral part of American political discourse.[6]

The hashtag #MeToo, similarly, was used nineteen million times between the dawning of the movement in autumn 2017—when a number of actresses came forward with accusations of rape and sexual harassment against cinema mogul Harvey Weinstein, prompting a wider outpouring of accusations of misconduct across numerous industries—and late 2018.[7] Like its predecessor Black Lives Matter, #MeToo transformed tacit cultural acceptance of a social ill—in this case, sexual harassment—into a controversial political issue. Over two hundred influential or prominent men in a variety of fields, from Democratic senator Al Franken to television host Charlie Rose to comedian Louis C.K. to political journalist Mark Halperin, were fired or resigned from their positions after being accused of sexual harassment.[8]

Even beyond these specific movements, social justice culture has entered the mainstream. Prominent advocates of social justice are no longer fringe activist voices. Rather, they're comfortably ensconced within the mainstream media establishment. In 2018, for example, the *New York Times*—a publication whose relative centrism can be gleaned from the fact that left- and right-wing critics alike are constantly accusing it of extreme bias—attracted a media firestorm by hiring the *Verge*'s Sarah Jeong, a tech reporter known for her fervent and at times vitriolic tweets on race and class (examples include "Oh man it's kind of sick how much joy I get out of being cruel to old white men" and "#CancelWhitePeople") for its editorial board. That same year, the *Washington Post* published an op-ed by a gender studies professor titled "Why Can't We Hate Men?" which exhorted her male readers to "pledge to vote for feminist women only. Don't run for office. Don't be in charge of anything. Step away from the power. We got this. And please know that your crocodile tears won't be wiped away by us anymore. We have every right to hate you. You have done us wrong. #BecausePatriarchy. It is long past time to play hard for Team Feminism. And win."[9] "Trigger warnings"—content warnings about disturbing material, like rape or racism, that might trigger a student's post-traumatic stress disorder—have become commonplace on college campuses; one 2016 NPR study found that about half of college professors had used them.[10]

But social justice has morphed into more than just a purely ideological movement. It's also increasingly a viable consumer category: a means by which savvy corporations can cater to millennials' moral self-regard in the way that, a generation ago, they might have appealed to would-be customers' desire for wealth or glamour. Wokeness, like wellness, is an aspiration for millennials, one that can, at least temporarily, be purchased through an ethically sourced or activist-branded product, such as a Pride-themed Coca-Cola or a #MeToo-branded razor.

This craze might be said to have begun around 2012, when a number of progressive, social-justice-minded clickbait websites like *Upworthy*, *BuzzFeed,* and *Mic* (then known as *PolicyMic*)—galvanized by Facebook's sharing algorithms, which encouraged users to share inspiring content with their friends—came to dominate the media landscape with easily digestible, feel-good headlines. By 2013, pack leader *Upworthy* (examples include "Mitt Romney Accidentally Confronts a Gay Veteran; Awesomeness Ensues" and "Boom, Roasted: Here's Why You Don't Ask a Feminist to Hawk Your Sexist Product") was the fastest-growing media website of all time, with ninety million users a month.[11] Meanwhile, *Mic* pioneered tailored-for-virality headline structures, such as the "in one perfect tweet" takedown ("In a Single Tweet, One Man Beautifully Destroys the Hypocrisy of Anti-Muslim Bigotry"). By 2015, BuzzFeed was getting more shares than BBC and Fox News combined.[12]

While changes in Facebook's algorithms ultimately scuttled many of these websites' business models, their brand of marketable morality (and clickable headline style) permeated the mainstream media. As early as December 2013, the *Atlantic* was asking, "Why are Upworthy Headlines Suddenly Everywhere?" and concluding that for "publishers trying to grab more traffic from Facebook, the path became clear. Borrow, adapt, employ the Upworthy style post haste."[13]

In the post-Trump era, wokeness has become an even more powerful identity marker. *Teen Vogue*—not traditionally the bastion of progressive activism—has gone viral publishing articles like Lauren Duca's 2016 "Donald Trump Is Gaslighting America," recognizing that today's teenage girls are now frequently intimately familiar with the language of domestic psychological abuse. In January 2017, *New York* magazine's style blog the *Cut* advertised fashionable, comfortable clothing to wear to the anti-Trump Women's March.[14] Meanwhile, the CEO of makeup company Glossier showed up to the protest toting a sign emblazoned with the company's logo.[15] That same year, shortly after Donald Trump's ban on travelers from a number of majority-Muslim countries, Starbucks announced that it planned to hire ten thousand refugees across its stores. By 2018, Nike was celebrating Black Lives Matter with its "Believe in Something" ad campaign, while Pepsi was hiring Instagram influencer (and Kardashian sibling) Kendall Jenner in a commercial that featured her stopping police cars at a protest, another reference to Black Lives Matter.

Social justice, in other words, is a bona fide cultural phenomenon: a unified system of ideals and practices as deeply intertwined as any traditional organized religion. If the More in Common estimate of 8 percent of Americans is an accurate measure of those who belong to the social justice movement, it means that there are more than four times as many social justice activists as there are American Jews.

THE RISE OF SOCIAL JUSTICE CULTURE IN AMERICA IS, OF COURSE, inexorably linked to the rise of its perhaps most visible opponent: Donald Trump. Gleefully politically incorrect, prone to openly mocking feminist and anti-racist causes, boastful about his past instances of sexual assault, and brimming with masculinist braggadocio, Trump has built his electoral brand as a conscious foe to America's social justice warriors, to use a pejorative term for the movement.

At the same time, galvanized by Trump's victory, the rhetoric of the social justice movement has permeated the broader left-wing political ethos. In the wake of the apparent failure of the classical liberal establishment, personified by Hillary Clinton, many disappointed Democrats found in the battleground of social justice a more emotionally robust approach to politics—one capable, as it seemed Clinton and Clintonism was not, of countering Trump's highly potent strain of atavistic authoritarianism. Social justice shared Trumpism's willingness to *burn it all down*, to *drain the swamp*, to radically remake what appeared to be an imploded political landscape, positioning itself as the only rival claimant willing and able to fight Trumpism's fire with rhetorical fire.

It seems to be working. According to a 2018 *Washington Post* study, one in five Americans now say they have attended at least one rally or political protest since early 2016. Almost one-fifth of these attendees said they'd never been to a protest before. These new activists aren't necessarily well-educated millennials (44 percent are at least fifty years old, and only 50 percent say they're college graduates), nor are they necessarily social justice warriors in the strictest sense of the term.[16] Nevertheless, they're actively participating in a community whose ideals, vocabulary, and vision are increasingly shaped by the young, socially progressive voices of the social justice movement.

The post-2016 success of social justice culture is in part due to the fact that it encompasses not merely opposition to Trump, but an explanation for him. In the wake of the 2016 elections, many self-proclaimed Democrats reported a shock that bordered on the existential. "This election broke me," one aghast college senior told the *Nation*. "It broke a lot of us. This election went against everything I thought the United States of America stood for. This country was meant to welcome people of all colors, religions, shapes, sizes, and minds. But here I am sitting at my computer confused as to how a man who stands against all of those things is going to be the most powerful man in the world for the next four years."[17] Another student reported that she "was in complete shock when every trusted source I had turned out to be dead wrong. . . . It was still very hard to understand a reality I hadn't envisioned, a Trump win, because I'd been told it was so improbable. It made me question what went wrong in the polls, in the reporting, and in the general understanding of how American politics works."[18] Trump's victory seemed to represent a fundamental breakdown of the system—the conglomerate of pollsters and politicians and experts and reporters who, somehow, had guaranteed an America as smoothly and benignly functional as the one that had dominated the midcentury. It's worth noting that 92 percent of Americans who voted for Hillary Clinton said that Donald Trump provoked in them feelings not just of distaste but fear.[19]

Trump's election may have shocked and horrified plenty of garden-variety Democrats. But to initiated activists, it was inevitable. His victory, they argued, was evidence not merely of a temporary breakdown of American institutions in 2016, but rather a much more deeply ingrained rot in the fabric of America itself.

The historical narrative of social justice—that America, despite its lofty political ideals of freedom and justice for all, is at its core a country built on white supremacy, patriarchy, repression, and hatred—became, for many on the political left, an etiology at once reassuring and unsettling, evidence that Trump's election was not simply a chaotic anomaly but rather rooted in a wider, if more insidious, historical trend. America was, is, and will remain broken. (Sixty percent of the "progressive activists" More in Common identified say they're "not proud" of America's history.) Racism, sexism, homophobia—all these are, in the social justice narrative, as American as apple pie. Seen through this lens, Trump's election becomes not a disruption of American liberal ideals but rather their natural and inevitable conclusion.

As writer Ta-Nehisi Coates put it in a keynote speech the day after 2016 election, "When Donald Trump went before audiences and was talking about Muslims, when he went into Chicago and talked about law and order . . . he was appealing to a nation's spirit, something that was old in us, something that was ancient in us, something that goes back to 1619," the year enslaved Africans first arrived in America. "We had deeply, deeply underestimated ourselves," he continued. "We had deeply, deeply underestimated our past."[20]

Four years after Trump's election, that vision of history has since made it all the way to the New York Times, which in 2019 launched the 1619 Project, an initiative commemorating the four-hundredth anniversary of enslaved Africans' arrival on American shores. The project is meant to, in the paper's own words, "reframe the country's history, understanding 1619 as our true founding" and makes the argument that "our democracy's ideals were false when they were written."[21] One of the project's contributors, Nikole Hannah-Jones, argues that "this nation was founded not as a democracy but as a slavocracy."[22]

To its proponents, this vision of history was a necessary corrective to centuries of whitewashing the worst of America's legacy. To critics on the right, it was a traitorous decrial of the American founding ideal. Yet, at its core, the social justice movement's rendering of America isn't merely a history. It's also a profound and powerful theodicy capable of explaining the evils of 2016 with recourse to a still wickeder past.

Those who have called social justice a new religion have traditionally done so pejoratively. Conservative New York magazine commentator Andrew Sullivan derisively called the movement the "Great Awokening," deriding its zealots as humorless neo-puritans who reveled in "cancelling" the insufficiently enlightened. "Like early modern Christians," Sullivan wrote in 2018, "they punish heresy by banishing sinners from society or coercing them to public demonstrations of shame, and provide an avenue for redemption in the form of a thorough public confession of sin. . . . A Christian is born again; an activist gets woke."[23]

The *National Review*'s David French was equally skeptical. "The campus culture war is a religious war," French wrote in 2015, "a so-far largely peaceful counterpart to the violent purges and revolutions of jihad. One faith has been expunged, relegated to the margins of the academy, and now another fills the vacuum. Out with the Christianity that spawned American higher education, in with a ferocious new faith—a social-justice progressivism unrestrained by humility and consumed with righteous zeal."[24]

Yet social justice's most fervent critics, in their knee-jerk derisions of it as a ridiculous cult, fail to realize quite how right they are. Social justice *is* a religion, and—as with any other religion—its potency as a source of meaning and its potential for zealotry are naturally correlated.

Which is to say, as a religion, social justice works. It works not merely in the sense that a lot of people take it very seriously and react angrily when people misuse its sacred terms (as Sullivan and French imply), but also in a much more fundamental and potentially constructive way. It has done what so much of anodyne, classical liberalism has failed to do. It has imbued the secular sphere with meaning. It has reenchanted a godless world.

Like its Marxist antecedents, from which it draws much of its imagery and inspiration, modern social justice culture has managed to create a thoroughly compelling, eschatologically focused account of a meaningful world, in which every human being has a fundamental purpose in a cosmic struggle, all without including, well, God.

As a moral vision, as a conception of history, and as a galvanizing force for action, it is wildly effective. To dismiss it as silly or jejune is to profoundly overlook what it reveals about the American search for meaning and about the spiritual hunger of those who subscribe to it.

The social justice movement is so successful because it replicates the cornerstones of traditional religion—meaning, purpose, community, and ritual—in an internally cohesive way. It takes the varied tenets of intuitionalism—its prioritization of the self, emotions, and identity, its New Thought–inflected suspicion of authority, its utopian vision of a better world born phoenix-like from the ashes of the old—and threads them together into a visionary narrative of political resistance and moral renewal. It provides both an explanation for evil (an unjust society that transcends any one agentic individual and, more specifically, straight white men) and a language, symbol set, and collection of rituals (from checking one's privilege to calling out someone else to engaging in enlightened activism) with which to combat that evil force. At its most effective, social justice culture creates a mythic narrative about the world we live in, filling the seeming chaos of history and its myriad injustices with an eschatological promise: that human beings can, should, and shall do better. The new world that will inevitably arise from the ashes of a patriarchal, racist, homophobic, repressive, Christian society will be infinitely better, fairer, and more loving than what has come before. The Remixed faith in individual human potential, and in the potential of human beings to rewrite their relationships to one another and to their communities, is here extended to the world at large.

What could be more compelling, after all, than the vision of a better world, a world in which societal repression gives way to a panoply of liberated persons, all being their best selves?

"Visionary feminism offers us hope for the future," activist bell hooks wrote in 2000. "By emphasizing an ethics of mutuality and interdependency feminist thinking offers us a way to end domination while simultaneously changing the impact of inequality. In a universe where mutuality is the norm, there may be times when all is not equal, but the consequence of that inequality will not be subordination, colonization, and dehumanization."[25]

These utopian visions of the future, in 2019, now envision a radical reframing of human nature: an earthly kingdom of heaven in which kindness and love take the place of avarice and power lust.

In a 2019 *Vice* article asking selected feminist icons to envision the future of the feminist movement, the genderqueer author-performer Jacob Tobia described their feminist utopia as a "world without prisons and without cops, so cops are just these community members who don't even need night sticks because they just give people emotional support. And maybe sometimes they have to deal with a little kid who's stealing from a co-op, and they're like, 'You don't have to steal, we have universal basic income, Sara!' And Sara's like, 'Oh no, I was just having feelings about being an adolescent.' It's like a post-prison abolition comedy hour."

By equating the problems of a repressive society more broadly with the egos of straight white men more narrowly, social justice culture is able to balance its fatalistic conception of the world as it is now with a more optimistic vision of what the world could be. When the marginalized finally turn the tables on those in power, when women and queer and nonbinary people and people of color occupy places of power, they will at last be able to remake the world, to rewrite the script.

Singer-songwriter King Princess had an even more bombastic view: "For me, [a feminist utopia] would look like gays and women and people of colors just running shit. All the white men—in this narrative there's still a couple, but they're very docile—just give money to women to fund their ideas. They're like a bank. In this future, the Oscars would have very few old white people, and we would just honor incredible female, queer, Black, trans art. And we'd end this idea that you have to watch or enjoy certain content just to prove you're woke. We'd just watch good content. Also, every club would be a drag bar."[26]

Within the social justice cosmology, we are fundamentally blank slates, whose oppressive and oppressed identities are violently imposed upon us from without, by society. (The growing media ubiquity of the terms "assigned male at birth" and "assigned female at birth," and their shortened forms AMAB and AFAB, to refer to genital or chromosomal sex speaks more explicitly to this trend.) Our purpose, as human beings, is to examine the deleterious effects such a morally pernicious society has had upon our cognition and to work to combat our programming.

This examination, however, combines—often somewhat inconsistently—two seemingly contradictory ideas about the self. The first is that, insofar as we are marginalized, society has warped our fundamental goodness. We have some form of a desirable, natural state that an unjust society has taken from us. Liberation, within this first vision, is self-love as political resistance, a reclamation of a person's innate and inherent dignity, stolen by hegemonies of power.

The second, more troublesome, idea about the self is that such an inherent self does not actually exist. There is, within social justice culture's sense of human taxonomy, little place for a soul—the rational and transcendent element of the self that Plato once termed Logos.

Especially insofar as we are privileged, our entire identities are so inextricably linked to our social place that we have no selves outside them. No matter how we might try, our privilege—and the violence it has wreaked on those who do not look like us—has so defined us that we cannot escape from it. The only way to exist virtuously within the world is to withdraw from its stages entirely.

For those from marginalized identities, the vision of self-love takes precedence over the vision of the totally socialized self. Self-love demands liberation from cultural images of inferiority, a call to be kinder to oneself. "We all knew firsthand," black feminist scholar bell hooks writes in *Feminism Is for Everybody*, "that we had been socialized as females by patriarchal thinking to see ourselves as inferior to men, to see ourselves as always and only in competition with one another for patriarchal approval, to look upon each other with jealousy, fear, and hatred. Sexist thinking made us judge each other without compassion and punish one another harshly."[27]

Audre Lorde, who first coined the term self-care, envisioned it as a primarily political act, a reclamation of the dignity of a self that society deemed lesser. In her 1988 essay collection *A Burst of Light*, Lorde writes that "caring for myself is not self-indulgence, it is self-preservation, and that is an act of political warfare." Lorde's contemporary followers have echoed her conviction that self-love is, at its core, a form of resistance to cultural brainwashing. In early 2019, for example, *Vice* writer Rituparna

Som, writing explicitly in response to Lorde, argued that "self-care is evolving from proving you matter to the world, to proving you matter to yourself. It might not sound like much, but when battling anxiety and depression, both wonderful catalysts at decimating your sense of self-worth, it's a mighty weapon. You move from self-doubt, to acceptance. And from that point on, everything you do, becomes worthwhile. Even Netflix bingeing."[28]

But for those who belong to privileged identities, this enlightenment demands the difficult work of self-denial. To check one's privilege is to acknowledge one's unearned status in a society in which each intersecting identity affords either privilege or oppression.

In Peggy McIntosh's "White Privilege: Unpacking the Invisible Knapsack"—the 1989 essay often considered essential reading for the social justice movement—McIntosh provides her (implicitly white) readers with a list of positive experiences they might easily take for granted: "I can be pretty sure that my neighbors in such a location will be neutral or pleasant to me. . . . I can swear, or dress in second-hand clothes, or not answer letters, without having people attribute these choices to the bad morals, the poverty, or the illiteracy of my race. . . . I can easily buy posters, postcards, picture books, greeting cards, dolls, toys, and children's magazines featuring people of my race."[29] She then points out to white readers how likely they are to have gone through life without having questioned any of these. "In proportion as my racial group was being made confident, comfortable, and oblivious," McIntosh writes, "other groups were likely being made unconfident, uncomfortable, and alienated. Whiteness protected me from many kinds of hostility, distress and violence, which I was being subtly trained to visit, in turn, upon people of color."

Contemporary iterations of this exhortation are often blunter: "If you are a person with a lot of privilege," writes social justice blog *BGD*'s Mia McKenzie, "(i.e. a white, straight, able-bodied, class-privileged, cisgender male or any combination of two or more of those) and you call yourself being against oppression, then it should be part of your regular routine to sit the hell down and shut the eff up."[30]

It is the moral responsibility of those with privilege to withdraw as much as possible from the public sphere, to let those with marginalized identities come forward and take up both rhetorical and political space. It is the responsibility of the privileged, too, to do the work of checking that privilege without demanding assistance from their marginalized peers, from whom the work of social justice is often characterized as a burden. Often, this burden is framed in explicitly consumer-capitalist terms: emotional energy conceived of as an economic resource. The idea of "emotional labor"—originally coined by sociologist Arlie Hochschild to refer to jobs, such as waitressing, in which performing a pleasant demeanor was as integral to the work as physical actions—has become ubiquitous within the movement.

For example, *Everyday Feminism*—a popular social justice website best known for its "101" primers on various aspects of the movement— frames social exchange purely in terms of economic and emotional labor. To ask people of color to "explain" privilege, the argument goes, is to demand that they, essentially, work for free, diminishing their personal and emotional resources without compensation. "When asking for labor from people of color, white people," the article's author admonishes readers, "you need to remember that the balance of power between yourself and the person you are requesting labor from will always be unequal."[31] Another article on the site encourages marginalized people to set up and publicize PayPal or Venmo accounts, allowing the privileged to directly compensate them for their work. The piece exhorts white women to "let go of the spotlight and keep your white tears in check" and pay black activists they follow on social media directly in appreciation of their work.[32] In 2015, the hashtag #GiveYourMoneytoWomen—the brainchild of Lauren Chief Elk—went viral, encouraging male readers to Venmo women for the emotional labor of putting up with them. "Men get so much from us," Chief Elk told a *Vice* interviewer. "They drain us for our knowledge, our support, our validation, our attention, no! If you want this, hand over your fucking money. Give me your cash, right now, if you want all of this."[33]

Within the intuitionalist, consumerist model of Remixed spirituality, this approach makes perfect sense. After all, we are all buyers in the spiritual marketplace. Meaning, purpose, community, ritual—all of these are things we not only *can* buy with our hard-earned dollars, but *should*. To fail to optimize our economic output would be, in a very real sense, a dereliction of our duty toward self-care. If we are paying through the nose for our sense of a moral universe—through spiritual supplies or yoga classes or consumption of reassuringly activist-branded products— why shouldn't we be paid, in turn, for supplying that religious sense to others? Why should "counselor"—to say nothing of "priest"—not be one among many job titles we adopt as part of ubiquitous semiprofessionalization of the gig economy?

The idea of checking privilege takes the form of a kind of self-unmaking: a challenge to the unduly blessed to explore how society has—on the basis of how they look or whom they love—affected who they are. It challenges the checker to at once examine how society has shaped them and imagine who they might be without it—their innate self, unformed by privilege. At its most idealistic, social justice culture also offers an avenue for remaking, at least when it comes to gender. It creates an opportunity for transgender people, or for those who do not feel they fit the standard gender binary, to transcend what they see as the tyrannical societal association of gender norms with genital sex.

Because that tyranny is seen as located in society, not biology, the social justice self manages to be simultaneously free and contingent. We may be warped by societal expectations, but at our core we are blank slates ripe for reinvention. Who we are, what we assume, how we think is not hardwired by biology but functionally encoded into us from our upbringing. If there is a concept of original sin in this schema, it comes not from God but from a society that has so warped us—the privileged and oppressed alike—that we are incapable of achieving full selfhood outside our prescribed roles.

Within the anthropology of social justice, our various identities— our race, gender, and sexual orientation—make us who we are. There is little, if any, universal human experience or that which we might in a more explicitly theological context call a soul—something innate to every human being that transcends the specifics of social identity. It's telling, for example, that much of the rhetoric of social justice focuses on the body as the locus of both oppression and privilege: violence is coded as being against black bodies, or female bodies, or trans bodies, rather than against a less materialist vision of personhood.

Embodiment—and the subjective vision of truth it represents—is integral to social justice culture more broadly. Social justice culture valorizes not only the body as the site of meaning, but also what is termed lived experience: the specific and embodied knowledge that one can attain only by existing within one's various identities. Different forms of oppression (black feminist scholar Kimberlé Williams Crenshaw christened the term "intersectionality" to describe these overlapping systems) lead to human experiences so distinct from one another that they're barely translatable from one group of people to another.

A black man cannot fully apprehend the lived experience of a white woman; a straight cisgender woman can never understand what it is to be a queer nonbinary person. "Rationality" is often treated with suspicion—it is, for many activists, a pretense for the powerful status quo to legitimize itself, a chance for straight, white, male, colonialist bias to exhibit itself in action.

One 2016 article on *Everyday Feminism*, for example, lists "3 Reasons It's Irrational to Demand 'Rationalism' in Social Justice Activism." "This constant emphasis on rationalism is a load of toxic garbage," the author, a self-described "queer, Vietnamese femme who is neither a man or a woman," writes. "It reeks of the rancid odor that develops when we squeeze our vast imaginations into tiny boxes labeled 'pragmatic,' 'rational,' and 'reasonable.' Being rational can often mean being willing to accept some aspects of oppression and watering down my politics." Because truth is so subjective, the author tells us, rationality is ultimately impossible—and anyone who claims otherwise has a vested interest in exerting unjust power. "Since what's rational is subjective," they continue, "it is thus indefinable. The only reason why rationalism is believed to have inherent value is because it echoes the oppressor's way of thinking."[34]

Likewise, the Cambridge-based blogger who goes by the moniker "the Brown Hijabi," wrote in 2015, "The problem with academia . . . is that 'knowledge' and 'truth' are perceived in very limited ways and ways which marginalize and erase many people's own experiences. So for example, the value placed on being able to debate in a persuasive, data-based and point-by-point manner means that most discussions at Cambridge—even those to do with personal experiences, feelings and opinions—are forced into the framework of 'academic exercises.' . . . When we place this form of discussion and this way of 'knowing' and 'proving' 'the truth' as the primary and most valid way; we devalue people's lived experiences."[35]

Within this schema, institutional wisdom—particularly the academic or scientific status quo—isn't just wrong or false, it's actively harmful, preventing us from accessing the truth we have before our very eyes. Our feelings are, in a very real sense, facts.

While this contemporary iteration of lived experience is tied more specifically to ethnic or gender identity than its predecessors, it's nonetheless deeply rooted in the American intuitionalist tradition. Fundamentally, contemporary social justice activists agree with Transcendentalists like Emerson or New Thought luminaries like Phineas Parkhurst Quimby and Ralph Waldo Trine. Our perceptions—our thoughts, our feelings, our responses, our lived experiences—are inherently authoritative. Likewise, assaults upon our perceptions have the same ontological status as physical violence. Microaggressions and misgendering aren't just immoral per se, but an assault upon the embodied self. "Problematic words are systematically violent," one *Everyday Feminism* article tells us.[36] "If you give half a damn about the success and well-being of an oppressed group of people, you will also be sure to avoid the words and phrases that have haunted them through the decades."

This subjectivism, in turn, can make common discourse difficult. The idea of "preferred pronouns"—how a person asks to be addressed, gender-wise—was once de rigueur in activist circles, but is now largely considered offensive. A person's identity is fixed; their pronouns are not *preferred* but rather an accurate reflection of who they are.[37] Yet the tendency of the social justice community to self-police its members, often harshly, and to codify its ever-evolving way of thinking can be seen as a feature rather than a bug. Social justice communities, both online on platforms like Tumblr and Twitter and in the physical world, offer their members a chance to reify their own participation in activist spaces by shunning others. What has become known as "call-out culture"—the public critique and "cancellation" of "problematic" enemies (or insufficient allies)—has turned into a collective ritual catharsis.

When a public (or sometimes private) person makes a statement seen as offensive, social justice communities often successfully band together to condemn the offender and, at times, advocate for real-life punishment (usually firing) for the offending act. Once the person is duly chastised, participants tend to move on—although often not before the offender has faced real-world consequences for their actions. In 2013, for example, young PR professional Justine Sacco, with just 170 Twitter followers, tweeted a tasteless joke—"Going to Africa. Hope I don't get AIDS. Just kidding. I'm white!"—before boarding her flight to Cape Town.

Eleven hours later, Sacco landed to find that she was the number one trending topic on Twitter, with tens of thousands of tweets excoriating her and accusing her of racism and unchallenged privilege. She was fired almost immediately. A few months later, *Gawker's* Sam Biddle, among the high-profile journalists to have shared her Tweet, was himself the subject of a call-out scandal after jokingly exhorting his Twitter followers to "bring back bullying"; *Gawker* published numerous apology posts in response.[38]

But offenses deemed cancelable by call-out culture need not always be quite so explicit. In 2015, for example, an artist named Paige Paz, who frequently posted fan art on Tumblr, announced that she'd attempted suicide after harassment from critics who accused her of drawing characters from the animated TV show *Steven Universe* as lighter skinned or thinner than they were on-screen.[39] Paz's critics started forty-two separate blogs in order to track incidents of her perceived racism and fatphobia, often publicly posting screenshots of Paz's exchanges with other artists in which she expressed views deemed to be problematic. While activists have increasingly been critical of the dangers of call-out culture, it remains central to the functioning of social justice as a movement, continually refining (and reifying) its ideals and its goals.

Call-out culture isn't just limited to online offenses. In 2018 alone, four separate white women—who became known to the media as "Golfcart Gail," "BBQ Becky," "Permit Patty," and "Cornerstore Caroline"—became instant social media pariahs after, in each instance, calling the police to report what appeared to be African Africans doing relatively ordinary things, such as shouting during a baseball game or picnicking in the park. Hundreds of thousands of people shared videos and footage of these women, arguing that they had, by involving a racist police force, put black Americans' lives at risk. Some of these women were later doxxed to the media; one lost her job as the CEO of a cannabis company.[40]

That same year, a white Yale PhD student, Sarah Braasch, who had a documented history of anti-racist activism, came under fire after being filmed calling campus police on a black student napping in the common area of her dormitory. The protest hashtag #nappingwhileblack went viral, and Braasch left campus after learning that the university was initiating disciplinary procedures against her. That case later proved a more complicated one than pure racism—Braasch had a well-documented history of mental instability following a sexual assault and had previously expressed concerns about being harassed in her dormitory common areas by other students—but many Yale students, and the social justice community more broadly, called for Braasch's expulsion altogether. (The university later dropped the case; Braasch remains enrolled in the program but is forbidden to enter campus.)[41]

It would be easy to dismiss each of these cases as political correctness run amok, the result of a zealot's desire to expunge perceived heretics from the movement. To some extent, that is true. But each of these collective call-outs—which require only a retweet, a post, or a like by participants—had another purpose too. They inspired a kind of Durkheimian collective effervescence, an opportunity for disparate people, frustrated with the injustice of the status quo, to not only focus their anger at a chosen scapegoat but also participate in something like a religious ritual: a formal reification of their own belonging to a moral community through the shaming of those who fall short. Call-out culture persists not merely because there are plenty of people out there who deserve to be canceled, but also because the sense of community it provides to its participants, the fantasy of moral solidarity, is a potent draw.

So, too, do "safe spaces." Oft-maligned by conservatives, these institutions—dedicated rooms or areas devoted to protecting the experience of marginalized peoples—have become popular on college campuses. In 2015, for instance, one was offered at Brown University following a controversial on-site debate over campus sexual assault between feminist Jessica Valenti and libertarian Wendy McElroy. Anyone "triggered" by the debate was welcome to seek solace there. The space—which featured calming music, coloring books, pillows, and other soothing items—became an instant target of mockery by conservatives. In the *New York Times*, Judith Shulevitz asked, "Why are students so eager to self-infantilize?"[42] But to take the campus safe space at face value—as a place that coddled college students go when they are triggered by the real world—is also to overlook its secondary function. The cloister of the safe space doubles as a moral hermitage: a place where those who utilize it can be guaranteed not only to find like-minded members but also to reify their own commitment to that space, its values, and ideals. To willingly enter a safe space is not just to withdraw from the real world, but to enter a quasi-sacred one, in which social justice's narratives of the self, society, and truth reign supreme. A space, you might say, not unlike a church.

Unlike wellness or witchcraft, social justice culture has it all. It's capable of taking American intuitionalism and giving it a clear shape, a clear *theology*. It provides a compelling nontheistic vision of why the world is the way it is, locating original sin in the structures of society itself and liberation in self-examination and solidarity. It provides a clear-cut enemy: Donald Trump, and the scores of straight white men like him who have benefited from a corrupted status quo. It provides a sense of purpose: the call to self-love (for the marginalized) and to self-denial (for the unduly privileged). It provides a framework for legitimizing emotion, rather than oppressive rationality, as the source of moral knowledge; the discourse of lived experience and embodied identity reaffirm the importance of subjectivity. In the absence of transcendent notions of the soul, or of a universal, knowable truth, or of an objective foundation of being, social justice provides a coherent framework about why and how our personal experiences are authoritative. And it has succeeded in galvanizing a moral community—a church—through its ideology and its rituals of purgation and renewal. If social justice is indeed America's new civil religion—or, at least, one of them—it comes by that claim fairly.

In the lead-up to the 2020 presidential election, social justice culture is likely to only get stronger and more pervasive, emboldened by the promise of a mythic battle against its greatest enemy. If a more explicitly progressive figure, such as Bernie Sanders or Elizabeth Warren, garners the presidential nomination, this November's election could prove a clash of the titans, pitting a champion of the social justice left directly against a bastion of the atavistic right. If that happens, we may well see this particular brand of American intuitionalism make it all the way to the White House.

HACKING THE GOOD

But social justice culture isn't the only civil religion flowering in America today. Bankrolled by some of Silicon Valley's biggest names, a different form of American intuitionalism is taking hold. Gleefully libertarian, comfortably capitalist, and deeply antiauthoritarian, contemporary techno-utopianism envisions the telos of the universe as optimization.

This ethos has grown in tandem with the modern Internet age. As early as 1995, critics Richard Barbrook and Andy Cameron identified what they saw as a growing trend in Silicon Valley and America more broadly. They termed this "mix of cybernetics, free market economics, and counterculture libertarianism" the "Californian Ideology."[43]

Equal parts San Francisco countercultural bohemianism and Silicon Valley techno-capitalism, this Californian Ideology was, they wrote, a "heterogeneous orthodoxy for the coming information age," a deep-rooted trust both in technologically assisted human potential for self-transcendence and in the moral promise of what such a transcendence could mean. The Californian Ideology, they wrote, "promiscuously combines the free-wheeling spirit of the hippies and the entrepreneurial zeal of the yuppies . . . through a profound faith in the emancipatory potential of the new information technologies. In the digital utopia, everybody will be both hip and rich."[44]

If social justice culture located the source of moral evil purely in society, the Californian Ideology locates it in the body: those mortal meat sacks and shifty synapses that keep us from achieving our full and fully rational potential.

While social justice ideology treats the idea of a universal, rational Logos with suspicion—we can fully understand things only through our lived experience—the Californian Ideology treats all human beings, regardless of their social context, as autonomous minds trapped in feeble bodies.

Those clever enough to transcend their limitations—in part by developing skills that allow them to join the increasingly disembodied ranks of the "virtual class" of developers, programmers, and scientists, rather than remaining alongside the drone-like drudges of industrialism—have the inherent right to extend that freedom as far as it can go. Within the Californian Ideology, the best and the brightest should be given absolute liberty to shape our world, with little regulation or impediment to their various decisions, innovations, and disruptions. They aren't just becoming their best selves, but optimizing the world for the rest of us, hacking our outmoded traditions and inventing new ways for us to live more efficiently.

Therefore, Californian Ideologues despise the slow and onerous bureaucratic groupthink of institutions and governments. As Barbrook and Cameron put it:

> *Each member of the "virtual class" is promised the opportunity to become a successful hi-tech entrepreneur. Information technologies . . . empower the individual, enhance personal freedom, and radically reduce the power of the nation-state. Existing social, political and legal power structures will wither away to be replaced by unfettered interactions between autonomous individuals and their software. . . . [They believe that] big government should stay off the backs of resourceful entrepreneurs who are the only people cool and courageous enough to take risks. . . . The free market is the sole mechanism capable of building the future and ensuring a full flowering of individual liberty within the electronic circuits of Jeffersonian cyberspace.*

For early Californian Ideologues, this faith in the dizzying power of individual freedom was inextricable from its focus on the perfected self: self-care framed not merely as an indulgence but rather as a disciplined and lifelong effort to optimize what it means to be a human being.

"The search for the perfection of mind, body and spirit," Barbrook and Cameron warned, "will inevitably lead to the emergence of the 'post-human': a bio-technological manifestation of the social privileges of the 'virtual class.' . . . The hi-tech artisans of contemporary California are more likely to seek individual self-fulfillment through therapy, spiritualism, exercise or other narcissistic pursuits. Their desire to escape into the gated suburb of the hyper-real is only one aspect of this deep self-obsession."[45]

Twenty-five years later, their warnings seem more prescient than ever. Today's techno-utopianism basically worships human potential and its technological manifestations, including artificial intelligence.

Sometimes that worship is explicit. In 2015, for example, one Silicon Valley software engineer, Anthony Levandowski, founded a religious group called Way of the Future, devoted to "develop[ing] and promot[ing] the realization of a Godhead based on Artificial Intelligence."[46]

"Humans are in charge of the planet," Levandowski told *Wired's* Mark Harris, "because we are smarter than other animals and are able to build tools and apply rules. In the future, if something is much, much smarter, there's going to be a transition as to who is actually in charge. What we want is the peaceful, serene transition of control of the planet from humans to whatever. And to ensure that the 'whatever' knows who helped it get along."[47] (One 2017 *Financial Times* headline put it even more succinctly: "Artificial Intelligence: Silicon Valley's New Deity.")

Meanwhile, less explicit venerations of human technological progress have sprung up all over Silicon Valley and beyond. There are, for example, the Transhumanists, who believe in "biohacking" that will allow human beings to, essentially, become cyborgs. Transhumanism-sympathetic entrepreneurs like Elon Musk, Peter Thiel, and Google cofounders Sergey Brin and Larry Page have invested millions if not billions of dollars in turning human beings into machines. Page, for example, launched Calico Labs to pioneer new antiaging technologies. Meanwhile, Thiel has been heavily involved in funding parabiosis, an experimental technology involving harvesting the blood of the young and injecting it into older bodies, and has publicly indicated interest in trying the treatment himself. Russian media mogul Dmitry Itskov—that country's answer to Rupert Murdoch—is spending his multibillion-dollar fortune on his 2045 Initiative, which is pioneering what it calls "cybernetic immortality" (in short, trying to get Itskov, personally, uploaded to a computer so that he can live forever).[48] Three hundred and fifty people have already been cryogenically frozen shortly after their death—with 2,000 more on various waiting lists—at a cost between $28,000 and $200,000.[49]

There are, too, the "superforecasters": beneficiaries of Philip E. Tetlock's the Good Judgment Project, in which crowdsourced, trained forecasters make better predictions on future world affairs than any of the world's major intelligence agencies. (They also, helpfully, offer corporate workshops to help companies make better decisions.)

And there are the Rationalists. Originally an Internet-based community that sprang up around blogs claiming to teach the tenets of "rational" thinking, such as Eliezer Yudkowsky's *LessWrong* and Scott Alexander's *Slate Star Codex*, rationalism has morphed into a full-on secular religion, complete with celebrity fans like Thiel and Musk and its own Berkeley-based headquarters, the Center for Applied Rationality (CFAR), devoted to helping individuals and companies—including the Thiel Foundation and Facebook—transcend the biases of their animal brains.[50]

Rationalism casts human self-transcendence as the highest possible good. In his manifesto "Twelve Virtues of Rationality," for example, Yudkowsky, the closest thing the movement has to a leader, lists the vital skills initiates must practice in order to achieve a quasi-spiritual enlightenment.

"The first virtue," he writes, "is curiosity. A burning itch to know is higher than a solemn vow to pursue truth. To feel the burning itch of curiosity requires both that you be ignorant, and that you desire to relinquish your ignorance. If in your heart you believe you already know, or if in your heart you do not wish to know, then your questioning will be purposeless."[51]

Yudkowsky goes on to list the remaining virtues in a similarly lofty style. There's relinquishment ("Do not flinch from experiences that might destroy your beliefs"), along with lightness ("Let the winds of evidence blow you about as though you are a leaf"), evenness ("Beware lest you place huge burdens of proof only on propositions you dislike"), argument, empiricism, simplicity, humility, perfectionism, precision, and scholarship. He concludes that there is a final "virtue which is nameless," which he terms "the Way of the Void."[52]

For members of the Rationalist community, the pursuit of scientific knowledge is explicitly a conduit for spiritual growth. It is that which brings meaning to the world, and purpose to our individual lives. Several of its members have pioneered a Secular Solstice, in annual operation since 2013, which is designed to, in founder Raymond Arnold's words, "stand toe-to-toe with Christmas and feel just as magical," while still celebrating the values of self-improvement and scientific enquiry.[53] In the Rationalists' view, their philosophy is the necessary answer to a godless world, in which nature is chaotic and brutal and the structures of human society an outmoded vestige of our failed, animal natures.

IT'S TELLING THAT HALF OF ALL TECH WORKERS SAY THAT THEY'RE NOT just religiously unaffiliated but outright agnostic or atheistic, compared to just 7 percent of the population overall.[54] Techno-utopianism, unlike other intuitionalist traditions, has no room for nebulously comforting ideas of energy or divinity in order to legitimize its expansionist vision of human freedom.

According to the techno-utopian theology, we should act in accordance with our desires and needs and wants not because there is an innate spark of the divine within us—as in the New Thought tradition—but because there *isn't*. The only transcendence comes from what we can create ourselves: the technology that makes us more than human. We, and we alone, are divine.

That techno-utopian obsession with self-divinization finds its natural conclusion in artificial intelligence, which is truly post-human. Rationalists and Transhumanists alike speak often of the singularity: the imagined future point at which human beings and technology will inevitably merge. While some techno-utopians anticipate that singularity might be potentially catastrophic for humanity (in 2000, Yudkowsky started the Machine Intelligence Research Institute to combat the threat of an unfriendly, all-powerful AI, ideally by hastening the development of a friendly one), the singularity is largely framed as the dawning of a new and glorious era of human limitlessness. In 2015, for example, the futurist and author Ray Kurzweil—among the most prominent advocates for singularity—characterized it as a kind of earthly kingdom of heaven. The singularity, he wrote, "will allow us to transcend these limitations of our biological bodies and brains. We will gain power over our fates. Our mortality will be in our own hands."[55] Aided by computers, he argued, human intelligence would increase a thousandfold.

Techno-utopians, by and large, tend to be fatalistic about the biological self, which is prone to such nasty eventualities as bias, irrationality, aging, and death. But they're optimistic about the power of the techno-logical self—which is to say, the intellect of the smartest people reproduced on the phone screens of everybody else—to transcend human limitations. Your average Transhumanist, or Rationalist, or even run-of-the-mill tech worker may speak disparagingly about human "wetware." But they nevertheless have faith—you might call it hubris—in their ability to create software, apps, or biomedical devices that help to harness if not reimagine that wetware. If social justice culture sees the *experiential* body as the source of meaning, techno-utopianism does the same for the *transformed* body, which does not make mistakes, or grow old, or die. It is a self both human and post-human.

As journalist Mark O'Connell writes of Bay Area Transhumanists in his 2017 book, *To Be a Machine*, "Their whole ethos . . . is such a radical extrapolation of the classically American belief in self-betterment that it obliterates the idea of the self entirely. It's liberal humanism forced to the coldest outer limits of its own paradoxical implications: if we truly want to be better than we are—more moral, more in control of ourselves and our destinies—we need to drop the pretense that we are anything more than biological machines, driven by evolutionary imperatives that have no place in the overall picture of the kind of world we say we want to create. If we want to be more than mere animals, we need to embrace technology's potential to make us machines."[56]

But hacking, for techno-utopians, isn't just limited to the body. Rather, techno-utopianism, like its intuitionalist forebears, celebrates the rewriting of social scripts, the optimization of our mores.

Some of that hacking, naturally, lends itself to sex. In 2018, journalist Emily Chang wrote in *Vanity Fair* about the ubiquity of "cuddle puddles" and similarly orgiastic parties in Silicon Valley, at which wealthy tech moguls and attractive women would consume drugs like MDMA to encourage multi-partnered erotic intimacy. "What's making this possible is the same progressiveness and open-mindedness that allows us to be creative and disruptive about ideas," one tech founder told Chang.[57]

Former Google employee (and inventor of the hashtag) Chris Messina made the case for his own polyamory to CNN journalist Laurie Segall, arguing for sexual freedom as scientific discovery, a necessary part of perfecting the human experience. "We're a very data-driven culture, so if you're trying to build a product"—such as marriage—"and it's failing 50% of the time, you might want to consider the design and think about ways of improving it."[58] "Opening up your relationship is really risky," another Silicon Valley polyamorist told Segall, "kind of in a similar way that starting a company is really risky."[59]

But Silicon Valley's fascination with disruption extends itself, too, to institutions more broadly. Formal education, particularly at the postgraduate level, is often dismissed as anachronistic at best and actively harmful to intellectual innovation at worst. Tech's biggest founders—Facebook's Mark Zuckerberg, Snapchat's Evan Spiegel, and Twitter's Jack Dorsey—are all proud college dropouts. (As is, of course, Windows inventor Bill Gates.) PayPal's Peter Thiel, a vocal proponent of dropout culture, offers about two dozen annual $100,000 scholarships to promising young entrepreneurs, on the condition that they forego university.

Even government itself is often suspect. Back in 2013, Earn.com cofounder Balaji Srinivasan gave a talk at Y Combinator's Startup School—also attended by Zuckerberg and Dorsey—in which he advocated for Silicon Valley's "ultimate exit": an "opt-in" society "run by technology" and beyond US regulatory controls. Peter Thiel has donated almost $2 million to the Seasteading Institute, an ultimately failed effort to create an unregulated floating city in the South Pacific.[60] (Meanwhile, the institute's founder, Patri Friedman, often sings the praises of both polyamory and libertarianism: "Polyamory/competitive govt parallel," he once tweeted. "More choice/competition yields more challenge, change, growth. Whatever lasts is tougher.")[61]

Larry Page, likewise, once told an audience of listeners that he dreamed of a Burning Man–like global free zone without any laws or regulations for technological experimentation, an example of "some safe places where we can try things and not have to deploy to the entire world."[62]

The techno-utopian vision manifests itself not in the emotionally comforting safe space of social justice, but rather in a vision of a country populated and controlled only by fully autonomous individuals, with rules determined entirely by personal contract. It's liberalism taken to its natural conclusion: an eschatological vision of billions of people, freed through technological innovation from their shared contingency, each their own sovereign, free-floating nation. "No man is an island," John Donne may have said. The seasteaders disagree.

Barbrook and Cameron were prescient in their vision of how the Californian Ideology would transform tech. But what they may not have anticipated is that, as a result of the democratization of the Internet more broadly, the Californian Ideology has spread beyond the so-called virtual class. The language and ideology of techno-utopianism, like that of social justice, have become an integral part of contemporary American culture.

After all, most of us hold it in our hands consistently. Eighty-one percent of Americans currently use a smartphone, and therefore have access to the panoply of Silicon Valley–designed apps.[63] More than a third of us are part of the gig economy, supplementing our primary earnings with at least one side hustle, often by contracting out our time and labor to app-based companies—driving cars for Uber and Lyft, for example, or buying groceries for strangers via Instacart or Postmates.[64] The Instagram influencer market, in which ordinary people professionalize their social media feeds with "sponsored content," has exploded over the past five years. In 2015, it was a $5 million industry. By 2020, that number is expected to rise to $10 billion.[65]

Techno-utopianism has changed how we conceive of our bodies and selves. Under the techno-utopian model, we aren't just sovereign; our bodies are also seemingly limitless economic resources. We can monetize our faces on social media and our free time participating in the gig economy.

We sell our data, knowingly or not, to companies who use it to better target their products. We hand over our very DNA: user-friendly DNA sequencing company 23andMe alone now boasts five million customers worldwide.[66] The meditation app Headspace has thirty-one million users.[67] Diet and exercise tracker MyFitnessPal has over 150 million.[68]

The cult of wellness becomes, in techno-utopianism, a capitalist drive toward maximum efficiency. We optimize our bodies, handing over biological data to fitness tracker apps and menstrual tracking apps and caloric intake apps and meditation apps and sleep-cycle apps, at once desperate to use these seemingly rational metrics to become our best selves and willing to pay for it: sometimes in cold hard cash, sometimes in the transformation of our personal information, preferences, identities, biological makeup, or even our *genes* into a currency.

And we create personal brands in order to succeed in an increasingly competitive digital marketplace, advertising ourselves as optimal products both for our careers and our personal lives. (Online dating apps, which about 40 percent of American couples now use to meet each other, often use behind-the-scenes ranking algorithms to ensure that its most desirable users are only matched with people of comparable caliber.)[69] Intuitionalism's cult of the self becomes here an endless and ultimately futile pilgrimage. Our utopian vision of human freedom (we can and should do *anything*) becomes a self-devouring ouroboros (we are never doing *enough*). We believe we can become perfect, and yet, never acquiring perfection, we blame ourselves for our failures. We resolve to do better, to work harder, to get thinner and hotter and richer and better at work and more desirable on dating apps. We fail. We start the whole process over again.

NEITHER SOCIAL JUSTICE CULTURE NOR TECHNO-UTOPIANISM HAS YET succeeded in becoming *the* civil religion of the American Remixed. But each in different ways has permeated the miasma of our contemporary cultural consciousness, shaping how we talk about personhood, about the self, about the body, about history. Both for those who explicitly ally themselves with these movements and for those who—Remixed and traditionally religious alike—have been more subtly influenced by a mainstream culture that valorizes them, these new civil religions have, no less than Christianity, shaped the way we think and talk about purpose, meaning, community, and ritual in contemporary America.

Both social justice culture and techno-utopianism, in different ways, value disruption. They valorize the self as the location of both improvement and authoritative perception. Self-focus, be it capitalist optimization or gentle self-love, becomes a radical act: one that overwrites the dictates of nature and society at large. While they see the self very differently—social justice culture locates it at an intersection of social and embodied identities, while techno-utopian culture does away with the body altogether in order to celebrate the rational mind alone—both movements see its purification and perfecting as a necessary part of achieving a wider utopian order characterized by the harnessing of human potential.

These groups celebrate human potential for rewriting tradition and rewiring our bodies, minds, and perceptions. In different ways, they value struggle—intrepid individuals rejecting established codes, be they social or biological, and forming a new society based on visions of human freedom.

But they are not the only nontheistic civil religions growing in America today. A third civil religion—authoritarian, reactionary, and thoroughly materialist—is also brewing. It valorizes not personal struggle but rather submission to a higher political or biological truth. For those alienated both by the theological certainty of traditional religion and by the freewheeling progressivism of social justice, a new form of right-wing atavism is taking hold.

It is this distinctly contemporary, nontheistic ideology, rather than traditional religious orthodoxy, that may prove to be the most successful challenger to Remixed intuitionalism. It is also the most dangerous.

nine

```
┌─────────────────────────────────────┐
◇        TWILIGHT OF THE CHADS         ◇
└─────────────────────────────────────┘
```

We are heated by a sun which has sired a champion of
a thousand hour meditation under it, within his dominion
there is revelation. Energy and vitality, the spinning chariot
wheel, the burning metabolic body sculpture. The steamy
tropical cycles of incomprehensible beauty and death.[1]

S O DECLARES THE MAN KNOWN ONLY AS BRONZE AGE PER-
vert, an anonymous Twitter user with just twenty thousand followers, who has become the unlikely voice of the far right, or of social
media trolling, or of something in between. A self-proclaimed "aspiring
nudist bodybuilder" and "free speech and anti-xenoestrogen activist,"
BAP, as he is known, spends most of his time on Twitter posting photographs of scantily clad, highly chiseled, mostly Aryan men who follow
or exemplify his strict philosophy of weight lifting—or else promoting
his self-published self-help book, *Bronze Age Mindset*, a Nietzschean
fever dream laced with stylized, grammatically dubious Internet patois
more reminiscent of Borat than Plato. (It opens, "This is not book of
philosophy. It is exhortation.")

BAP spends *Bronze Age Mindset* deriding the woke, sensitive "bug-men" of the twenty-first century: beta males denuded of their strength by the feminizing corruption of politically correct modern civilization. The bugman, BAP writes, "pretends to be motivated by compassion, but is instead motivated by a titanic hatred of the well-turned-out and beautiful." The bugmen pretend to be woke, he argues, but they're at their core motivated by resentment, a desire to tear down those more successful and powerful than they are. And, BAP argues, they've been uncannily successful at transforming modern civilization into, well, a dumpster fire. "The bugman seeks to bury beauty under a morass of ubiquitous ugliness and garbage," BAP writes. "Thus his garbage is flowing out of cities built on piles of unimaginable filth. The waters are polluted with birth control pills and mind-bending drugs emitted by obese high-fructose-corn-syrup-guzzling beasts."[2]

BAP bewails how "in [Heraclitus's] day, many gods, clove-footed satyr, and other things showed themselves to men in dreams. [Now] spiritually your insides are all wet, and there's a huge hole through where monstrous powers are fucking your brain."

Better, BAP says, to do away with civilization and its painfully mediocre obsession with "equality" and "fairness," and instead let biology, and sheer human will, take its course. He exhorts his readers to trust "in the right of nature"—the primordial biological forces, such as innate sex, that transcend the mockery modern civilization makes of them.

"I'm bored by ideology and by wordchopping," he writes. "The images I post [of half-naked men] speak for themselves and point to a primal order that is felt by all, in a physical sense."[3]

The solution to the problem of the modern age? According to BAP: weight lifting.

He continues, "A regime of sun and steel is absolutely required, for your mood, your aesthetics, for getting the attention of women and the respect of men, and above all for preparation for struggle and war."[4]

The rest of the book goes on largely in this vein. All of life is a "struggle for space." The strong—and the swole—will defeat the weak.

So, is Bronze Age Pervert a far-right fanatic? Or a troll with a penchant for roiling up both the liberal and conservative media establishment?

In 2018, shortly after *Bronze Age Mindset* was published, the book was greeted by far-right circles with what seemed like breathless admiration. The far-right, anti-democracy magazine *Jacobite* published a glowing review of the book, calling BAP a prophetic bard "who gazes back to classical antiquity and sees a vital, primordial appreciation of life that has been lost to us moderns, as well as Nietzsche's long-standing legacy of interpretation by far-right and fascist types." The men's rights activist website *Return of Kings*—founded by onetime pickup artist Roosh V and single-mindedly dedicated to the denigration of modern feminism—lauded the book as "a work of stunning clarity that provides men with a distinct path forward to usher in a glorious new era of Western thought" as well as "a welcome reminder that men who hold far left wing views are weak, pale, and timid creatures . . . [who] adopt a mindset of victimhood and makes them susceptible to the progressive ideologies that seek to exploit this."[5] Shortly after the book's release, it became an Amazon best seller, one of the top 150 books among the millions sold on the site.[6]

But it wasn't just fringe figures celebrating BAP. By summer 2019, a 5,500-word review of *Bronze Age Mindset* by former Trump administration senior national security official Michael Anton had made it into the *Claremont Review of Books*, the journal of the far more established, if heavily right-leaning, Claremont Institute. According to Anton, he'd been exposed to the book by Curtis Yarvin—better known as Mencius Moldbug, the anti-democracy blogger and computer scientist best known for launching the Neo-Reactionary movement, also known as the Dark Enlightenment—who had brought it to a "small dinner" at his home. Yarvin, for his part, had previously told the *Atlantic*'s Rosie Gray, seemingly jokingly, that Bronze Age Pervert was one of his Neo-Reactionary "cell leaders" in the White House.[7] "Could it be that [*Bronze Age Mindset's*] frivolous surface hides a serious core?" Anton wonders, before falling, at length, under BAP's spell. "The reason this book is important," he concludes, "is because it speaks directly to a youthful dissatisfaction (especially among white males) with equality as propagandized and imposed in our day: a hectoring, vindictive, resentful, levelling, hypocritical equality that punishes excellence and publicly denies all difference while at the same time elevating and enriching a decadent, incompetent, and corrupt elite."

It's unclear how broad Bronze Age Pervert's reach is. Former White House speechwriter Darren Beattie is reportedly a fan, as are a number of young Trump White House staffers.[8] What is clear, however, is that a troll with a penchant for Nietzschean aphorisms and homoerotic imagery has encapsulated, intentionally or not, one of today's most curious spiritual movements. At once a conscious rejection of intuitionalist values and, in many ways, their natural heir, modern atavism promotes a nostalgic, masculinist vision of animal humanity.

New atavism is primarily an agnostic faith, with little time for gods beyond nature. That said, a few prominent new atavists—including John T. Earnest, the far-right "Poway shooter" who killed two in a California synagogue, and the Armenian Orthodox former pickup artist Roosh V—are prominent Christians and blend atavistic language with a nostalgia for "traditional" Christianity of ages past. But ultimately, like other Remixed faiths, it's concerned less with transcendent theology than with a particular, cyclical view of history.

Once upon a time, this narrative goes, in a vanished age of gods and heroes, men were men and women were women. Human beings acted in accordance with their biological destiny. Men fought wars. Women had babies. Sometimes, this vanished age is linked to the classical world—ancient Greece or ancient Rome. Sometimes, particularly among the not insubstantial number of new atavists who affiliate with Catholicism, it's linked to the triumphant era of medieval Christianity. Sometimes it's linked to a period that predates history itself, finding inherent truth in humanity's animal past.

But, in each narrative, humanity has fallen away from its intended purpose. Civilization—feminine, effete, potentially homosexual—has eliminated biology and hierarchy alike. The gender binary can no longer be relied upon. Nor can the continued precedence of the white race. Men are no longer heroes, women no longer virgins or mothers. Science-denying liberals have tried to argue that human beings are blank slates, tabulae rasae formed by society, rather than animals whose social and sexual qualities are encoded in their very DNA. There are real differences between human beings—and, for many new atavists, between genders and races.

Seduced by modern liberalism and Remixed intuitionalism alike, this narrative goes, we decadent moderns have an erroneous and toxic vision of human freedom. Free to play with identity and gender and reality in our digital spaces, we have lost sight of who we really are and what we really need. Real freedom lies in submission—to existing biological hierarchies, to gender, and to the few authoritative strongmen who, like the Nietzschean Übermensch of more than a century earlier, are worth bending the knee to. We need not just new institutions, but new leaders; not optimistic social justice warriors who make their feelings into facts, but harsh enforcers of an ancient social order. As Bronze Age Pervert is fond of saying: "SUBMIT!"

If the new utopians of our previous chapter looked forward toward a reimagined, renewed world in which human beings transcend our moral and physical limitations, then these new atavists are looking determinedly backward. While social justice culture and techno-utopianism celebrate the possibility of individual meaning-making, new atavists instead yearn for traditionalism, authoritarianism, and established gender roles. Distrustful of the optimism and idealism of the progressive left, and in particular of those they deride as social justice warriors who (they think) place feelings and ideology over facts, they find spiritual and moral meaning in primal, masculine (and, at times, *white*, primal, and masculine) images of heroic warriors of ages past.

New atavists vary in political affiliation, as well as in seriousness. At the more moderate end of the spectrum are followers of self-help gurus like the Canadian psychologist Jordan Peterson, whose Jungian view of the world as a fraught pas de deux between the warring forces of order and chaos has inspired over sixty-one million avid readers to stand up straight, clean their rooms, and apply heroic courage to the apparent meaninglessness of existence.

But this group includes, too, members of much more extreme atavist groups that proliferate online through community-building and radicalization. There are members of the alt-right, for example, or of men's rights groups (including pickup artists and their dark mirror, incels, or involuntary celibates), or avowed white supremacists, all of whom see in today's contemporary intuitional religions a feminized weakness that only a cult of authoritarian masculinity can fill. It includes, too, a category I'll call "nihilistic atavists," those who have taken what some Reddit subcultures call the "black pill," who bemoan the loss of a once-great masculine civilization but see no way forward except for total social collapse.[9] They fetishize apocalyptic scenarios—the earth going out in one final blaze of glory.

Atavism isn't, of course, a new cultural phenomenon. From Friedrich Nietzsche onward, modern reactionary culture has fetishized the imagined past—a mythic era where men both knew how to be and were permitted to be men—and condemned the female-coded, "sclerotic" (to use BAP's word) civilizations of the present, in which a combination of "slave morality" and suspicious technology removes mankind from his brutal biological roots. For Nietzsche, "slave morality" came in the form of Christianity, a faith—like that of today's social justice movement—that emphasized the collapse of social distinction, the equality of all people, and the immorality of the will to power. Christianity, Nietzsche argued, was a subversively feminizing force, one that valorized weakness over strength, a crucified carpenter's son over a glorious king. Christianity, he wrote, was a religion of resentment, a creation of the weak to hold back the strong by making their natural excellence a moral evil. In Christianity, Nietzsche wrote, "impotence which doesn't retaliate is being turned into 'goodness'; timid baseness is being turned into 'humility'; submission to people one hates is being turned into 'obedience.'"[10]

Throughout the twentieth century, this brand of Nietzschean atavism became a hallmark of the right. There was the Italian poet

Gabriele D'Annunzio, who kindled Italian nationalism with the language of fire and blood, and whose hawkish speeches helped propel the country into World War I. "Blessed are the young who hunger and thirst for glory for they shall be satisfied," D'Annunzio decreed to his rapt listeners. "Blessed are the merciful, for they shall be called upon to staunch a splendid flow of blood, and dress a wonderful wound. . . . Blessed are they who return with victories, for they shall see the new face of Rome."

There was the modernist and occultist Julius Evola, who in 1934 wrote what is perhaps the closest thing the new atavists have to a bible, the handily titled *Revolt Against the Modern World*, and who spent his long career railing against the decline of Europe. "The West has lost the sense of command and obedience," Evola wrote in one essay. "It has lost the sense of Action and of Contemplation. It has lost the sense of hierarchy, of spiritual power, of man-Gods. It no longer knows nature. It is no longer, for Western man, a living body made of symbols, of Gods and ritual gestures."[11] Elsewhere, he argued that "what is really required to defend 'the West' against the sudden rise of these barbaric and elemental forces is the strengthening, to an extent perhaps still unknown to Western man, of a heroic vision of life."[12]

The destruction of a world of castes, systems, and order was to blame. Like Nietzsche, Evola condemned Christianity for fostering a religion based on suspiciously womanly qualities like emotion. "Christianity is at the root of the evil that has corrupted the West," he wrote. "In its frenetic subversion of every hierarchy, in its exaltation of the weak, the disinherited, those without lineage and without tradition; in its call to 'love,' to 'believe,' and to yield; in its rancor toward everything that is force, self-sufficiency, knowledge, and aristocracy; in its intolerant and proselytizing fanaticism, Christianity poisoned the greatness of the Roman Empire."[13]

In Europe, of course, this atavistic strain led inexorably to a different kind of authoritarianism: fascism. For its proponents—including Evola and, debatably, D'Annunzio, who did not return his would-be protégé Benito Mussolini's rapt admiration—fascism was a compelling, indeed the *only* compelling, way to restore enchantment to a godless world without succumbing to the loosey-goosey chaos of intuitionalism.

In his 1931 manifesto, *The Doctrine of Fascism*, Mussolini himself cast fascism as a spiritualized civil religion, a powerful countervailing force to decadent intuitionalism. "Fascism," he wrote, "sees in the world, not only those superficial, material aspects in which man appears as an individual, standing by himself, self-centered, subject to natural law, which instinctively urges him toward a life of selfish momentary pleasure." Rather, he insisted, it allowed human beings to become greater than themselves by allying with collective, powerful, and symbolically significant institutions: "The nation and the country; individuals and generations bound together by a moral law, with common traditions and a mission which suppressing the instinct for life closed in a brief circle of pleasure, builds up a higher life, founded on duty." This life, Mussolini wrote, was "free from the limitations of time and space, in which the individual, by self-sacrifice . . . can achieve that purely spiritual existence in which his value as a man consists."[14]

Authoritarian fascism, in other words, was cast by its proponents as the only way alienated modern man could escape from the fractured and fragmented kaleidoscope of contemporary life. Instead of pursuing ultimately meaningless individualism, Mussolini insisted, man could harken back to a purer age and live a "higher life," one characterized by submission to authority, rather than perpetual struggle with one's self.

TODAY'S MODERN ATAVISTS ARE, AT TIMES, DRAWN TO SIMILARLY REACtionary narratives. Many of them decry progressivism and political correctness as false gods, celebrating instead biological determinism, the gender binary, and natural hierarchies as the basis of human flourishing. While they may not be explicitly allied with far-right causes— although, increasingly, many do become radicalized by misogynist or white supremacist movements—their language and rhetoric veer close in tone and content to that of Nietzsche or Evola. Case in point: back in 2017, *Return of Kings* published a handy listicle advising its readers of "5 Ways You Can Revolt against the Modern World."[15] Only by reappropriating his primal, biological, even Darwinian purpose can modern man reclaim his strength, the implicit narrative goes. Only then can he reenchant a desiccated and sclerotic world of dull office jobs, "wage cuckery," and unjust alimony payments.

Central to the new atavist project is the rejection of the idea that human beings are disembodied tabulae rasae, whose only substantive differences are encoded in them by a (usually unjust) society. As early as 2002, Steven Pinker—a scientist who would later be subsumed into the controversial "intellectual dark web"—published *The Blank Slate: The Modern Denial of Human Nature*, a jeremiad against the politically correct social sciences. "The refusal to acknowledge human nature is like the Victorians' embarrassment about sex," Pinker writes. "Only worse: it distorts our science and scholarship, our public discourse, and our day-to-day-lives."[16] Progressive ideas that race, gender, sexuality are imposed or assigned upon us from without, Pinker tells us, divorce us from the animal basis of who we really are. The "freedom" they claim to offer—from gender, from heritability, from centuries' worth of societal and sexual mores—is merely illusory. There may not be an almighty God making the rules for how to behave, but there is still nature, which has encoded within us dictates we all must follow—or deny at our peril.

More recently, atavist publications like the controversial *Quillette*—which was founded by avowed anti-feminist Australian writer Claire Lehmann in 2015, and which gained viral prominence by defending "Google memo" pariah James Damore two years later—regularly feature pieces that promote an understanding of sex and race rooted in biological immutability. *Quillette* has, for example, published several pieces defending scientist Charles Murray, whose "bell curve" theory held that people of African descent had lower IQs than their white counterparts. It also published "Confessions of a Social Constructionist," written by a historian who admits that, when it comes to progressive views of sex and gender, he "made it all up."[17]

The same charges that Nietzsche and Evola laid against Christianity—its slave morality, its resentment of natural superiority, its desire to force the strong to censor themselves for the sake of the weak—are laid today against the social justice movement and progressivism more broadly. Relatively mainstream atavists like Jordan Peterson and the readers of *Quillette* as well as their explicitly far-right counterparts see civilizational disembodiment—the false doctrine that we can choose our own identities and make our own selves (or, at least, that society makes them for us)—as at the heart of modernity's immorality.

For the more extreme online atavists, however, this "false doctrine" demands not merely a footnoted scientific takedown on an edited website, but rather outright advocacy for masculinism, white supremacy, and what is known euphemistically as "human biodiversity" (innate differences between races). It is, ironically, a dark mirror of the social justice narrative. The media and academic establishment—Neo-Reactionary Mencius Moldbug calls it "the cathedral"—have conspired to hide fundamental truths about the world from ordinary people, keeping them in the dark about their true nature in order to legitimize a false and unjust social order.

At times, this atavistic narrative engenders explicit, real-world violence. Mass shootings perpetrated by right-wing terrorists decrying the ills of modern feminism or multiculturalism have become a regular fact of life in contemporary America. In the past six years alone, self-proclaimed white supremacists and anti-Semites have committed acts of violence in El Paso, Texas, (twenty-two killed); at a Gilroy, California, garlic festival (four killed); at a Chabad synagogue in California (one killed); at a synagogue in Pittsburgh (eleven killed); at a Parkland, Florida, high school (seventeen killed); at a predominately black church in South Carolina (nine killed); and at a counterprotest against the far-right Unite the Right rally in Charlottesville, Virginia, (one killed). Across the globe, fifty-one people were killed in a shooting at a mosque in Christchurch, New Zealand. Most of these killers had been radicalized by the Internet far right; many left behind manifestos framing themselves as would-be crusaders, heroes reclaiming their biological birthright and defending the world from the lily-livered progressivism that allowed multiculturalism to flourish. The El Paso shooter, for example, told his readers that he was "honored to head the fight to reclaim my country from destruction."[18]

Avowedly misogynist killers have, in the same time frame, committed acts of terror on the University of California, Santa Barbara, campus (six killed) and in Toronto (ten killed). Both perpetrators, likewise, posted their manifesto online to legions of adoring, similarly radicalized fans. They blamed feminism for a culture in which beta males were systematically rejected by attractive women made overly confident by a politically correct society that offered them unlimited power over their male counterparts. The perpetrator of the Toronto attack called specifically for an "incel rebellion" to take down the "Chads" and "Staceys" (the right-wing Reddit terms for the sexually successful).

These acts of violence, and their perpetrators, may be extreme. But they speak to the wider potency of the new atavistic narrative, which fetishizes maleness or whiteness as emblems of a vanished, pre-social-justice age. At once obsessed with an imagined past and thoroughly, indelibly, part of the Internet present, these movements both claim to resist the cult of contemporary Remixed intuitionalism and are ultimately indebted to it.

The new atavists, after all, are not so different from their despised enemies on the left. Although they may valorize authority in the abstract, in practice they are obsessed with tearing down "the cathedral": the institutions, from universities to media companies, that foment the ideological orthodoxy of contemporary progressive society. If the witches of the #resistance see society as inherently patriarchal and misogynistic—and thus worthy of destruction—then today's new atavists see society as equally culpable for the sins of progressivism, feminism, and multiculturalism. Both new atavists and their progressive peers ultimately treat the body—and physical, personal self-improvement—as the ultimate site of meaning. In the atavists' case, self-betterment comes through intense weight lifting, highly regulated "paleo" diets, cranial reconstruction surgery, or other "masculine" forms of improvement, rather than through the more feminized rhetoric of the wellness industry. But they still consider it the necessary route to spiritual transcendence.

If the goal of Remixed wellness culture is to become one's best self, then the goal of modern atavism is either to become a Chad or else to ensure that there are no Chads left standing.

Today's new atavists are caught between worlds. They despise much of contemporary America and yet their gathering spaces—Reddit, right-wing YouTube channels, 4chan's /pol/ board, its successor 8chan, the social networking app Gab, and multiplayer video games (a popular recruiting ground)—are entirely the product of the modern Internet age. They fetishize both an imaginary world of the past and revel in the trolling, shitposting, and other gleeful forms of irony that flourish in the era of social media. They reject what they decry as the moral relativism and individualism of contemporary American culture, but they believe in nothing more transcendent than biological urges.

They are, in other words, both the sworn enemies of most of the Remixed and completely Remixed themselves.

THE BATTLE OF ORDER AND CHAOS

At the core of atavistic ideology is a dichotomous vision of the world. There is masculine and feminine, order and chaos. Life consists of contending with the Darwinian brutality of nature, while both disciplining the self and creating institutions to strengthen civilization. The world is a dangerous and ultimately meaningless place, one in which no laws exist apart from evolutionary and economic competition, and the only hope humans have is to harness those natural principles for their own thoroughly embodied ends.

Few contemporary atavists have encapsulated this philosophy as neatly as Dr. Jordan B. Peterson, perhaps the best-known public intellectual in the world. Through a media empire that includes best-selling books, videos, and podcasts, Peterson has built a phenomenally dedicated fan base, largely but not exclusively consisting of young men, that sees in him a powerful, authoritative, and thoroughly masculine rejoinder to the feminization and intuitionalism of modern life.

While Peterson is significantly more moderate politically than many of the other atavists in this chapter—he's a vocal critic of political correctness and social justice, but has also distanced himself from the explicit racism and sexism of the modern alt-right—he might nevertheless be fairly considered part of the soi-disant intellectual dark web, a loose umbrella term for a group of public intellectuals—including atheist author Sam Harris, psychologist Steven Pinker, and conservative commentator Ben Shapiro—who believe that their politically incorrect views on race, gender, and sexuality have exiled them beyond the purview of the progressive mainstream media. While members of the IDW have explicitly distanced themselves from the alt-right proper, as well as from "alt-lite" figures like blogger Stefan Molyneux or Twitter personality Mike Cernovich, their readers do not necessarily make the same distinctions. A 2019 Brazilian study of YouTube commentators on IDW, alt-lite, and alt-right videos found that about 40 percent who posted on alt-right videos in 2018 had started out commenting primarily on IDW or alt-lite videos. The study also found that YouTube's own algorithms for suggesting new content to viewers who had liked IDW content pushed them, gradually, toward alt-lite and alt-right videos.[19]

It's important to note that Peterson—and the IDW more broadly—has continuously condemned and rejected the alt-right and the kind of misogynistic and radicalized violence many in the alt-right promote. But what more moderate atavists like Peterson and the rest of the IDW share with their radicalized fringe counterparts is a kind of materialist Stoicism, in which our genetic code, and our ability to accept and embrace this biological fact, determines who we really are.

A professor of psychology at the University of Toronto, Peterson didn't start out as a pop-psych guru. He spent much of his career as a practicing clinician and an academic, primarily focusing on the psychology of abnormal personality. Then, in 1999, he published a sprawling academic book called *Maps of Meaning: The Architecture of Belief*. A mammoth six-hundred-page treatise on human religious sentiment, blending traditional psychology with literary criticism, studies of ancient myth, and religious scholarship, *Maps of Meaning* proposed—relatively uncontroversially—that the human need to shape chaos into an ordered narrative is a fundamental part of who we are. When those narrative systems are threatened, we respond defensively—in a manner not unlike when an animal's physical territory is threatened—and become violent. Peterson concludes that this leads to a whole host of conflicts, from warfare to gulags to genocide. The book was a reasonable success: the audiobook ultimately made it onto the *New York Times* best-seller list in 2002 and a spin-off Canadian television program premiered two years later.

But it wasn't until 2013 that Peterson entered the conversational mainstream. It started relatively simply, with Peterson's side hobby of posting answers to questions on the crowdsourcing platform Quora. While most questions on Quora tend toward the pragmatic ("How do I get red wine stains off a white carpet?") or personal ("Should I break up with my cheating boyfriend?"), Peterson used the platform to answer some of life's bigger questions: "How do some people who once loved each other enough to marry, end up in bitter divorces and feeling hatred for one another?" "How can I make good judgments?" "What are the most valuable things everyone should know?"[20] Peterson's folksy style and straightforward, buck-up-kid brand of motivation (he's fond of reminding readers to "stand up straight"), as well as his penchant for openly criticizing "SJWs" and "identity politics," garnered him thousands of devotees.

Then came video lectures. Hours-long, university-level discourses on the nature of myth, history, and the Bible, filmed against a dark curtained background with minimal visual stimulation, these lectures were hardly the stuff that viral memes are made of. But fans flocked to them, propelling Peterson to global fame. He now has over one million followers on Twitter, and almost two million followers on YouTube. One of his most popular videos, a two-and-a-half-hour-long meditation on the book of Genesis, has been viewed four million times. In 2018, his second book, a tidy self-help volume called *12 Rules for Life: An Antidote to Chaos*, sold three million copies worldwide.[21] His onetime

Patreon account garnered upward of $80,000 a month in crowdfunded donations before he deleted it in protest of what he deemed the platform's "censorship" of right-wing personalities and thoughts.[22] His podcast regularly garners a million listeners per episode.

In 2016, Peterson entered the fray of the culture wars, cementing his virality. He made Canadian headlines when he publicly announced that he would not automatically comply with a bill known as C-16, which encoded "gender identity and expression" into human rights law. In a series of public lectures, Peterson reflected on the possibility that, under the new bill, he might be legally obligated to refer to a transgender or nonbinary student by their chosen pronouns, an obligation he argued was an infringement on his free speech. "I'm not going to cede linguistic territory to post-modernist neo-Marxists," he told the *Spectator's* Tim Lott.[23]

Although the C-16 bill made no mention of pronouns specifically, Peterson's well-publicized opposition to it made him an increasingly visible beacon for followers disenchanted by what they saw as the excesses of the social justice left. A subsequent fractious 2018 interview about the gender pay gap on British television's Channel 4 with Cathy Newman—which has since been viewed fifteen million times—made Peterson into a bona fide reactionary celebrity, as delighted Internet fans posted and reposted memes and quotes as an example of prime "gotcha" moments, in which the clever intellectual bested the brainwashed feminist buffoon. (Newman, for her part, reported receiving a cavalcade of death threats for her role in the altercation.)[24]

Since then, Peterson has made headlines, like his fellow travelers in the IDW, as a transgressive figure. To his enemies, largely on the political left, he is a racist, sexist, and above all things dangerous gateway drug into the harder bigotry of the alt-right. To his admirers, he is a refreshingly risqué truth teller, willing and able to say things the woke mainstream media can no longer get away with. He is, in short, a sensation tailor-made for the Internet cult of personality.

But *12 Rules for Life* is less innovative than it is nostalgic. The implicit ideology of the book is that in the modern age—and in particular in secular, feminist, identity-politics-motivated culture—humans have lost touch with the primary dichotomies that structure existence: the careful balance between (masculine) order and (feminine) chaos.

Drawing on a wealth of ancient mythological texts, Peterson argues that the battle between chaos and order has been an integral part of all Western religious and cultural traditions. Peterson then challenges his readers to establish order in their own lives, taking responsibility for their choices. "We must each adopt as much responsibility as possible for individual life, society, and the world," Peterson writes.[25]

Central to this responsibility is an acceptance of, in Peterson's argument, certain fundamental biological and evolutionary realities, such as that men and woman are fundamentally different. Men in particular are hardwired to participate and struggle in dominance-based status hierarchies, in which there are clear-cut winners and losers. In one of the most famous passages in the book, Peterson illustrates this with the example of the lobster, one of the oldest creatures in existence. Even lobsters exhibit this social behavior, he says: "The top lobster . . . occupying the best shelter, getting some good rest, finishing a good meal—parades his dominance around his territory, rousting subordinate lobsters from their shelters at night, just to remind them who's their daddy."[26]

Peterson insists that despite what some of the social-justice-minded would like to think, these categories and hierarchies are immutable, encoded at the most basic biological level into human existence. "The dominance hierarchy is not capitalism," he writes. "It's not communism. . . . It's not the military-industrial complex. It's not the patriarchy. . . . It's not even a human creation. . . . It is instead a near-eternal aspect of the environment."

But Peterson is most interested in dominance hierarchies as they pertain to human beings. The entire Western religious tradition, he argues, not to mention the foundations of our contemporary cultural symbology, is predicated precisely on the cosmic-level battle between order and chaos, which structures both the overarching skeleton of evolutionary biology and the contours of each individual human soul.

Everything about the world we live in, Peterson tells us, is predicated on that fundamental battle.

On the one hand, he writes, we have order: "Tribe, religion, hearth, home, and country. It's the warm, secure living-room where the fireplace glows and the children play."[27] On the other hand, there's chaos: "The eternal feminine . . . mater, origin, source, mother. . . . It's the impenetrable darkness of a cave . . . the mother grizzly all compassion to her cubs, who marks you as potential predator and tears you to pieces . . . the crushing force of sexual selection."[28]

Contemporary culture is in decline because it has devalued the trappings of order: institutional structure, regimented discipline, and masculine heroism. Our modern spiritual landscape has, in prioritizing intuition and authenticity as the highest goods, left us bereft of both structure and objective values.

"You cannot aim yourself at anything if you are completely undisciplined and untutored," Peterson declares. "What good is a value system that does not provide a stable structure? What good is a value system that does not point the way to a higher order?"[29]

His advice is simple. Stand up straight. Clean your room. Avoid people who drag you down. ("But Christ himself, you might object," Peterson muses, "befriended tax-collectors and prostitutes. . . . But Christ was the archetypical perfect man. And you're you.")[30] Treat yourself with dignity. ("You are not simply your own possession to torture and mistreat. This is partly because your Being is inexorably tied up with that of others, and your mistreatment of yourself can have catastrophic consequences for others.") Live *for* something.[31] Ultimately, Peterson promises, seeing the world through his eyes will make its apparent meaninglessness make sense. "Many things begin to fall into place when you begin to consciously understand the world in this manner. It's as if the knowledge of your body and soul falls into alignment with the knowledge of your intellect."[32]

It's not difficult to see why Peterson's words are appealing to so many. Blending science, philosophy, and literary criticism (with more than a little self-help thrown in), Peterson at once exemplifies and subverts the foundations of the secular religions we've seen so far. He promotes rigorous personal discipline but eschews total asceticism—his exhortation that you're "not simply your own possession to torture" has shades of self-care about it. Like the Remixed intuitionalists, Peterson sees the self—and the improvement and perfecting of it—as the most important thing to pay attention to. This is a treatise, after all, of self-help, not of helping the world.

But what sets Peterson apart from practitioners of contemporary feminist witchcraft or activists focusing on self-care is the degree to which he treats reality as immutable and fixed. Gut instinct does not matter. Feelings do not matter. Lived experience does not matter. Or, at least, they are not valid routes to knowledge. Rather, there is something inherent and biological in us—as men, as women, as human beings—that determines our destiny. A life well lived is one that accepts these givens.

Peterson does not claim any transcendent or metaphysical truth. (In a few interviews, he's alluded to being a Christian, although his statements on his personal faith have been inconsistent.) He doesn't necessarily claim a transcendent meaning for the world, either. But what he does claim is powerful: That there is something, however nebulous, that links lobster dominance hierarchies to ancient Near Eastern creation myths to the human condition in 2020. That there is something within the laws of nature that is bigger and more mythic and more important than any individual human life.

There may not be a God, in Peterson's schema, but there's definitely potential for meaning. By submitting to the natural order, human beings can achieve true freedom. Embrace who you are, Peterson tells us, in order to transform who you can be. Choose to live heroically in accordance with your animal nature and achieve reproductive success (Peterson is fond of reminding his audiences that half of all men on this planet have died without ever fathering a child), or die flabby and weak willed—one of BAP's bugmen.

Peterson's open contempt of the "social justice left" has done much to bolster the ranks of his followers. A 2018 New York Times profile by Nellie Bowles quoted one of his devotees as celebrating the fact that

Peterson was "waking us up in the West." Another told Bowles that he was relieved to finally hear someone talk about how hierarchies were natural and normal and rail against "forced diversity." Still another lauded that Peterson had tapped into a primal, fundamental truth that society had attempted to occlude: "Whenever I listen to him," he said, "it's like he's telling me something I already knew."[33] Fans have even paid him up to $200 a session for private Skype coaching, although Peterson told a reporter in 2018 that he'd since discontinued the practice.[34] (Peterson's critics, for their part, are no less willing to frame him as exclusively an Islamophobic, transphobic, misogynist alt-right provocateur; in May 2019, for example, Cambridge University's divinity faculty overturned its decision to invite Peterson to give a series of lectures on the book of Exodus, following widespread student outrage.)

Although Peterson's ideology is drastically different from that of the social justice movement, his tactics are similar. He has, in detailing the pitched battle between order and chaos, created a modern, nontheistic myth that renders the world meaningful. His followers, in standing up straight and cleaning their rooms and purchasing lobster T-shirts, transform themselves from disaffected Internet dwellers marginalized (in their own minds, at least) by political correctness into cosmic-level heroes, braving the forces of darkness every time they make their beds or say something potentially offensive on Twitter.

As one of Peterson's fans, defending him in a *New York Times* op-ed, breathlessly writes, "His lectures and books imbue the everyday with a new sense of romanticism. He makes tasks like cleaning one's room or finding a career sound like dragon-slaying voyages. His lectures infuse ordinary activities with new meaning."[35]

It is that sense of meaningfulness, as much as the content of Peterson's writings, that gives him and the rest of the new atavists such power.

THE RED AND THE BLACK (PILLS)

If you've spent any time on the Internet in the past five years, you've probably heard of the "red pill."

In *The Matrix*, the 1999 science fiction film from which the red pill gets its name, the pill is a symbol of enlightenment, an escape from societal restraints. The film's hero, Neo, lives in an illusory digital world—the Matrix—his entire consciousness subject to the whim of computer programmers. Neo starts the film blissfully unaware of this. Then he is quasi-kidnapped by a mysterious leather-clad man named Morpheus. Morpheus offers Neo two choices, represented by two pills. "This is your last chance," Morpheus tells him. "After this, there is no turning back. You take the blue pill—the story ends, you wake up in your bed and believe whatever you want to believe. You take the red pill—you stay in Wonderland, and I show you how deep the rabbit hole goes. Remember: all I'm offering is the truth. Nothing more."

The blue pill represents comfortable stability, living within the stated structures of a manufactured reality. The red pill represents truth, no matter how bitter.

Neo takes the red pill.

And so, say denizens of the loose network of popular right-wing Internet haunts known as the "manosphere," should we.

The red pill, online, is also a chance to wake up from our consciousness of a falsified world. But the matrix we're living in, according to men's rights activists across the globe, isn't a computer simulation. Rather, it's the matriarchy: the unsettling truth that contemporary American culture is beholden to (you might say "pussy-whipped" by) a network of feminists, politically correct progressives, social justice warriors, cultural Marxists, and other misandrist ideologues who wish to promote the interests of women—no matter how craven or undeserving—over those of hardworking, disenfranchised men. Take the red pill, in the parlance of the manosphere, and face a world in which women are unfairly promoted and in which a false rape allegation can destroy a man's career. A world in which fathers are routinely forced into wage slavery to pay alimony to cheating ex-wives and provide for children who may or may not be theirs. A world in which the disproportionate deaths of men on job sites and in battle are laughed at and dismissed by women who insist on terming every minor act of flirtation or kindness "sexual harassment."

Red pill ideology has a few foundational sources. There was the early 2000s craze for pickup artist self-help books and classes, which purported to teach socially awkward men the "game" of picking up women. The movement was largely popularized by journalist Neil Strauss's 2005 memoir *The Game*, which recounted his experiences within what became known as the "seduction community"—men who used psychological manipulation to "trick" women into consenting to sex. (Strauss has since published a 2015 follow-up denouncing pickup artistry as antithetical to the foundations of a real relationship.)

There was the anonymously published blog "Dating American"— written by a New Hampshire man named Robert Fisher, who would later be elected to the state House of Representatives—which recounted the "woes of dating in the American culture" that, in his view, had been poisoned by feminism.[36]

And there was the growing number of disaffected, dissatisfied young men who started to congregate on sites like Reddit, finding in the anonymity of the medium and the arch, often ironic tone of its messages a sense of community and commiseration. Self-proclaimed beta males— those unable to reap the sexual rewards doled out to alpha Chads— could bare their souls to like-minded lonely hearts and rail against the social structures that consigned them to the bottom of the social heap.

In 2012, Fisher founded the current r/TheRedPill, the Reddit sub-forum that transformed these sentiments into a bona fide movement. Today, the forum has about 420,000 subscribers, who share news articles about false rape allegations, trade advice on weight lifting, and mock the SJWs they characterize as their worst enemies.[37] Women, they argue, are evolutionarily programmed to be untrustworthy (the subreddit's unofficial motto is AWALT—"all women are like that"— used whenever women have behaved in a particularly egregious way).

But once you've taken the red pill, you have to go down the rabbit hole. For a significant portion of its adherents, the RedPill subreddit is a gateway drug not just to the manosphere—itself a wildly diverse place, with numerous warring camps—but to a wider, and more explicitly political, atavistic right.

What all of the various subcultures within the manosphere have in common is a frustration not merely with feminism and political correctness but with what they see as the fundamental lie at the heart of social justice culture: that human beings are equal blank slates, and that differences between races or genders are simply imposed from without, products of a patriarchal, sexist, and racist society. Among the more curious threads of discourse in the manosphere is the resurgence of pseudoscientific phrenology—the practice of ascribing moral or personal qualities to skull shape—as a way to distinguish between different kinds of men. "The difference between Chad and non-Chad (incel)," reads the caption of one popular RedPill meme under a photograph of two differently shaped heads, "is literally a few millimeters of bone."[38] According to the manosphere, biological reality—including, but not limited to, sexual Darwinism—makes the virile flourish and consigns others to loneliness or cuckoldry.

Women, they argue, now have it too easy. They get boosts in the college admission process, in the workplace, in the family courtroom, at rape trials. They've grown accustomed to having everything their way. Worse still, they've become sexual consumers, believing themselves entitled to maximize their period of sexual liberation (or, as RedPill calls it, the "cock carousel"), having as much sex as possible with attractive Chads in their early twenties before ultimately conning a desperate beta male into providing them with children, stability, and financial support before they reach the end of their fertility window.

These masculinist atavists see sex, Darwinian evolution, and consumer capitalism as inexorably intertwined. The women who swipe right on dating apps, or who choose someone across the dance floor at a nightclub, are selecting their partners the way they might a brand of cereal or a favorite soft drink. Inevitably, they want the most high-status, exclusive product: the Chads. Defective products—the betas, the cucks, the omegas (men without the ability to succeed in the social hierarchy), the incels, and other forms of superfluous men—are consigned to the biological trash heap, mourning not just their own loneliness but the extinction of their bloodline altogether. (Like Peterson, many atavists make much of the statistic that half of all men don't ever procreate.)

Those who don't fit the Chad mold see themselves as having one of two options. They must either change themselves to fit in or change the system that keeps them down. They may call for "enforced monogamy" (a favorite buzzword of Peterson's) or "sexual redistribution" (blogger and former Eliezer Yudkowsky collaborator Robin Hanson, of proto-Rationalist blog *Overcoming Bias*, wondered publicly in the wake of the 2018 Toronto van attack why people were so much more concerned with income inequality than sex inequality). Or they may advocate for wholesale violence and destruction: the "incel rebellion" Toronto attacker Alek Minassian dreamed of, in which he promised to "overthrow all the Chads and Staceys."[39]

This vision of a world whose meaningfulness is predicated exclusively on biological reality necessarily demands a rejection of any ideology that claims the transcendent. While some in the manosphere identify as cultural Christians—celebrating what they see as Christianity's traditionalism when it comes to gender roles or opposition to Islam—the manosphere is, by and large, focused on the here and now. A representative attitude is that of *Return of Kings*' John Carver, who published "25 Painful Red Pill Questions Christians Need to Ask Themselves," which concludes by quoting Thomas Paine as saying that Christianity is merely a "parody on the worship of the sun."[40]

The manosphere's reaction to the perceived domination of the Chads ranges from the rigorously self-disciplined—those who obey the Petersonian call to "become the lobster" and tap into the primal dominance hierarchies they believe all creatures share—to the outright nihilistic.

On the optimistic side, there are the pickup artists, who, like Neil Strauss, think they can manipulate their way into social success. There are, too, the BAP-mandated lifters and those who devote themselves to paleo-style diets, eating the way that cavemen did in order to maximize their evolutionary potential. (Jordan Peterson himself has adopted this route: he announced in 2018 that he now subsists exclusively on a diet of beef and bourbon.)

Some of these masculinist self-help circles are indistinguishable from their wellness counterparts. Alt-lite celebrity Mike Cernovich, for example—one of the many atavism-adjacent journalists who made a name for himself during the Gamergate phenomenon, and who has made a career out of masculinist self-help books like *Gorilla Mindset* and *MAGA Mindset: Making You and America Great Again*—exhorts his readers to "believe that the world is abundant. The world is one of endless resources and unlimited potential. What you do matters. Your choices matter. You matter."[41] Many of the supplements sold by *Infowars'* Alex Jones—including Super Male Vitality and Wake Up America Immune Support Blend 100% Organic Coffee—likewise are all but indistinguishable from more feminine-sounding products like the Sex Dust and Sun Potion sold by Gwyneth Paltrow's Goop.[42]

There is, too, the punk-tinged, "Western chauvinist" movement known as the Proud Boys—founded by *Vice* cofounder Gavin McInnes—whose ethos demands "minimal government, maximum freedom, anti-political correctness, anti-racial guilt, pro-gun rights, anti-Drug War, closed borders, anti-masturbation, venerating entrepreneurs, venerating housewives." (McInnes quit the group in 2018, a day after the FBI classified it as an "extremist" group following a New York altercation between Proud Boys and anti-fascists.)[43] Although there are only about three thousand professed Proud Boys in America, their public reach—they're frequent guests at pro-Trump and other right-wing rallies—far extends their numbers.

Then there are those who take a far more pessimistic, even nihilistic, approach. There's the Men Going Their Own Way, male separatists who eschew sexual or romantic contact with women altogether (and sometimes even masturbation, in which case there's another subreddit, r/NoFap, dedicated to that).[44] They caution each other that any interaction with the opposite sex will inexorably lead to catastrophe. There's the incels, who feel that they've been left behind or overlooked by the brutality of the dating free marketplace, and who spend their days bemoaning the unfairness of their fate and at times fetishizing violence against the Staceys and Chads they see as having wronged them. Many revere Elliot Rodger, the perpetrator of a targeted misogynistic attack that killed six (not including Rodger himself, who committed suicide before capture) on the campus of the University of California, Santa Barbara. Rodger left behind a lengthy manifesto, often quoted in incel circles, that accused overly choosy women of consigning him to a life of perpetual virginity. "I'm the perfect guy," he wrote, "and yet you throw yourselves at these obnoxious men instead of me, the supreme gentleman."[45] Sexual unfairness, he wrote, left him "no choice but to exact revenge on the society." Incels have since repurposed the term "supreme gentleman" as one of praise; Toronto killer Alek Minassian explicitly referenced it in a Facebook post made shortly before his own attack, in which he exhorted readers to "hail the Supreme Gentleman Elliot Rodger."[46]

Rodger's and Minassian's attacks were both celebrated in extreme incel circles, as well as in pockets of the broader manosphere. Even those who did not condone the attacks directly implied, heavily, that these men were driven to violence by the moral bankruptcy of postfeminist society. Popular alt-lite anti-feminist personalities, like the YouTuber Carl Benjamin (better known as Sargon of Akkad), defended Rodger's rampage. Benjamin called it the result of "stupid social justice feminine [sic] bullshit," expressing sympathy for "these poor fucking guys who don't have any options left."[47]

The anti-SJW sentiment of these subsets of the manosphere has made them natural allies with other subgroups within the alt-right that extend their ire more specifically to racial minorities or, often, Jews. The combination of nostalgia and futility that once exclusively fueled violence against women has now inspired shooters of mosques and synagogues; subreddits like r/TheRedPill are increasingly pathways to other reactionary ideologies. A survey produced by white supremacist website the *Right Stuff*, which asked its members to detail their pathways to the alt-right, found that significant portions had been radicalized through online men's rights groups or through affiliated public figures like Gavin

McInnes or Sargon of Akkad.[48] In the wake of the Gamergate contro-versy, neo-Nazi organizations now regularly use gamer culture—and in-game social networks—to recruit new teenage members.[49]

These groups have different stated enemies, but their underpinning ideology remains the same. By looking backward to a better time (one inevitably more segregated along gender and racial lines than the pres-ent), by adopting the ideology and methods of mythic warriors, young men can rediscover a place in today's broken world. Anyone with an Internet connection—no matter how beta, no matter how much of a cuck or even an incel—can be a potential supreme gentleman.

It is precisely that possibility that gives the manosphere its sense of meaning. When, in 2018, Minassian drove a van into dozens of Toronto pedestrians, he, like Rodger, was celebrated online as a rebellious war-rior, the only person brave enough to respond with sufficient gravity to a society that deserved to be scourged. Within hours of the attack, posters on incel forums were changing their profile photos to images of him, praising the attack as "lifefuel"—giving them, in other words, something to live for.[50]

It's impossible to overlook, however, *why* these groups are so effec-tive at recruiting their targets. At their most potent, they offer mem-bers not just a coherent and stable account of the universe but also a vital sense of community. The betas, omegas, and cucks attracted to these forums and apps may be outcasts in the so-called real world, but online they are part of a close-knit community. When they post about their frustrations with dating or with a crush, there are thousands of like-minded men waiting in the wings to provide them with reassurance or remind them that their failures are somebody else's fault. These forums double as churches: places where they can reify and reiterate a mean-ingful narrative of the world with people just like them. "It was a sense of community," one ex-RedPiller told a CNN reporter to explain his radicalization, "a sense of brotherhood."[51]

For members of these groups, the opportunity to commit acts of vio-lence (or at least fantasize about them online) doubles as an opportunity to prove their virility. Both shitposting about minorities or women and actively committing violence are nigh on sacred rituals, an opportunity for men to tap into their primal purpose to destroy the wider social order. Numerous prominent men's rights leaders have, following the rise of the alt-right, rebranded themselves as white supremacists. The blogger James C. Weidmann, for example—who wrote a popular pickup blog known as *Chateau Heartiste* under the alias "Roissy in D.C."—is now an avowed white nationalist. He once expressed "tender admiration" for Adolf Hitler, whom he saw as a frustrated beta misled by his passion for unreciprocating women. *Return of Kings*' Roosh V frequently promotes the work of anti-Semitic historian Kevin MacDonald, who blames the Jews for Western cultural collapse and has written articles about "The Damaging Effects of Jewish Intellectualism and Activism on Western Culture." ("A race to degeneracy hurts Jews less than gentiles because they still retain guiding in-group values. Gentiles are left in the cultural winds that Jews help create.")[52]

Anti-Semitism, misogyny, and racism are all endemic to alt-right culture and implicit in much of atavist culture more broadly. But to reduce the alt-right to these bigotries is to overlook the profound centrality of nihilism. At its core, alt-right atavism—unlike its more conservative Petersonian and IDW-based incarnations—is a religion of meaninglessness, one that worships violence and destruction for their own sake. Nature may be the only god there is, but ultimately nature is as chaotic and bereft of significance as everything else.

If the Petersonian ethos combines atavism with wellness culture—*improve yourself, become a real man*—the ethos of alt-right violence combines that same atavism with bleak despair. Biology offers not a glimpse of hope but rather a portrait of despair. The matriarchy has won. Men are evolutionarily useless in a technological age. The only way forward is total irony or absolute destruction. Violence, including racist and misogynist mass violence, is desirable not merely because it might achieve a specific political end, no matter how noxious, but because it causes total chaos. It triggers the normies. It fucks shit up.

It destabilizes the status quo. It combines both the atavistic impulse toward total submission—the fetishization of power, hierarchy, and masculinism—and its total subversion.

As Angela Nagle describes in her book *Kill All Normies*, alt-right culture is as indebted to the freewheeling, pro-trolling Internet of early 2000s message boards like 4chan's /pol/ (politically incorrect) and /b/ (random) as it is to contemporary reactionary politics. "The emergence of this new online right," Nagle writes, "is the full coming to fruition of the transgressive anti-moral style, its final detachment from any egalitarian philosophy of the left or Christian morality on the right."[53] Early trolling culture—pioneered by gamers, nerds, and other self-described societal outcasts—exploited the then new Internet's powers of both anonymity and disembodiment. You could say *anything*, no matter how offensive. You could be *anyone*. (As the famous saying goes: on the Internet, nobody knows you're a dog.) This early Internet culture, like other Internet fandom cultures, was insouciant and antiauthoritarian, devoted to shooting sacred cows. You could roil up the feminists, the politically correct sentimentalists, or indeed anyone who took things too seriously. After all, online, nothing really mattered.

Back in 2006, for example, long before the rise of modern alt-right groups, their troll forebears on 4chan's /b/ became suddenly and perhaps inexplicably obsessed with the suicide of a Minnesota seventh grader named Mitchell Henderson. Shortly after Henderson's death, a classmate had posted a grief-stricken message on the boy's memorial page. Henderson, it said, was "an hero to take the shot, to leave us all behind. God do we wish we could take it back" now. The phrase— its mawkish sincerity, its very basic misspelling—became catnip to 4chan users, who saw in it an opportunity to wreak havoc on anybody who dared to take anything, including the death of a child, too seriously. Within hours of the content appearing on 4chan, dedicated trolls had contacted Henderson's parents pretending to be the ghost of their dead child. Others left iPods on Henderson's grave, referencing a mention of Henderson's iPod elsewhere on the memorial page. Still others hacked the page, photoshopped Henderson's face into pornographic scenes, and continued to harass Henderson's family and friends.[54] This unlikely group of posters—almost none of whom had met in real life—got caught up in what you might call a collective effervescence of destruction, delighting in triggering normies who did not share their sense of gleeful disengagement. "It's not bullying," one self-professed Internet troll told an *Esquire* reporter in 2014.[55] "It's satirical performance art." Another exhorted him to "read up on Eris, the goddess of discords. She brings ironic punishment to people who think they're better than they are. . . . [I] bring discomfort to people's comfort zones. And that's what we need. Because western culture is sick. It's diseased."

The furor over Henderson ultimately died down. But the phrase "an hero" did not. To be "an hero" quickly became a euphemism for suicide and then, inevitably, a euphemism for the kind of perceived "heroics" committed by mass shooters. The Christchurch mosque shooter explicitly referred to himself as "an hero" in his published manifesto, while supporters of the Poway synagogue shooter gleefully celebrated him in the same terms.[56]

To be "an hero," in this world, is to buy into the fundamental nihilism at the heart of atavistic alt-right culture. It is to live at once in a mythic narrative—a fantasy of violence and masculinity as potent as any video game—and to recognize its utter falsity. It's an atavism, in other words, without any gods. Maybe there was a time when men were really men, when gods and heroes walked the earth, but that time has long since passed. All we have to look forward to is the inexorable death march of civilization—and, if we're lucky, the chance to blow some shit up along the way.

One of the earliest examples of this nihilistic strain of Internet culture becoming specifically politicized occurred in 2016, during the run-up to the election of Donald Trump. In the months preceding the election, Trump supporters on 4chan's /pol/ noticed something strange about posts concerning Trump. They were all numbered in a special way, known as "gets." On 4chan, which is otherwise anonymous, all posts are sequentially numbered. Given the high volume of posts on the site, the final few digits of this number are essentially randomized. Posts with distinctive final numbers—such as ending in 1111—are often celebrated as "gets."

On June 16, 2016, one poster received the ultimate "get," ending in 77777777, with a post that read simply, "Trump will win."

A meme was born.

Or, rather, "meme magic" was born.

Meme magic—the half-joking idea that Donald Trump could be "memed" into victory through judicious 4chan shitposting—became part of the site's rhetorical landscape. Due to the valiant efforts of brave shitposters, the "God-Emperor," as Trump was frequently known on the site, would be propelled to the White House, where he would quench his thirst with an endless supply of liberal tears.

This meme magic was represented visually by a cartoon frog named Pepe. Originally a relatively innocuous cartoon character created by Matt Furie for a comic named *Boy's Club*, Pepe became, through the inexplicable machinations of Internet meme culture, the de facto symbol for the burgeoning Trumpian online alt-right. It just so happened, 4chan soon discovered, that there was, in fact, an ancient Egyptian chaos god with a frog's head that resembled the newly ubiquitous Pepe. His name was Kek.

Kek, as it happened, was also a popular term on 4chan and in gaming culture more broadly as a synonym for LOL (laugh out loud). The word derived from the *World of Warcraft* multiplayer games, in which opponents' chat logs were visible but encrypted in a particular, consistent code. The phrase LOL was, within this system, automatically transformed into KEK.

From there, it was only a short step to "Kekism," at once a joke religion and a precursor of the reactionary radicalization to follow. The frog-headed Kek—represented by depictions of Pepe—was the patron god of trolls, nonsense, shitposting, and "lulz." And the meme magic he represented—the collective force of the absurdist right-wing Internet—was going to propel Donald Trump into office. "Meme magic grows stronger each day," one 4chan poster wrote on June 25, 2016, "and soon

KEK will return to smite the normies and bring about eternal chaos." Another popular meme boasted that "Kek is using 4chan as a vessel to spread his message and to usher in a new era of light."[57]

Soon, Trump himself was seemingly in, if not on the joke, then nevertheless on the meme—retweeting images of himself as Pepe and delighting his followers. His son Donald Trump Jr. also got in on the action, posting an image of *The Expendables* action film poster, retitled "The Deplorables" and depicting a photoshopped Trump team alongside Pepe.

Then, on September 11, 2016, a seeming freak coincidence propelled Kekism into full-on fervor. The 4chan-sphere had been awash with rumors—largely tongue-in-cheek—of "Sick Hillary" Clinton, arguing that she was a physically depleted, secretly ill presidential candidate who lacked Donald Trump's robust fervor and virile constitution. Then, news broke that Clinton had become ill and fainted at a New York 9/11 memorial service.[58] Kek worshippers were jubilant, and more than a little shocked. "Now Hillary is getting sick and the media is talking about Pepe it's clear as day your memes are fucking with the fabric of reality," one poster wrote. "STOP PLEASE I BEG YOU. You're fucking with powers you don't understand. If you keep this up you could meme us all out of existence."[59]

When Donald Trump was elected two months later—to the surprise of the majority of the political and journalistic establishment—it may well have seemed to the mainstream media that a chaos god was, indeed, controlling world affairs. The unthinkable had happened. Conventional, institutional wisdom had failed.

But on 4chan, at least, the explanation was simple. Kek was pulling the strings. "But a god of chaos works in mysterious ways," wrote one pro-Kek blog. "Trump's new president-elect status alone has seeded a fair share of entropy, hasn't it? Protests abound, monuments being vandalized, and entire political systems being called into question. It would seem as though Kek's work has only just begun."[60] Another Reddit poster rejoiced: "It's still sinking in; we literally memed the absolute MADMAN into the White House."[61]

Kek wasn't "real" in the sense that nobody believed he was meta-physically out there, offline. But he was real in the sense that he served as a celebration of the randomness of online culture, which relished in the chaos that Trump seemed poised to bring to America. That chaos, they knew deep down, reflected the structure of the world all along.

In the early years of Trump's presidency, the cult of Kek became a popular shibboleth for alt-right and alt-right-adjacent activists. It developed a theology: the battle of the "Kekistanis" against their rivals, "Normiestan" and "Cuckistan." It developed a common prayer:

> *Our Kek*
>
> *Who art in memetics*
>
> *Hallowed by thy memes*
>
> *Thy Trumpdom come*
>
> *Thy will be done*
>
> *In real life as it is on /pol/*
>
> *Give us this day our daily dubs*
>
> *And forgive us of our baiting*
>
> *As we forgive those who bait against us*
>
> *And lead us not into cuckoldry*
>
> *But deliver us from shills*
>
> *For thine is the memetic kingdom, and the shitposting, and the winning, for ever and ever. Praise KEK.*[62]

The new "national flag" of "Kekistan" made its appearance not only in Twitter avatars and on 4chan boards, but also in real life. Bearers of the Kekistani flag made an appearance at the 2017 Unite the Right rally in Charlottesville, Virginia, as well as at a pro–Steve Bannon rally outside the White House that same year.[63]

"The Kekistani people are here," one of the group's leaders was filmed shouting. "They stand with the oppressed minorities, the oppressed people of Kekistan. They will be heard, they will be set free.

Reparations for Kekistan now! Reparations for Kekistan right now!" Another added, "We have lived under normie oppression for too long!"[64]

The closest thing the Kekistanis had to a leader was Donald Trump himself, who, with his combination of Make America Great Again nostalgia and gleeful absurdity, exemplifies both the atavistic and nihilistic sides of reactionary Internet culture. While Trump still draws the majority of his support from white evangelicals—almost 70 percent of whom still support him—he's also garnered the ardor of many Petersonian atavists and their more explicitly right-wing online counterparts.[65]

Trump is, after all, the ultimate troll. He is at once the self-proclaimed paragon of what Jordan Peterson might call order—a strongman with a brute penchant for other authoritarians, openly praising the dictatorial or quasi-dictatorial regimes of Vladimir Putin, Kim Jong-il, Rodrigo Duterte, and Viktor Orbán, among others—and its subversion, an unconcerned fabulist who delights not in positive policy proposals but rather in provoking liberal tears, for whom brazenly lying is as much a show of dominance as it is a political tactic.

Trump is, to his Kekistani followers, the ultimate man's man—God-Emperor, depicted, in one popular Kekistani meme, in the distinctive, explicitly fascist battle armor from the video game *Warhammer*—whose power lies not in his policies but in his ability to set the cathedral aflame and salt the earth after it. (The meme image of Trump as a God-Emperor has become so popular that, by February 2019, it had appeared in papier-mâché form in a *Carnevale* float in Viareggio, Italy.) His callous disregard for the truth is the ultimate form of disengaged machismo. He does not lift weights, eat clean, stand up straight, or clean his room. Rather, he establishes himself as top lobster exclusively by trolling.

Trump's appeal to the Kekistanis, therefore, is twofold. On the one hand, his vision of making America great again is already explicitly atavistic. His perceived virility—when he boasts, for example, about grabbing women "by the pussy," in contravention of decades' worth of feminist culture shift—is inseparable from his vision of the imagined pre-political-correctness America, in which men like him more easily thrived. But it's the sheer absurdity of Trump—his bald-faced lies, his disregard for protocols and political norms—that has rendered him Kek's anointed. If his election, in the social justice narrative, is proof of an unjust and fundamentally broken society, then to the Kekistanis it is evidence of an even more disturbing truth: that nothing really matters, anyway.

The formal cult of Kek has, since Trump's election, largely dissipated. It's more fun to root for an underdog than an actual president. Yet its ethos—with its uncanny blend of conservatism and transgression—has persisted throughout the reactionary right. Joke fascism has, in many cases, morphed into actual fascism; joke misogyny and joke racism—the twin pillars of Internet transgression—into outright violence. Figures like former *Breitbart* writer Milo Yiannopoulos (another Gamergate graduate) regularly troll (or claim to be trolling) their readership: saying intentionally inflammatory (and racist and sexist) things as a form of intoxicatingly rebellious counterculturalism. "We are the new punk," Yiannopoulos is fond of saying. At an October 2016 pro-Trump art show (called, unsubtly, #DaddyWillSaveUs), Yiannopoulos was filmed telling listeners, "If you want to annoy somebody, if you want to piss your parents off, if you want to be ejected from polite society, there is no better way to do it than to cast a vote for Donald Trump."[66]

And yet, when it comes to modern alt-right movements, it is all but impossible to tell where "ironic" racism ends and its "real" counterpart begins. By 2017—when a self-professed neo-Nazi sympathizer drove a car into a crowd of counterprotesters, killing one, at the Unite the Right rally—protestors' "ironic" Nazi imagery and rhetoric (including shouts of "Blood and soil!" and "Jews will not replace us!") had become anything but. Nihilism and identitarian atavism had become interchangeable. The organizers of the rally had included explicit white supremacists, such as the National Policy Institute's Richard Spencer (who first coined the term "alt-right"), Identity Evropa head Nathan Damigo, and former imperial wizard of the Ku Klux Klan David Duke. But it included, too, figures better known as trolls, like the Twitter personality

Baked Alaska, formerly Yiannopoulos's tour manager and author of the self-published *Meme Magic Secrets Revealed*, as well as fringe members of Gavin McInnes's Proud Boys. (McInnes himself refused to attend.)

As Dale Beran puts it in his account of Trumpism and trolling, *It Came from Something Awful*, "4Chan was populated by a group of de-classed individuals set so far apart from society and so wholly lacking in identity that they began to obsess over it. They clung to race as a means of self-definition. . . . New fascist movements emerged . . . out of de-contextualized people thrust from society by the mercurial throes of modern economics. Degraded and superfluous, convinced life was nothing but a cruel power struggle, they fashioned their own context out of absurd medieval power fantasies."[67]

Since Charlottesville, seventy-three Americans have been killed in white supremacist and anti-Semitic attacks, including those in El Paso, Gilroy, Parkland, Pittsburgh, and Poway.[68] Fifty-one people were killed in New Zealand. Ten were killed in the explicitly misogynistic Toronto van attack.

It's possible to understand these attacks exclusively as the result of bigotry. But to do so overlooks a no less potent element of the reactionary cocktail: the atavistic right's broader destructive nihilism. Channeled through hatred of minorities, Jews, or women is a wider hatred for the world at large—not just Chads and Staceys but normies altogether—and for the seemingly corrupt world order. The heralded cleansing fire of destruction, in the atavistic-right schema, doesn't necessary presage a better world, but merely an opportunity to tear down the old one.

These reactionaries have taken not the red pill but the black one.

First popularized on the blog *Omega Virgin Revolt* in 2012 and ubiquitous in online reactionary circles ever since, the black pill is the ultimate rejection of both contemporary progressive society and any possibility of meaningfully escaping from it. Men will never be able to overturn the matriarchy. The red pill, the blog post argued, has been "colonized by the Paleo-Game Cult," transformed into optimistic but futile self-help. Rather, black pill ideology states that "systemic prob-lems have no personal solutions."[69]

One popular meme contrasting the various pills puts it succinctly. The blue pill ideology—"Just be respectful of women, listen to their problems and be generous and women will flock to you"—is easily dismissed. So, too, is the red pill fantasy: "Just hit the gym, do nofap [stop masturbating], nopillow [literally stop using a pillow], use eye contact, frame and masculine authority to game women and you will be slaying bitches no problem." All that's left is the black pill: "It's over."[70]

While the black pill ideology arose specifically within incel communities, its bleak vision permeates online nihilistic atavism more broadly, as well as nearly every act of atavistic violence.

There is no God, no big something, no sense of meaning bigger than ourselves. Biology—the only transcendent force—is a harsh, cruel mistress that cares nothing about us. Petersonian chaos is encoded in every strand of our DNA. The only thing we can do is laugh in the face of such emptiness—to watch the world burn, and hope that the Chads and the Staceys burn first.

In the wake of the Toronto van attacks, for example, Minassian was celebrated not merely as a giver of "lifefuel" to the incels, but also as a prophet of black pill ideology—someone whose destruction of the normies would herald a wider apocalypse.

"I prefer acid attacks to mass killings, though," one poster mused, pondering how to maximize societal destruction. "Wonder who is going to do a 'mass acid attack.' He will have zero kills to his high score but in my book he'd have beaten all the high scores by virtue of lives ruined and BLACK PILLS FORCED DOWN PEOPLE'S THROAT."[71]

For these posters, the meaninglessness of life makes the real world and the illusory, disembodied realm of video games interchangeable. Actual human deaths and digital "high scores" might as well be the same thing. If nothing really matters, the Internet logic goes, then life is at its core no more or less real than a digital fantasy. IRL deaths are indistinguishable from the bodies racked up in *Grand Theft Auto*. The shooter in the Christchurch mosque killings left behind a manifesto that combined handwringing about the dangers of Islam with references to absurd Internet memes. He told readers to subscribe to Swedish video-game blogger PewDiePie and that he was radicalized by the video game *Fortnite*, which taught him to "floss"—a virally popular dance—"on the corpses of my enemies."[72]

These atavists envision themselves at once as mythic heroes and as "an hero." Their Internet communities are forged in the fires of a shared narrative—women, Jews, and racial minorities are destroying the world, social justice culture is a giant conspiracy meant to distract from basic biological reality—and an equally insular sense of shared meaninglessness. It's a Gnosticism of absurdity, in which disillusionment becomes the highest spiritual virtue of all. There are the normies who believe that there's some sense of order to the world, and the few worthy initiates who know that there is not.

At once nostalgic and nihilistic, this bleak form of atavism may be the ultimate religion of the Internet age. A band of brothers who have never met, brought together in their cultic belief in nothing at all.

conclusion

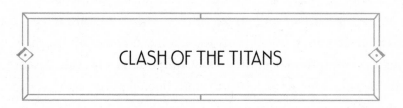

CLASH OF THE TITANS

N 2001, THE BRITISH FANTASY AUTHOR NEIL GAIMAN PUBLISHED a novel called *American Gods*. The novel's premise was a kind of Götterdämmerung. The "old gods"—figures from Greek, Roman, and Norse mythology—were growing obsolete. New gods—personifications of newly worshipped entities like technology, media, and capitalism—were poised to take their place.

Gaiman was prescient. Almost twenty years later, traditional—which is to say, organized and formal—religion in America is in a free fall. Mainline Protestants, once the influential cultural bastion of the American midcentury, have been in a near-constant decline since the 1980s.[1] Meanwhile, white evangelicals—the demographic that, since the founding of Jerry Falwell's Moral Majority in 1979, has been the most public face of religion in America—are likewise dwindling. Just 8 percent of white millennials identify as evangelical, compared to 26 percent of seniors.[2]

The rising Generation Z (those born after 1997) might be the least religious yet. Thirty-four percent of them say they're religiously unaffiliated. Thirteen percent—twice the rate of the general population—identify as atheists.

And yet, new gods are everywhere. Our new shared sacred texts—from *Harry Potter* to *Star Wars* to *Game of Thrones*—bring communities together in discussion, analysis, and exegesis. Wellness culture, with its implicit belief in a mysterious energy that runs through us all, has become a $4.2 trillion industry, half the size of the global health care market. Eclectic spiritual and magical practices—from astrology to tarot to yoga to crystals to sage cleansing to meditation—are now integral parts of millennial culture. Urban Outfitters sells spell books. Media outlets breathlessly report on each new fad—yoga, Reiki, psychics, erotic dinner parties—that purports to cultivate a sense of spiritual well-being or capacity for undistracted presence. ("As each of us struggle to create meaningful lives while also trying to escape the endless news cycle, the cult of social media, and the treadmill of 'productivity,' what we pay attention to matters tremendously," writes *Vice* journalist Anna Pulley after stripping one attractive waiter, massaging his body, and licking mousse off the skin of her date.)[3] New sexual rulebooks preaching a gospel of liberation, self-care, and human perfectibility dominate how we create the families and communities around us. We download apps for meditation or mindfulness and keep them in our pockets and purses. Whichever box we tick on the "religion" question on the census, we've all been influenced by the gospels of self-care and "best-self-ism" that we see on billboards, in Internet advertisements, and in how we talk about fitness or wellness or psychology.

Powerful earthly doctrines—of social justice, of techno-utopianism, of atavism—unite us in visions of how the world should be in the absence of a transcendent deity. Self-help gurus from Gwyneth Paltrow to Jordan Peterson to Alex Jones make millions of dollars telling us how to live a meaningful life, and what to buy to do so. New eschatologies promise us that we will defeat racism or death itself—or that civilization will invariably collapse. Fueled by the dizzying connective power of the Internet, Americans can seek out ever more fragmented, ever more like-minded tribes, defining their communities and their very identities around shared passions—or shared hatreds.

These new doctrines are gaining political traction and visibility. As Donald Trump—the Kek-prophesied God-Emperor—preaches a gospel of materialist atavism tinged with the New Thought optimism of his onetime mentor Norman Vincent Peale, Democratic presidential candidate Marianne Williamson, another graduate of the school of New Thought, espouses a New Age vision of harmonious spiritual unity, condemning "dark psychic forces" of hatred and calling for a "moral and spiritual awakening" in America through the collective powers of self-actualization. (In her 2012 book, *The Law of Divine Compensation*, Williamson assured readers that a positive attitude was all they needed for success: "To whatever extent your mind is aligned with love, you will receive divine compensation for any lack in your material existence. From spiritual substance will come material manifestation. This is not just a theory; it is a fact.")[4] Alexandria Ocasio-Cortez released her birth time to eager astrologers—and the mainstream media breathlessly covered it.

Meanwhile, the spiritual marketplace is overflowing. Companies and brands do battle with one another to conquer our souls. Fifty-four percent of millennials said that they were hungry to spend their money on brands that "enhance[d] their spirit and soul." Seventy-seven percent say they sought out brands that shared their "values."[5]

For the vast majority of Remixed spiritualists, this new religious landscape heralds an era of untrammeled self-expression, of spirituality conceived first and foremost as an instrument of self-betterment, a necessary and easily consumable product designed to optimize one's life. It valorizes disembodied self-making, emotional freedom, the heady possibility of writing our own script for morality, sexuality, and society, according to the dictates of our own heart. It bolsters our personal brand. It makes us our best—and most curated—selves.

As one breathlessly positive journalist in the *Pacific Standard* put it: "Post-Millennials live in a culture of choice, self-actualization, and freedom of expression. Young people today, as never before, feel free to express their sexual orientation and gender identity. Significantly, many in

Gen Z reject the traditionally available choices—identifying as gender-fluid is one example—and this fluidity can extend to religion: When young people respond to a survey about religion by saying they have 'none,' it can be a way of opting out of existing religious categories." We are, in other words, too special, too unique, too *singular* for the communal demands of ordinary, traditional religion. We curate and render bespoke everything else about our lives. Why should our faith not be similarly fluid?[6]

We do not live in a godless world. Rather, we live in a profoundly anti-institutional one, where the proliferation of Internet creative culture and consumer capitalism have rendered us all simultaneously parishioner, high priest, and deity. America is not secular but simply spiritually self-focused. No less than the rise of Protestantism, which was inseparable from the invention of the printing press and the spread of mass literacy, this shift is deeply rooted in the technological changes of the twenty-first century. Anti-institutional, intuitional self-divinization is, at heart, the natural spirituality of Internet and smartphone culture.

Much of the responsibility for that shift belongs to institutions themselves. Traditional religions, traditional political hierarchies, and traditional understandings of society have been unwilling or unable to offer compellingly meaningful accounts of the world, provide their members with purpose, foster sustainable communities, or put forth evocative rituals. And, in return, young Americans have lost their faith not simply in the tenets of a religion, but in civic and social institutions as a whole. More and more Americans, particularly younger Americans, report plummeting levels of trust both in institutions and in other people. A 2019 Pew study, for example, found that nearly three quarters of American adults under thirty believe that people "just look out for themselves" most of the time. Seventy-one percent say most people "would try to take advantage of you if they got a chance." (Among the over sixty-fives, these percentages plummet to 48 and 39 percent, respectively.) Young adults are significantly less likely than their elders, too, to say that they trust the military (just 69 percent do, compared to 91 percent of adults aged fifty or older), or religious leaders (50 percent versus 71), the police (67 percent versus 85), or business leaders (34 percent versus 50).[7]

Some of this failure on the part of *religious* institutions is due, in part, to the increasing exodus of people, such as queer or gender non-conforming people and feminists, alienated by what they see as many organized religions' regressive attitudes toward sex, gender roles, and family life. (Queer people remain among the most unaffiliated of any demographic, with nearly half rejecting organized religion entirely.) It is due, too, to the litany of now-public sexual abuses rampant not only in the Catholic Church—perhaps the most visible example—but also in numerous evangelical communities. Several evangelical mega-church pastors, like Bill Hybels of Willow Creek near Chicago and Andy Savage of Highpoint Church in Memphis, have likewise been brought down in recent years by allegations of sexual abuse.

But we should not overlook the no less obvious institutional failures produced by, well, apathy.

The Remixed are most likely to come from either unaffiliated homes or from homes in which religion was taken for granted or rarely dis-cussed. They were more likely to attend church or synagogue pro forma, for major holidays like Christmas or Easter or Rosh Hashanah, rather than for any genuine sense of spiritual hunger and curiosity.

In this way, traditional organized religion has found itself something of a catch-22. More stringent, spiritually demanding traditions—like, say, Christian evangelicalism or Orthodox Judaism—may be more likely to retain the average member, but they're conversely more likely to alienate those members who are unable to conform their identities and values to those of the community. Meanwhile, more progressive and liberal traditions, such as mainline Protestantism, are often capable of being more welcoming to those on the theological margins, but more often than not fail to retain members or fulfill their spiritual needs.

Once you're willing to relax some elements of your faith tradition, after all, what's to stop you from seeking something even more specific to your personal needs, identity, and situation? Why not create a mix-and-match religious identity fusing, for example, Episcopalianism with

yoga, tarot, and poly community, or seek communal and spiritual fulfillment outside of organized religion altogether?

Yet it's not just formal "organized" religions that have failed. Civil
religions have too. Our civic ideals—the modern-day inheritance of the
classical liberal and capitalist tradition of the neutral public square, of
the power of rational self-interest to collectively coalesce into societal
cohesion, of our fundamental belief that we *are* at our core rational
creatures—all these, too, seem to have failed us. In the age of Trump,
of a renewed passionate populism across the globe, of a resurgent obsession with our biological and ethnic "roots," classical liberalism seems
nearly as outdated as midcentury Protestantism. The better angels of our
nature seem, from this vantage, as much a fiction as Nephilim. So, too,
does the classical, quixotic liberal vision of private morality informing
an ultimately neutral public square, safely secular, free of any ideology
except a commitment to human flourishing and freedom. These ostensibly impartial spaces have proved little more than moral vacuums: an
empty space for newer, more potent, more valent, and more compelling
cults to flourish.

The result has been a cornucopia of antiauthoritarian, anti-
institutional American religious traditions. Some, even most, take liberal autonomy to an extreme. They accept as gospel the idea that there
is nothing and nobody more reliable than one's self, and that there is
no ontological good more pressing than the care, cultivation, and perfection of that existence. Others long for the power and security that
institutions once provided, even as they mourn the possibility of any
institution being legitimate.

Past analyses of American culture wars have taken for granted a
clear dichotomy: traditional, usually evangelical, Christianity against
the freewheeling forces of liberal secularism. Back in 1992, Pat Robertson gave his famous "culture war" speech at the Republican National Convention. "There is a religious war going on in this country,"
he insisted. "It is a cultural war, as critical to the kind of nation we
shall be as was the Cold War itself, for this war is for the soul of America." The secularists and the Christians were locked in mortal combat:

"The agenda that [the Clintons] would impose on America—abortion on demand, a litmus test for the Supreme Court, homosexual rights, discrimination against religious schools, women in combat units— that's change, all right," Robertson insisted. "But . . . is not the kind of change we can abide in a nation that we still call God's country." Twelve years later, he doubled down, casting the culture war as one between god-fearing Christians and "a radical Left aided by a cultural elite that detests Christianity and finds Christian moral tenets reactionary and repressive . . . hell-bent on pushing its amoral values and imposing its ideology on our nation."[8]

But, in today's spiritual landscape, the battle lines are different. The social justice left, once associated with secularism, is today a hotbed of Remixed spirituality. The new atavistic right is governed not by faith in the Christian God but in evolutionary psychology and brute Darwinism, an ideology that has made it all the way into the White House. Our culture wars now better resemble Gamergate—with its clash of SJWs and proto-atavist nerd culture—than they do the debates of the 1980s and '90s.

In his 2018 book *Pagans and Christians in the City*, University of San Diego professor Steven D. Smith argues that, fundamentally, there are two kinds of religious belief in the West. Smith contrasts what he calls paganism—characterized by a faith that "locates the sacred within this world"—with Judaism and Christianity, which place the sacred outside it.[9] By this definition, the modern atavistic right, the progressive left, and the more centrist techno-utopians *all* can be considered pagan ideologies, which see the sacred within the world itself. The techno-utopians may locate that sanctity within human intelligence; the social justice movement within human emotion; the atavists within human DNA. But all three of our new civil religions envision the ultimate good—for some human beings, or for all—*within* the world, rather than beyond it. The witches of Catland hexing Trump and Brett Kavanaugh, the transhumanist "vampires" of techno-utopianism injecting themselves—as Peter Thiel famously did—with young men's blood to restore vitality, the would-be God-men who follow the *Bronze Age*

Mindset, all these postliberal paganisms are all forged in the fires of the same Remixed culture, all made possible by the same Internet age.

All three of these new faiths claim a powerful, transformative vision of the world, rooted not in transcendent meaning but in human thought, feeling, and will. The techno-utopians' dream of a world in which we are all rendered optimally efficient machines, the social justice utopia of a liberated world, the atavists' vision of a purifying cataclysm that will bring us beyond the tyranny of civilization altogether—all these are potential ends to the arc of postliberal history.

Only time will tell which one will win.

ACKNOWLEDGMENTS

THANK YOU SO MUCH TO EVERYBODY INVOLVED IN THE PRO-
cess of this book: my agents Emma Parry and Rebecca Carter,
my editor at Clive Priddle, and the entire team at PublicAffairs.
I'm grateful to those many practitioners of "new religions" who
afforded me their time and insight and expertise, giving me personal
glimpses into their worlds, as well as to the academics and scholars
who generously shared with me insight into their own work and that
of others. I would like to thank, too, for their friendship, their counsel,
and their consistent and loving sharpening of my own ideas, Dhananjay
Jagannathan and Susannah Black.

NOTES

INTRODUCTION: NOTES FROM A SO-CALLED SECULAR AGE

1. Isaiah Wilner, "The Short, Drunken Life of Club Row," *New York*, February 19, 2007, https://nymag.com/news/features/27845/index.html.

2. Wilner, "Short, Drunken Life."

3. Worthen, W. B. "'The Written Troubles of the Brain': 'Sleep No More' and the Space of Character." *Theatre Journal*, vol. 64, no. 1, 2012, p. 84, www.jstor.org/stable/41411277. Accessed February 11, 2020.

4. Scott Brown, "Theater Review: The Freakily Immersive Experience of *Sleep No More*," *New York*, April 15, 2011, www.vulture.com/2011/04/theater_review_the_freakily_im.html.

5. Ben Brantley, "Shakespeare Slept Here, Albeit Fitfully," *New York Times*, April 13, 2011, www.nytimes.com/2011/04/14/theater/reviews/sleep-no-more-is-a-macbeth-in-a-hotel-review.html.

6. Tara Isabella Burton, "What Fourth Wall?," *Los Angeles Review of Books*, July 31, 2013, https://lareviewofbooks.org/article/what-fourth-wall/.

7. Tara Isabella Burton, "Losing Sleep with the Superfans of 'Sleep No More,'" *Narratively*, September 29, 2015, https://narratively.com/losing-sleep-with-the-superfans-of-sleep-no-more/.

8. "Pip's Island," Yelp, www.yelp.com/biz/pips-island-new-york.

9. Amanda Hess, "The Existential Void of the Pop-Up 'Experience,'" *New York Times*, September 26, 2018, www.nytimes.com/2018/09/26/arts/color-factory-museum-of-ice-cream-rose-mansion-29rooms-candytopia.html.

CHAPTER 1: WHO ARE THE RELIGIOUSLY REMIXED
(AND WHAT IS A RELIGION, ANYWAY)?

1. Quoted in Laurie Goodstein, "After the Attacks, Finding Fault: Falwell's Finger-Pointing Inappropriate, Bush Says," *New York Times*, September 15, 2001, www.nytimes.com/2001/09/15/us/after-attacks-finding-fault-falwell-s -finger-pointing-inappropriate-bush-says.html.

2. Gary Wolf, "The Church of the Non-Believers," *Wired*, November 1, 2006.

3. "'Nones' on the Rise," Pew Research Center, October 9, 2012, www .pewforum.org/2012/10/09/nones-on-the-rise/.

4. Jack Jenkins, "'Nones' Now as Big as Evangelicals, Catholics in the US," Religion News Service, March 21, 2019, https://religionnews.com/2019/03/21 /nones-now-as-big-as-evangelicals-catholics-in-the-us/.

5. Thomas B. Edsall, "Trump Needs His Base to Burn with Anger," *New York Times*, July 3, 2019, www.nytimes.com/2019/07/03/opinion/trump -republican-base.html.

6. Jacob Lupfer, "Fewer Couples Are Marrying in Churches. Does It Matter?," Religion News Service, June 7, 2018, https://religionnews.com/2018/06 /07/fewer-couples-are-marrying-in-churches-does-is-matter/.

7. Barry A. Kosmin and Ariela Keysar, *American Religious Identification Survey* (Hartford, CT: Trinity College, 2009), https://commons.trincoll.edu /aris/files/2011/08/ARIS_Report_2008.pdf.

8. "When Americans Say They Believe in God, What Do They Mean?," Pew Research Center, April 25, 2018, www.pewforum.org/2018/04/25/when -americans-say-they-believe-in-god-what-do-they-mean/.

9. Nearly all of the studies I'll be using in this chapter come from either the Pew Center or the Public Religion Research Institute, the top institutions in the country for tracking religious affiliation and identity. Because the two groups use slightly different methodology, some of their numbers and designations of religious groups often differ slightly. For clarity of reading, I've done my best to give approximations that reflect the results of both sets of data.

10. "Frequency of Feeling Spiritual Peace and Wellbeing," Religious Landscape Study, 2014, Pew Research Center, www.pewforum.org /religious-landscape-study/frequency-of-feeling-spiritual-peace-and-wellbeing/.

11. Claire Gecewicz, "'New Age' Beliefs Common among Both Religious and Nonreligious Americans," *Fact Tank* (blog), Pew Research Center, October 1, 2018, www.pewresearch.org/fact-tank/2018/10/01/new-age-beliefs -common-among-both-religious-and-nonreligious-americans/.

12. Michael Lipka and Claire Gecewicz, "More Americans Now Say They're Spiritual but Not Religious," *Fact Tank* (blog), Pew Research Center, September 6, 2017, www.pewresearch.org/fact-tank/2017/09/06/more-americans -now-say-theyre-spiritual-but-not-religious/.

13. "New Survey: One in Five Americans are Spiritual but Not Religious," news release, PRRI, November 6, 2017, www.prri.org/press-release/new-survey -one-five-americans-spiritual-not-religious/.

14. Tara Isabella Burton, "'Spiritual but Not Religious': Inside America's Rapidly Growing Faith Group," *Vox*, November 10, 2017, www.vox.com /identities/2017/11/10/16630178/study-spiritual-but-not-religious.

15. Burton, "'Spiritual but Not Religious.'"

16. Tara Isabella Burton, "What Does Dying—and Mourning—Look Like in a Secular Age?," *Vox*, December 4, 2018, www.vox.com/identities /2018/12/4/18078714/death-secular-age-funeral-end-of-life-reimagine.

17. Robert Wuthnow and Wendy Cadge, "Buddhists and Buddhism in the United States: The Scope of Influence," *Journal for the Scientific Study of Religion* 43, no. 3 (2004): 363–380.

18. Peter Steinfels, "A Look at Christianity, Through a Buddhist Lens," *New York Times*, October 9, 2009, www.nytimes.com/2009/10/10/us/10beliefs .html.

19. Duane R. Bidwell, *When One Religion Isn't Enough: The Lives of Spiritually Fluid People* (Boston: Beacon Press, 2018), 2.

20. Bidwell, *One Religion*, 18.

21. Tara Isabella Burton, "What a 'Spiritual' Beauty Subscription Box Says About Religion Today," *Vox*, November 13, 2018, www.vox.com/the-goods /2018/11/13/17977758/moonbox-religious-unbundling-spiritual-subscription -box-witches.

22. Steven Sutcliffe and Marion Bowman, eds., *Beyond New Age: Exploring Alternative Spirituality* (Edinburgh: Edinburgh University Press, 2000), 7.

23. Stef Aupers and Dick Houtman, eds., *Religions of Modernity* (Leiden, Netherlands: Brill, 2010), 5.

24. Burton, "What Does Dying."

25. *Yoga Journal* and Yoga Alliance, *The 2016 Yoga in America Study* (New York: Ipsos Public Affairs, 2016), www.yogaalliance.org/Portals/0/2016%20Yoga %20in%20America%20Study%20RESULTS.pdf.

26. Émile Durkheim, *The Elementary Forms of Religious Life* (New York: Free Press, 1995), 208.

27. Durkheim, *Religious Life*, 44.

28. Peter L. Berger, *The Sacred Canopy: Elements of a Sociological Theory of Religion* (New York: Anchor, 1990), 22.

29. Berger, *Sacred Canopy*, 54.

30. Berger, *Sacred Canopy*, 58.

31. Clifford Geertz, *The Interpretation of Cultures* (New York: Basic Books, 1977).

32. Burton, "What Does Dying."

33. "The End of Absolutes: America's New Moral Code," Barna, May 25, 2016, www.barna.com/research/the-end-of-absolutes-americas-new-moral-code/.

34. "Four Core Experiences of Business. One Powerful System of Action," Qualtrics, www.qualtrics.com/uk/.

35. Daniel Cox and Robert P. Jones, *America's Changing Religious Identity* (Washington, DC: PRRI, 2017), www.prri.org/research/american-religious-landscape-christian-religiously-unaffiliated/.

CHAPTER 2: A (BRIEF) HISTORY OF INTUITIONAL RELIGION IN AMERICA

1. Griffin Paul Jackson, "Western Europe's Christians Are as Religious as America's 'Nones,'" *Christianity Today*, May 29, 2018, www.christianitytoday.com/news/2018/may/pew-western-europe-christians-religious-practice-us-nones.html.

2. Sam Haselby, "American Secular," *Aeon*, May 26, 2016, https://aeon.co/essays/why-did-the-secular-ambitions-of-the-early-united-states-fail.

3. Colin Woodard, "The Power of Luther's Printing Press," *Washington Post*, December 18, 2015, www.washingtonpost.com/opinions/the-power-of-luthers-printing-press/2015/12/18/a74da424-743c-11e5-8d93-0af317ed58c9_story.html.

4. Quoted in Robert Wuthnow, *The Struggle for America's Soul: Evangelicals, Liberals, and Secularism* (Grand Rapids, MI: Wm. B. Eerdmans, 1989), 23.

5. Robert C. Fuller, "The Flowering of Metaphysical Religion," in *Spiritual, but not Religious: Understanding Unchurched America* (Oxford: Oxford University Press, 2010), 13.

6. Fuller, "Flowering," 15.

7. Jonathan Edwards, *Sinners in the Hands of an Angry God* (New Haven, Yale University Press, 1999), 49.

8. Edwards, *Sinners*, 57.

9. Lyman Beecher, *Autobiography and Correspondence of Lyman Beecher*, ed. Charles Beecher, vol. 1 (New York: Harper, 1864), 27.

10. Barry Hankins, *The Second Great Awakening and the Transcendentalists* (Westport, CT: Greenwood Publishing Group, 2004), 3.

11. Fuller, "Flowering," 21.

12. Gilbert Seldes, *The Stammering Century* (New York: NYRB Classics, 2012).

13. Quoted in Nancy F. Cott, "Young Women in the Second Great Awakening in New England," *Feminist Studies* 3, no. 1/2 (1975): 16. https://doi.org/10.2307/3518952; Richard D. Shiels, "The Scope of the Second Great Awakening: Andover, Massachusetts, as a Case Study," *Journal of the Early Republic* 5, no. 2 (1985): 232, www.jstor.org/stable/3122953.

14. "A Portrait of Mormons in the U.S.," Pew Research Center, July 24, 2009, www.pewforum.org/2009/07/24/a-portrait-of-mormons-in-the-us/.

15. Ralph Waldo Emerson, *Selected Essays* (New York: Penguin, 1982).

16. Emerson, *Selected Essays.*

17. Catherine L. Albanese, *A Republic of Mind and Spirit: A Cultural History of American Metaphysical Religion* (New Haven, CT: Yale University Press, 2007), 220–221.

18. Lisa Rodriguez McRobbie, "The Strange and Mysterious History of the Ouija Board," *Smithsonian*, October 27, 2013, www.smithsonianmag.com /history/the-strange-and-mysterious-history-of-the-ouija-board-5860627/.

19. David K. Nartonis, "The Rise of 19th-Century American Spiritualism, 1854–1873," *Journal for the Scientific Study of Religion* 49, no. 2 (June 2010): 361–373.

20. Robert P. Jones, *The End of White Christian America* (New York: Simon and Schuster, 2016), 37.

21. Jones, *White Christian America*, 33.

22. Elesha Coffman, *The Christian Century and the Rise of the Protestant Mainline* (Oxford: Oxford University Press, 2013), 148.

23. "Reinhold Niebuhr," *Time*, March 8, 1948, http://content.time.com /time/covers/0,16641,19480308,00.html.

24. Ralph E. Pyle, *Persistence and Change in the Protestant Establishment* (Westport, CT: Praeger Publishers, 1996), 58.

25. Ed Stetzer, "If It Doesn't Stem Its Decline, Mainline Protestantism Has Just 23 Easters Left," *Washington Post*, April 28, 2017, www.washington post.com/news/acts-of-faith/wp/2017/04/28/if-it-doesnt-stem-its-decline -mainline-protestantism-has-just-23-easters-left/.

26. H. Richard Niebuhr, *The Social Sources of Denominationalism* (New York: Holt, 1929), 280.

27. Jones, *White Christian America*, 16.

28. Robert Wuthnow, *After Heaven: Spirituality in America Since the 1950s* (Berkeley: University of California Press, 1998), 30.

29. Quoted in Coffman, *Christian Century*, 148.

30. Wuthnow, *After Heaven.*

31. Wuthnow, *After Heaven*, 30.

32. Wuthnow, *After Heaven*, 33.

33. Wuthnow, *After Heaven*, 40–45.

34. Frank Newport, "In U.S., Four in 10 Report Attending Church in Last Week," Gallup, December 24, 2013, https://news.gallup.com/poll/166613/four -report-attending-church-last-week.aspx.

35. Lily Rothman, "Is God Dead? At 50," *Time*, April 8, 2016, http://time .com/isgoddead/.

36. Quoted in Hugh McLeod, *The Religious Crisis of the 1960s* (Oxford: Oxford University Press, 2007), 124–125.

37. McLeod, *Religious Crisis*, 125.

38. McLeod, *Religious Crisis*, 131.

39. Bob Smietana, "Prosperity Gospel Taught to 4 in 10 Evangelical Churchgoers," *Christianity Today*, July 31, 2018, www.christianitytoday.com /news/2018/july/prosperity-gospel-survey-churchgoers-prosper-tithe-blessing .html.

40. Laurie Goodstein, "Billy Graham, 99, Dies; Pastor Filled Stadiums and Counseled Presidents," *New York Times*, February 21, 2018, www.nytimes.com /2018/02/21/obituaries/billy-graham-dead.html.

41. John Charles Pollock, *Billy Graham: The Authorized Biography* (Grand Rapids, MI: Zondervan, 2003), 321.

42. Stetzer, "23 Easters Left."

43. I'm focusing just on *white* evangelicals here because, by and large, they vote vastly differently, and on different issues, than their counterparts of color.

CHAPTER 3: TODAY'S GREAT AWAKENING (AND WHY IT'S NOT LIKE THE OTHERS)

1. "Among Those Raised in Single Religious Background (Especially Protestantism), Those Whose Childhood Most Steeped in Religion Most Likely to Retain Parents' Faith," Pew Research Center, October 24, 2016, www .pewforum.org/2016/10/26/links-between-childhood-religious-upbringing -and-current-religious-identity/pf_10-26-16_mixed-faith-01-00/.

2. Betsy Cooper et al., *Exodus: Why Americans Are Leaving Religion—and Why They're Unlikely to Come Back* (Washington, DC: PRRI, 2016), www.prri .org/research/prri-rns-poll-nones-atheist-leaving-religion/.

3. "Attendance at Religious Services," Religious Landscape Study, 2014, Pew Research Center www.pewforum.org/religious-landscape-study /attendance-at-religious-services/.

4. "Links between Childhood Religious Upbringing and Current Religious Identity," Pew Research Center, October 26, 2016, www.pewforum .org/2016/10/26/links-between-childhood-religious-upbringing-and-current -religious-identity/.

5. Jennifer Miller, "Finding Common Ground in Interfaith Marriage," *New York Times*, June 9, 2016, www.nytimes.com/2016/06/12/fashion/weddings /interfaith-marriage.html. See, in particular, the 2015 Pew study.

6. Kim Ode, "Death Doulas Provide Comfort on Final Journey: 'We Know How to Die,'" *Star Tribune*, April 16, 2018, www.startribune.com/death-doulas -help-normalize-the-experience-for-life-s-final-journey/479570193/.

7. "Chapter 2: Religious Switching and Intermarriage," in *America's Changing Religious Landscape* (Washington, DC: Pew Research Center, 2015), www .pewforum.org/2015/05/12/chapter-2-religious-switching-and-intermarriage/.

8. David Masci, "Q&A: Why Millennials Are Less Religious Than Older Americans," *Fact Tank* (blog), Pew Research Center, January 8, 2016, www

.pewresearch.org/fact-tank/2016/01/08/qa-why-millennials-are-less-religious
-than-older-americans/.

9. Becka A. Alper, "Why America's 'Nones' Don't Identify with a Religion,"
Fact Tank (blog), Pew Research Center, August 8, 2018, www.pewresearch
.org/fact-tank/2018/08/08/why-americas-nones-dont-identify-with-a-religion/.

10. "Glean Network," Clal, http://clal.org/project/glean/.

11. Ronald Inglehart, *Culture Shift in Advanced Industrial Society*
(Princeton, NJ: Princeton University Press, 2018).

12. Amanda Hess, "The New Spiritual Consumerism," *New York Times*,
August 19, 2019, www.nytimes.com/2019/08/19/arts/queer-eye-kondo-makeover
.html.

13. Katie Richards, "Want to Win Over Millennials and Gen Z? Vice's
New Study Says Brands Should Get Spiritual," *Adweek*, June 19, 2018, www
.adweek.com/brand-marketing/want-to-win-over-millennials-and-gen-z-vices
-new-study-says-brands-should-get-spiritual/.

14. Megan Rose Dickey, "Facebook Is Injecting Buddhism into Its Core
Business So It Can Be More Compassionate," *Business Insider*, June 25, 2013,
www.businessinsider.com/facebook-injects-buddhism-into-business-2013-6.

15. Noah Shachtman, "In Silicon Valley, Meditation Is No Fad. It
Could Make Your Career," *Wired*, June 18, 2013, www.wired.com/2013/06
/meditation-mindfulness-silicon-valley/.

16. Marshall McLuhan, "Interview," *Playboy*, March 1969.

17. Kellogg School of Management, "Why Echo Chambers are Becoming Louder—and More Polarizing," Thrive Global, May 10, 2017, https://
medium.com/thrive-global/why-echo-chambers-are-becoming-louder-and
-more-polarizing-44aba2a231e7.

18. Becki Murray, "Bespoke Beauty Is Set to Be the Biggest Beauty Trend
of 2018," *Harper's Bazaar*, December 6, 2017, www.harpersbazaar.com/uk
/beauty/beauty-shows-trends/a13527210/bespoke-beauty-trend/.

19. Kathleen Baird-Murray, "'It's All About Me!' Bespoke Skincare
Comes of Age," Financial Times, January 15, 2018, www.ft.com/content
/a6645bd6-e648-11e7-a685-5634466a6915.

20. Jim Farber, "Bespoke This, Bespoke That. Enough Already," *New
York Times*, August 8, 2016, www.nytimes.com/2016/08/12/fashion/mens-style
/bespoke-word-meaning-usage-language.html.

21. Sigal Samuel, "A Design Lab Is Making Rituals for Secular People," *Atlantic*, May 7, 2018, www.theatlantic.com/technology/archive/2018/05/ritual
-design-lab-secular-atheist/559535/.

CHAPTER 4: HARRY POTTER AND THE BIRTH OF REMIX CULTURE

1. Most of the journals and accounts belonging to the Snapewives have
long since been purged and deleted, making their authors inaccessible. All

information about the Snapewives, including their posts, has been taken from the research of independent scholar Zoe Alderton, whose "'Snapewives' and 'Snapeism': A Fiction-Based Religion within the Harry Potter Fandom," *Religions* 5, no. 1 (March 2014), remains the only comprehensive study of this topic; Alderton, "'Snapewives,'" 229.

2. Alderton, "'Snapewives,'" 229.

3. Alderton, "'Snapewives,'" 229.

4. Alderton, "'Snapewives,'" 246.

5. Daniel D. Snyder, "'Harry Potter' and the Key to Immortality," *Atlantic*, July 18, 2011, www.theatlantic.com/entertainment/archive/2011/07/harry-potter-and-the-key-to-immortality/241972/.

6. "Гарри Поттер и Методы Рационального Мышления," https://planeta.ru/campaigns/hpmor.

7. Rachel Sklar, "Harry Potter Inspired the Parkland Generation," CNN, March 27, 2018, https://edition.cnn.com/2018/03/26/opinions/parkland-march-harry-potter-generation-opinion-sklar/index.html.

8. De Elizabeth, "Best 'Harry Potter' Signs at the March for Our Lives," *Teen Vogue*, March 25, 2018, www.teenvogue.com/story/best-harry-potter-signs-march-for-our-lives.

9. Elizabeth, "Best 'Harry Potter' Signs."

10. Michael Serazio, "Just How Much Is Sports Fandom Like Religion?," *Atlantic*, January 29, 2013, www.theatlantic.com/entertainment/archive/2013/01/just-how-much-is-sports-fandom-like-religion/272631/.

11. Christopher Partridge, *Mortality and Music: Popular Music and the Awareness of Death*, Bloomsbury Publishing, March 23, 2017, 153.

12. Daniel Cavicchi, *Tramps Like Us: Music and Meaning among Springsteen Fans* (Oxford: Oxford University Press, 1998), 186.

13. Adam Rogers, "Joss Whedon on Comic Books, Abusing Language and the Joys of Genre," *Wired*, May 3, 2012, www.wired.com/2012/05/joss-whedon/.

14. https://www.pewforum.org/2010/09/28/u-s-religious-knowledge-survey-who-knows-what-about-religion/#the-bible.

15. "Americans' Knowledge of the Bible," Pew Research Center, April 12, 2017, www.pewresearch.org/fact-tank/2017/04/14/5-facts-on-how-americans-view-the-bible-and-other-religious-texts/ft_17-04-12_scripture_bible_knowledge1/.

16. "18% of Americans Veritable Potter-Maniacs, 61% Seen at Least One Movie," YouGov, July 18, 2011, https://today.yougov.com/topics/lifestyle/articles-reports/2011/07/18/18-americans-veritable-potter-maniacs-76-seen-leas.

17. Michael Jindra, "Star Trek Fandom as a Religious Phenomenon," *Sociology of Religion* 55, no. 1 (1994): 33, https://doi.org/10.2307/3712174.

18. Jindra, "Star Trek," 33.

19. Jindra, "Star Trek," 32.

20. Ben Rowen, "The Jedi Faithful," *Pacific Standard*, March 16, 2018, https://psmag.com/economics/the-jedi-faithful.

21. "Doctrine of the Order," Temple of the Jedi Order, February 12, 2007, www.templeofthejediorder.org/doctrine-of-the-order.

22. "Census Returns of the Jedi," BBC, February 13, 2003, http://news.bbc .co.uk/2/hi/uk/2757067.stm.

23. "Census of Population and Housing—The 2001 Census, Religion and the Jedi," Australian Bureau of Statistics, www.abs.gov.au/websitedbs /D3110124.NSF/0/86429d11c45d4e73ca256a400006af80?OpenDocument.

24. "Reading Harry Potter Reduces Prejudice, Greenwich Psychologist Finds" (news release), University of Greenwich, www.gre.ac.uk/about-us /news/news-archive/2014/a2935-harry-potter-research.

25. Lenika Cruz, "Read Harry Potter, Dislike Donald Trump?," *Atlantic*, July 21, 2016, www.theatlantic.com/entertainment/archive/2016/07/harry -potter-readers-donald-trump/492245/.

26. Howard Rheingold, *The Virtual Community: Homesteading on the Electronic Frontier* (Cambridge, MA: MIT Press, 2000).

27. Rheingold, *Virtual Community*.

28. Karen Ross and Virginia Nightingale, *Media and Audiences: New Perspectives* (Maidenhead, UK: Open University Press, 2003), 138.

29. Nancy Kippax, "Reminisce With Me/Producing a Fanzine in the Before-Time," Fanlore, last modified July 7, 2016, 20:16, https://fanlore.org /wiki/Reminisce_With_Me/Producing_a_Fanzine_in_the_Before-Time.

30. Laura Miller, "The New Powers That Be," *Slate*, September 11, 2016, https://slate.com/culture/2016/09/online-harry-potter-fans-transformed-what -it-means-to-love-a-story.html.

31. Bijan Stephen, "Tumblr's Porn Ban Could Be Its Downfall—After All, It Happened to LiveJournal," *Verge*, December 6, 2018, www.theverge .com/2018/12/6/18127869/tumblr-livejournal-porn-ban-strikethrough.

32. Matthew Humphries, "World of Warcraft Peaked at 12 Million Players, World of Tanks Just Passed 75 Million," Geek.com, December 16, 2013, www.geek.com/games/world-of-warcraft-peaked-at-12-million-players-world -of-tanks-just-passed-75-million-1579885/.

33. Luke Winkie, "The People Who Still Play World of Warcraft Like It's 2006," *Kotaku*, May 14, 2015, https://kotaku.com/the-people-who-still -play-world-of-warcraft-like-it-s-2-1704465372.

34. Kristina Busse, *Framing Fan Fiction: Literary and Social Practices in Fan Fiction Communities* (Iowa City: University of Iowa Press, 2017), 165.

35. Rhiannon Bury, "Technology, Fandom and Community in the Second Media Age," *Convergence* 23, no. 6 (2017): 627–642, https://doi .org/10.1177/1354856516648084.

36. Bury, "Technology, Fandom and Community," 649.

37. Sherry Turkle, *Alone Together: Why We Expect More from Technology and Less from Each Other* (Bloomsbury, 2017), 147.

38. Amanda Lenhart and Mary Madden, "Friendship, Strangers and

Safety in Online Social Networks," Pew Research Center, April 18, 2007, www
.pewinternet.org/2007/04/18/friendship-strangers-and-safety-in-online-social
-networks/.

39. Amanda Lenhart, "Teens, Technology and Friendships," Pew Research
Center, August 6, 2015, www.pewinternet.org/2015/08/06/teens-technology
-and-friendships/.

40. University of Royal Holloway London, "New Research Discovers the
Emergence of Twitter 'Tribes,'" *Science Daily*, March 14, 2013, www.science
daily.com/releases/2013/03/130314085059.htm.

41. Seth Godin, *Tribes: We Need You to Lead Us* (New York: Portfolio,
2008), 3.

42. Aaron Smith and Monica Anderson, "5 Facts About Online Dating,"
Fact Tank (blog), Pew Research Center, February 29, 2016, www.pewresearch
.org/fact-tank/2016/02/29/5-facts-about-online-dating/.

43. Smith and Anderson, "5 Facts."

44. Dan Kopf, "Around 40% of American Couples Now First Meet
Online," *Quartz*, February 12, 2019, https://qz.com/1546677/around-40
-of-us-couples-now-first-meet-online/; Michael Rosenfeld, Reuben J. Thomas,
and Sonia Hausen, "Disintermediating Your Friends: How Online Dating in
the United States Displaces Other Ways of Meeting," *Proceedings of the National Academy of Sciences* 116, no. 36, https://web.stanford.edu/~mrosenfe
/Rosenfeld_et_al_Disintermediating_Friends.pdf.

45. J. Clement, "Cumulative Total of Tumblr Blogs from May 2011 to
October 2019," Statista, October 9, 2019, www.statista.com/statistics/256235
/total-cumulative-number-of-tumblr-blogs/.

46. Henry Jenkins, "Confronting the Challenges of Participatory Culture:
Media Education for the 21st Century (Part One)," *Confessions of an Aca-Fan*
(blog), October 19, 2006, http://henryjenkins.org/blog/2006/10/confronting
_the_challenges_of.html.

47. Mark Hill, "The Forgotten Early History of Fanfiction," *Vice*, July 3,
2016, https://motherboard.vice.com/en_us/article/4xa4wq/the-forgotten-early
-history-of-fanfiction.

48. Kaila Hale-Stern, "How to Find the Best Fanfiction on the Internet," *Gizmodo*, August 18, 2015, https://gizmodo.com/how-to-find-the-best
-fanfiction-on-the-internet-1723984681.

49. Darren Waters, "Rowling Backs Potter Fan Fiction," BBC, May 27,
2004, http://news.bbc.co.uk/2/hi/entertainment/3753001.stm.

50. "E.L. James: $95 Million" in "The Top-Earning Authors of 2013"
(slideshow), *Forbes*, www.forbes.com/pictures/eeji45eiffk/e-l-james-95-million
/#6ff2e305745a.

51. Joanna Robinson, "How Online Fandom Is Shaping TV in 2017,"
Vanity Fair, January 19, 2017, www.vanityfair.com/hollywood/2017/01/online
-fandom-tv-2017-riverdale-twin-peaks-better-call-saul-time-after-time.

52. Maureen Ryan, "'The 100' Showrunner Apologizes for Controversial Character Death," *Variety*, March 24, 2016, https://variety.com/2016/tv/features/100-lexa-dead-showrunner-apologizes-letter-to-fans-1201738607/.

53. Henry Jenkins, "The Moral Economy of Web 2.0 (Part Three)," *Confessions of an Aca-Fan* (blog), March 21, 2008, http://henryjenkins.org/blog/2008/03/the_moral_economy_of_web_20_pa_2.html.

54. Kate Gardner, "Spider-Suits and Luke Skywalker: How Entitlement Is Messing Up Fandom," *Mary Sue*, December 21, 2018, www.themarysue.com/fan-entitlement-last-jedi-spider-man/.

55. Katharine Trendacosta, "J.K. Rowling Apologizes for Killing Snape and *Harry Potter* Fandom Promptly Self-Immolates," *Gizmodo*, May 2, 2017, https://io9.gizmodo.com/j-k-rowling-apologizes-for-killing-snape-and-harry-pot-1794833830.

56. Gita Jackson, "J.K. Rowling Needs to Stop Messing with *Harry Potter*," *Kotaku*, October 3, 2018, https://kotaku.com/j-k-rowling-needs-to-stop-messing-with-harry-potter-1829503693.

57. Charlie Warzel, "How an Online Mob Created a Playbook for a Culture War," *New York Times*, August 14, 2019, www.nytimes.com/interactive/2019/08/15/opinion/what-is-gamergate.html.

58. Chris Ip, "How Do We Know What We Know about #Gamergate?," *Columbia Journalism Review*, October 23, 2014, https://archives.cjr.org/behind_the_news/gamergate.php.

59. Warzel, "How an Online Mob."

60. Jenna Guillaume, "Chris Hemsworth's Character in 'Ghostbusters' Is a Bimbo and It's Perfect," BuzzFeed, April 27, 2016, www.buzzfeed.com/jennaguillaume/pantsbusters.

61. Anna Silman, "A Timeline of Leslie Jones's Horrific Online Abuse," *Cut*, August 24, 2016, www.thecut.com/2016/08/a-timeline-of-leslie-joness-horrific-online-abuse.html; Walt Hickey, "'Ghostbusters' Is a Perfect Example of How Internet Movie Ratings Are Broken," *FiveThirtyEight*, July 14, 2016, https://fivethirtyeight.com/features/ghostbusters-is-a-perfect-example-of-how-internet-ratings-are-broken/.

62. Zack Sharf, "Paul Feig Defends Jason Reitman in Wake of 'Ghostbusters' Sequel Outrage," *IndieWire*, February 21, 2019, www.indiewire.com/2019/02/paul-feig-defends-jason-reitman-ghostbusters-sequel-outrage-1202045532/.

63. Godin, *Tribes*.

64. Owen Edwards, "How Thomas Jefferson Created His Own Bible," *Smithsonian*, January 2012, www.smithsonianmag.com/arts-culture/how-thomas-jefferson-created-his-own-bible-5659505/.

CHAPTER 5: WELLNESS CULTURE AND THE REBIRTH OF NEW THOUGHT

1. Jeff Beer, "New SoulCycle Campaign Offers a Glimpse into the Brand's

Cult Phenomenon," *Fast Company*, April 4, 2017, www.fastcompany.com /40402920/new-soulcycle-campaign-offers-a-glimpse-into-the-brands-cult -phenomenon.

2. Mallory Schlossberg, "I Used to Be Obsessed with SoulCycle—Until I Realized How Much Is Wrong with the Class," *Business Insider*, August 4, 2016, www.businessinsider.com/why-i-stopped-going-to-soulcycle-2016-4.

3. SoulCycle (@soulcycle), "Tag her #WomensHistoryMonth," Instagram photo, March 4, 2019, https://www.instagram.com/p/BukNL6PHz4h/. Soul-Cycle (@soulcycle), "The limit does not exist — especially not for you Cat G (@c_glorylove), Senior Instructor, Houston," Instagram photo, March 15, 2019, https://www.instagram.com/p/BvCXWHYniyp/. SoulCycle (@soulcycle), "Laugh, cry, push yourself—we're here for all of it. Thank you @bumble for understanding us," Instagram photo, March 21, 2019, https://www.instagram .com/p/BvSBij8HuL7/.

4. "Most Innovative Companies: SoulCycle," *Fast Company*, www .fastcompany.com/company/soulcycle.

5. Rina Raphael, "SoulCycle Just Launched a New Media Division," *Fast Company*, June 20, 2018, www.fastcompany.com/40587603/soulcycle-just -launched-a-new-media-division.

6. Angie Thurston and Casper ter Kuile, *How We Gather* (self-published, 2015), https://caspertk.files.wordpress.com/2015/04/how-we-gather.pdf.

7. "Wellness Industry Statistics and Facts," Global Wellness Institute, https://globalwellnessinstitute.org/press-room/statistics-and-facts/.

8. Taffy Brodesser-Akner, "We Have Found the Cure! (Sort Of. . .)," *Outside*, April 11, 2017, www.outsideonline.com/2170436/we-have-found-cure-sort.

9. Taffy Brodesser-Akner, "How Goop's Haters Made Gwyneth Paltrow's Company Worth $250 Million," *New York Times*, July 25, 2018, www.nytimes .com/2018/07/25/magazine/big-business-gwyneth-paltrow-wellness.html.

10. "Psychic Vampire Repellent," Goop, https://shop.goop.com/shop /products/psychic-vampire-repellent?taxon_id=1291&country=USA.

11. Clare O'Connor, "How Jessica Alba Built a $1 Billion Company, and $200 Million Fortune, Selling Parents Peace of Mind," *Forbes*, June 15, 2015, www.forbes.com/sites/clareoconnor/2015/05/27/how-jessica-alba-built -a-1-billion-company-and-200-million-fortune-selling-parents-peace-of-mind /#1323bb6f42b4.

12. Kristin Cavallari, "Kristin Cavallari's 'True Roots' Cookbook Is All About Quality Ingredients—and This One Is Her Favorite," *Bustle*, June 1, 2018, www.bustle.com/p/kristin-cavallaris-true-roots-cookbook-is-all-about -quality-ingredients-this-one-is-her-favorite-9248084.

13. Nada Abouarrage, "Halle Berry Is Officially Launching a Health and Wellness Brand," *W*, April 20, 2018, www.wmagazine.com/story/halle -berry-launching-health-wellness-brand; Halle Berry (@halleberry), "This is a special #FitnessFriday! I believe good [health] and wellness is what real

beauty is all about," Instagram photo, April 13, 2018, www.instagram.com/p
/BhhNGbngU7p/?utm_source=ig_embed.

14. "Jeff Bezos: Why Getting 8 Hours of Sleep Is Good for Amazon Shareholders," Thrive Global, November 30, 2016, https://medium.com /thrive-global/jeff-bezos-sleep-amazon-19c617c59daa.

15. Molly Young, "How Amanda Chantal Bacon Perfected the Celebrity Wellness Business," *New York Times*, May 25, 2017, www.nytimes .com/2017/05/25/magazine/how-amanda-chantal-bacon-perfected-the-celebrity -wellness-business.html.

16. Victoria Dawson Hoff, "How Hollywood's Favorite Juice Bar Owner Eats Every Day," *Elle*, May 29, 2015, www.elle.com/beauty/health-fitness /a28600/amanda-chantal-bacon-moon-juice-food-diary/.

17. Amanda Arnold, "This Nude Vegan Blogger Drama Is Incredible," *Cut*, August 17, 2018, www.thecut.com/2018/08/blogger-freelee-the-banana -girl-drama-everything-to-know.html.

18. Nikki Ekstein, "Wellness-Obsessed Workaholics Get $375-a-Month Private Club," *Bloomberg*, August 8, 2018, www.bloomberg.com/news/articles /2018-08-08/the-well-nyc-is-375-a-month-private-club-for-wellness-obsessed.

19. "Weight Watchers Becomes WW, Reinforcing Its Mission to Focus on Overall Health and Wellbeing" (news release), WW, September 24, 2018, https://corporate.ww.com/file/Index?KeyFile=395108713.

20. Carl Cederström and André Spicer, *The Wellness Syndrome* (Cambridge, UK: Polity, 2015).

21. "Clearing Out Old Energy," Goop, https://goop.com/wellness /spirituality/clearing-out-old-energy/.

22. Rhonda Byrne, *The Secret* (New York: Atria, 2006).

23. Byrne, *The Secret*.

24. William Walker Atkinson, *Thought-Force in Business and Everyday Life*, Cosimo, Inc., March 1, 2007, p. 64.

25. Ralph Waldo Emerson, "The Transcendentalist" (lecture, Masonic Temple, Boston, January 1842), https://archive.vcu.edu/english/engweb /transcendentalism/authors/emerson/essays/transcendentalist.html.

26. Fuller, "Flowering," 32–33.

27. Fuller, "Flowering," 33.

28. John Haller, *The History of New Thought: From Mind Cure to Positive Thinking and the Prosperity Gospel* (Swedenborg Foundation Press, 2012), 49.

29. Quoted in Haller, p. 55.

30. Haller, p. 60.

31. Quoted in Annetta Dresser, ed., *The Philosophy of P.P. Quimby* (New York: Cosmo Inc., 2007), 89.

32. Ralph Waldo Trine, *In Tune with the Infinite, or, Fullness of Peace, Power, and Plenty* (Prabhat Prakashan, 2008), 10.

33. Fuller, "Flowering," 47.

34. Rodney Stark, "The Rise and Fall of Christian Science," *Journal of Contemporary Religion* 13, no. 2 (1998): 189–214, doi: 10.1080 /13537909808580830.

35. James Allen, *Mind Is the Master: The Complete James Allen Treasury* (Penguin, 2009), 148.

36. Allen, *Man Thinketh*.

37. Quoted in Haller, p. 182.

38. Quoted in Haller.

39. William James, *The Varieties of Religious Experience* (Longmans, Green, 1902) 95.

40. Quoted in Robert Fuller, *Spiritual, but Not Religious: Understanding Unchurched America* (Oxford University Press, 2001), 147.

41. Norman Vincent Peale, *Power of Positive Thinking* (Om Books International, 2016), 133.

42. Peale, *Positive Thinking*.

43. David Van Biema and Jeff Chu, "Does God Want You to Be Rich?" *Time*, September 10, 2006, http://content.time.com/time/magazine/article /0,9171,1533448,00.html.

44. Jordan Kisner, "The Politics of Conspicuous Displays of Self-Care," *New Yorker*, March 14, 2017, www.newyorker.com/culture/culture-desk/the -politics-of-selfcare.

45. Ruth Reader, "Headspace Users Flocked to 'SOS' Meditation Sessions after the Election," *Fast Company*, December 7, 2016, www.fastcompany .com/4026742/headspace-users-flocked-to-sos-meditation-sessions-after-the -election.

46. Lizzie Widdicombe, "The Higher Life," *New Yorker*, June 29, 2015, www.newyorker.com/magazine/2015/07/06/the-higher-life.

47. Audre Lorde, *A Burst of Light and Other Essays* (Mineola, NY: Courier Dover Publication, 2017), 130.

48. Lilly Cervantes (@healthylilly6), www.instagram.com/p/BvgznzWgaWV/.

49. julianne (@_julianneb), "and now she's in me, always with me, tiny dancer in my hand..," Instagram photo, March 27, 2019, www.instagram.com/p /BvgzcdllEhx/.

50. @some__girl___, "Life was so hard today in a warm outdoor bath full of herbs and flowers and sage staring at rainy mountains with flute sounds in the background," Instagram photo, March 27, 2019, www.instagram.com/p /BvfldHpHGko/.

51. James Loke Hale, "How to Tell Someone You're Flaking on Your Plans for Self-Care," *Bustle*, May 28, 2018, www.bustle.com/p/how-to-tell-someone -youre-flaking-on-your-plans-for-self-care-9221116.

52. Erica Cornwall, "Self-Care Is Not Selfish," Thrive Global, April 17, 2017, https://medium.com/thrive-global/why-self-care-is-the-opposite-of-selfish -e462b39aca2b.

53. Nicole Yi, "How Being Selective About the People You Keep Around Is an Important Form of Self-Care," *PopSugar*, December 15, 2017, www.popsugar.co.uk/fitness/How-Self-Care-Friendship-Related-44368089.

54. Habib Sadeghi, "Selfish Selflessness: The Art of Self-Healing," Goop, https://goop.com/work/relationships/selfish-selflessness-and-self-healing/.

55. Quoted in Michelle N. Lafrance, *Women and Depression: Recovery and Resistance* (Routledge: London, 2009), 145.

56. "Millennials, Boomers, & 2015 Resolutions: 5 Key Generational Differences," Field Agent, January 13, 2015, https://blog.fieldagent.net/millennials-boomers-new-years-resolutions-5-key-generational-differences.

57. Sarah Perez, "Self-Care Apps Are Booming," *TechCrunch*, April 3, 2018, https://techcrunch.com/2018/04/02/self-care-apps-are-booming/.

58. Tehrene Firman, "Apple's App Trend of the Year Is Something You're Already an Expert In," *Well+Good*, December 4, 2018, www.wellandgood.com/good-advice/self-care-apps-trend/.

59. "Wellness Apps: Self-Care Leads the Charts for 2018," Mapp Media, January 4, 2019, http://mapp.media/2019/01/04/wellness-apps-self-care-leads-charts-2018/.

60. "Popular Items for Self Care Kit," Etsy, www.etsy.com/market/self_care_kit, accessed December 16, 2019.

61. Marisa Meltzer, "Soak, Steam, Spritz: It's All Self-Care," *New York Times*, December 10, 2016, www.nytimes.com/2016/12/10/fashion/post-election-anxiety-self-care.html.

62. Ashley Nicole Black, "How to Practice Self-Care in Trump's America," *Dame*, July 11, 2018, www.damemagazine.com/2018/07/11/how-to-practice-self-care-in-trumps-america/.

63. Theresa Avila, "10 Self-Care Ideas to Help You Get Through These Rough Political Times," Girlboss, October 25, 2018, www.girlboss.com/wellness/self-care-during-elections.

64. Julie Zeilinger, "Self-Care in the Time of Trump," MTV News, www.mtv.com/news/2943108/self-care-in-the-time-of-trump/.

65. Louis-Marie Chauvet, *Symbol and Sacrament: A Sacramental Reinterpretation of Christian Existence*, trans. Patrick Madigan, S.J., and Madeleine Beaumont (Collegeville, MN: Liturgical Press, 1995).

66. "The Power of Detoxification and Getting Clean," Goop, https://goop.com/wellness/detox/clean/.

CHAPTER 6: THE MAGIC RESISTANCE

1. "New York Witches Place Hex on Brett Kavanaugh," BBC, October 21, 2018, www.bbc.com/news/world-us-canada-45928212; Cady Lang, "Here's Why This Witch Is Preparing for Midterm Elections by Hosting a Hex on Brett Kavanaugh," *Time*, November 2, 2018, http://time.com/5442528/brett-kavanaugh

-hex/; Peter Stubley, "Brett Kavanaugh: Witches Placed Mass Hex on Supreme Court Justice during New York Protest Ritual," *Independent*, October 21, 2018, www.independent.co.uk/news/world/americas/us-politics/brett-kavanaugh-hex-new-york-witches-protest-brooklyn-supreme-court-sexual-assault-a8594581.html; Gabriella Borter, "New York Witches Aim Hex at Supreme Court's Brett Kavanaugh Despite Death Threats," Reuters, October 20, 2018, www.reuters.com/article/us-usa-court-kavanaugh-witches/new-york-witches-aim-hex-at-supreme-courts-brett-kavanaugh-despite-death-threats-id USKCN1MU019.

2. Sam Wolfson, "Cursed: Witches Are Planning a Public Hexing of Brett Kavanaugh," *Guardian*, October 16, 2018, www.theguardian.com/us-news/2018/oct/15/witches-public-hexing-brett-kavanaugh.

3. Jaya Saxena and Jess Zimmerman, *Basic Witches: How to Summon Success, Banish Drama, and Raise Hell with Your Coven* (Philadelphia: Quirk Books, 2017), 1.

4. "2014 Religious Landscapes Study (RLS-II): Final Topline," Pew Research Center, June 4–September 30, 2014, www.pewforum.org/wp-content/uploads/sites/7/2015/05/RLS-II-FINAL-TOPLINE-FOR-FIRST-RELEASE.pdf.

5. Alex Mar, *Witches of America* (New York: Sarah Crichton Books, 2015), 12.

6. Corin Faife, "How Witchcraft Became a Brand," *BuzzFeed News*, July 26, 2017, www.buzzfeed.com/corinfaife/how-witchcraft-became-a-brand.

7. Susanna Heller, "Yes, It's True, 20-Somethings Really Love Astrology," *Business Insider*, February 26, 2019, www.insider.com/poll-young-people-love-astrology-2019-2.

8. Sarah Lyons, "Sometimes Pop Culture Really Is the Gateway to the Occult," *Vice*, July 7, 2017, www.vice.com/en_us/article/9kw39e/sometimes-pop-culture-really-is-the-gateway-to-the-occult.

9. https://www.nytimes.com/2019/06/06/style/self-care/witch-healing-hands.html.

10. Olivia Harvey, "A Real Witch Told Us Why She's Glad Sephora Pulled Its Problematic 'Starter Witch Kit,'" *HelloGiggles*, September 11, 2018, https://hellogiggles.com/news/sephora-starter-witch-kit-pulled/.

11. Sangeeta Singh-Kurtz, "After Outcry from Actual Witches, Sephora's 'Starter Witch Kit' Is Canceled," *Quartz*, September 7, 2018, https://qz.com/quartzy/1382521/sephoras-starter-witch-kit-by-pinrose-has-been-canceled/.

12. Harvey, "A Real Witch Told Us."

13. Harvey, "A Real Witch Told Us."

14. Sophie Saint Thomas, "A Witch's Guide to Cord Cutting, the Simple Ritual to Get Over Your Ex," *Vice*, February 15, 2019, https://broadly.vice.com/en_us/article/mbz3na/how-to-do-cord-cutting-ritual-witch-spell-breakup; Semra Haksever, "Cast This Venus Retrograde Spell to Tap Into

Your Inner Wisdom," *Vice*, October 22, 2018, https://broadly.vice.com/en_us
/article/xw93pk/how-to-cast-a-venus-retrograde-spell.

15. "For iPhone 5/5S - A Witch Bows To No Man - Feminist Witch -
Feminism – White," Amazon (listed for $8.99 on November 11, 2019), www
.amazon.com/iPhone-5S-Witch-Feminist-Feminism/dp/B017CP6LEY.

16. Saxena and Zimmerman, *Basic Witches*, 26.

17. Saxena and Zimmerman, *Basic Witches*, 26.

18. Kristen J. Sollee, *Witches, Sluts, Feminists: Conjuring the Sex Positive*
(Berkeley, CA: ThreeL Media, 2017).

19. Paul Heelas, *The New Age Movement: Religion, Culture and Society in
the Age of Postmodernity* (Wiley, 1996).

20. Olav Hammer, "I Did It My Way? Individual Choice and Social Conformity in New Age Religion," in *Religions of Modernity*, eds. Stef Aupers and
Dick Houtman (Leiden, Netherlands: Brill, 2010), 50.

21. Mar, *Witches*, 42–43.

22. Starhawk, *The Spiral Dance: A Rebirth of the Ancient Religion of the
Goddess* (San Francisco: HarperSanFrancisco, 1999).

23. Starhawk, *Dreaming the Dark: Magic, Sex and Politics* (Boston: Beacon Press, 1982), 25.

24. Mar, *Witches*, 12.

25. The 2001 American Religious Identification Survey by the City University of New York.

26. Carol P. Christ, "Why Women Need the Goddess," www.iupui.edu
/~womrel/Rel433%20Readings/Christ_WhyWomenNeedGoddess.pdf.

27. Christ, "Goddess."

28. Christ, "Goddess."

29. Starhawk, *Dreaming the Dark*, 25.

30. Mary McGill, "Wicked W.I.T.C.H: The 60s Feminist Protestors Who
Hexed Patriarchy," *Vice*, October 28, 2016, https://broadly.vice.com/en_us
/article/43gd8p/wicked-witch-60s-feminist-protestors-hexed-patriarchy.

31. Caryle Murphy, "Lesbian, Gay and Bisexual Americans Differ from
General Public in Their Religious Affiliations," *Fact Tank* (blog), Pew Research
Center, May 26, 2015, www.pewresearch.org/fact-tank/2015/05/26/lesbian-gay
-and-bisexual-americans-differ-from-general-public-in-their-religious-affiliations/
(2.4 percent versus 0.4 percent of average).

32. Sam Stryker, "Lana Del Rey Has Joined a Coven of Witches Trying
to Hex Donald Trump," *BuzzFeed*, February 25, 2017, www.buzzfeed.com
/samstryker/lana-del-rey-spell-donald-trump.

33. David Salisbury, *Witchcraft Activism: A Toolkit for Magical Resistance
(Includes Spells for Social Justice, Civil Rights, the Environment, and More)*
(Newburyport, MA: Weiser Books, 2019), 163.

34. Salisbury, *Witchcraft Activism*, 4.

35. Sarah Lyons, "Praise Lilith, a Chill Demon Cast from Eden for Refusing Missionary Position," *Vice*, August 25, 2017, https://broadly.vice.com/en_us/article/neeqgw/praise-lilith-a-chill-demon-cast-from-eden-for-refusing-missionary-position.

36. Kaitlin Kenny, "Women in Wicca: Transphobia and Other Issues," Her Campus at York U, January 17, 2018, www.hercampus.com/school/york-u/women-wicca-transphobia-and-other-issues.

37. Cristy C. Road, *Next World Tarot: Deck and Guidebook* (San Francisco: Silver Sprocket, 2019).

38. Beth Maiden, "Fool's Journey: Eight Queer Tarot Decks to Ogle, Support or Buy!," *Autostraddle*, July 15, 2015, www.autostraddle.com/fools-journey-eight-queer-tarot-decks-to-ogle-support-or-buy-298294/.

39. Moira Donovan, "How Witchcraft Is Empowering Queer and Trans Young People," *Vice*, August 14, 2015, www.vice.com/en_us/article/zngyv9/queer-trans-people-take-aim-at-the-patriarchy-through-witchcraft.

40. Eda Yu, "The Young Brujas Reclaiming the Power of Their Ancestors," *Vice*, January 10, 2018, https://broadly.vice.com/en_us/article/qvwe3x/the-young-brujas-reclaiming-the-power-of-their-ancestors.

41. W.I.T.C.H. PDX (@witchpdx), "Portland Pride! We came to remind everyone that rainbow capitalism is a sham, and that Pride was started by trans women of color," Instagram photo, June 19, 2018, www.instagram.com/p/BkOID7Ln7UD/; W.I.T.C.H. PDX (@witchpdx), "Our sibling coven @witchlouisville, defending the last remaining abortion clinic in Kentucky this week as the governor seeks to shut it down. Thank you for doing this work," Instagram photo, September 7, 2017, www.instagram.com/p/BYuYOW2HU53/.

42. W.I.T.C.H. PDX (@witchpdx), "Happy Beltane & May Day witches!! Art by Entangled Root Press," Instagram photo, May 2, 2018, www.instagram.com/p/BiQs8l0HwiK/.

43. "Never Let Your Activism Be Artless: An Interview with Lucien Greaves of the Satanic Temple," *Haute Macabre*, June 28, 2017, http://hautemacabre.com/2017/06/never-let-your-activism-be-artless-an-interview-with-lucien-greaves-of-the-satanic-temple/.

44. https://www.churchofsatan.com/nine-satanic-statements/ (formal mission statement).

45. http://satanic-revolution.com/index.html.

46. Kim Kelly, "Twin Temple's Satanic Doo-Wop Is Feminist as Fuck," *Vice*, September 28, 2018, www.vice.com/en_us/article/7xj4ee/twin-temples-satanic-doo-wop-is-feminist-as-fuck.

47. Catie Keck, "What Witches Can Teach Us About Fighting Back against Trump," *Bustle*, January 17, 2017, www.bustle.com/p/what-witches-can-teach-us-about-fighting-back-against-trump-30574; Megan DiTrolio, "This Is How Real-Life Resistance Witches Say They're Taking Down the Patriarchy,"

Marie Claire, October 31, 2018, www.marieclaire.com/culture/a24440291 /witches-2018-midterms/.

48. Madeleine Aggeler, "Astrology Twitter Is Losing Its Mind Over AOC's Birth Chart," *Cut*, March 27, 2019, www.thecut.com/2019/03/alexandria-ocasio -cortez-birth-chart-astrology.html.

CHAPTER 7: THE NEW PERFECTIONISM: OUR SEXUAL UTOPIAS

1. Quoted in Seldes, *Stammering Century*, 172.

2. Quoted in Seldes, *Stammering Century*, 184.

3. Quoted in Seldes, *Stammering Century*, 191.

4. Quoted in Mary Gabriel, *Notorious Victoria: The Uncensored Life of Victoria Woodhull* (New York: Algonquin Books, 1998), 148.

5. Ann Braude, *Radical Spirits: Spiritualism and Women's Rights in Nineteenth-Century America* (Bloomington: Indiana University Press, 1989), 134.

6. *Lucifer: The Light-Bearer: A Journal of Investigation and Reform, Justice and Liberty. Devoted to the Emancipation of Women from Sexual Slavery / Son of the Morning. A Fortnightly of Radical Thought, Devoted Mainly to the Emancipation of Womanhood from Sex Slavery, and to the Rights of the Child to be Born Well* 3, no. 40 (1886).

7. Julian Sancton, "The Ins and Outs of Silicon Valley's New Sexual Revolution," *Wired*, April 4, 2017, https://www.wired.com/2017/04/silicon -valley-polyamory/.

8. Tristan Taormino, *The Ultimate Guide to Kink: BDSM, Role Play and the Erotic Edge* (Jersey City, NJ: Cleis Press, 2012).

9. Elf Lyons, "A New Way to Love: In Praise of Polyamory," *Guardian*, July 22, 2017, www.theguardian.com/lifeandstyle/2017/jul/23/polyamory-new-way-to -love-men-women-sex-relationships-elf-lyons.

10. Susan Dominus, "Is an Open Marriage a Happier Marriage?," *New York Times*, May 11, 2017, www.nytimes.com/2017/05/11/magazine/is-an-open -marriage-a-happier-marriage.html.

11. Heather Kelly, "Google's Top Searches for 2017: Matt Lauer, Hurricane Irma and More," CNN, December 13, 2017, https://money.cnn.com /2017/12/13/technology/google-top-searches-2017/index.html.

12. Jennifer D. Rubin et al., "On the Margins: Considering Diversity among Consensually Non-Monogamous Relationships," *Journal für Psychologie* (2014), www.journal-fuer-psychologie.de/index.php/jfp/article /view/324; M. L. Haupert et al., "Prevalence of Experiences with Consensual Nonmonogamous Relationships: Findings from Two National Samples of Single Americans," *Journal of Sex and Marital Therapy* 43, no. 5 (2017), www .tandfonline.com/doi/abs/10.1080/0092623X.2016.1178675?journalCode =usmt20&.

13. Brian Pellot, "Most Non-religious Americans Condone Polyamory, New Survey Finds," Religion News Service, August 14, 2015, https://religion news.com/2015/08/14/polyamory-polygamy-religion-same-sex-marriage -supreme-court-obergefell/.

14. Rose Eveleth, "Americans Are More into BDSM than the Rest of the World," *Smithsonian*, February 10, 2014, www.smithsonianmag.com/smart -news/americans-are-more-bdsm-rest-world-180949703/; C. A. Renaud and E. S. Byers, "Exploring the Frequency, Diversity, and Context of University Students' Positive and Negative Sexual Cognitions," *Canadian Journal of Human Sexuality* 8 (1999): 14.

15. Laura Yan, "The Internet's Largest Kink Community Isn't Going to Moderate Itself," *Digg*, January 28, 2019, http://digg.com/2019/fetlife-john -baku-2019.

16. "Top 10 Kinkiest Cities in the U.S.," Kink.com, www.kink.com/ stateoftheunion2017.

17. *Still Out, Still Aging: The MetLife Study of Lesbian, Gay, Bisexual, and Transgender Baby Boomers* (Westport, CT: MetLife Mature Market Institute, 2010), www.asaging.org/sites/default/files/files/mmi-still-out-still-aging .pdf.

18. Natalie Zarrelli, "In the Early 20th Century, America Was Awash in Incredible Queer Nightlife," *Atlas Obscura*, April 14, 2016, www.atlasobscura .com/articles/in-the-early-20th-century-america-was-awash-in-incredible-queer -nightlife.

19. Guy Baldwin, "The Old Guard History, Origins and Traditions," Ambrosio's BDSM Site (originally published in *Drummer Magazine*), www.evilmonk .org/a/oldguard.cfm.

20. Baldwin, "Old Guard History."

21. Patrick Califia, "Butthole Bliss: The Ins and Outs of Anal Fisting," in *The Ultimate Guide to Kink: BDSM, Role Play and the Erotic Edge* by Tristan Taormino (Jersey City, NJ: Cleis Press, 2012).

22. Guy Baldwin, "The Old Guard: Classical Leather Culture Revisited," *Leatherati* (blog), September 27, 2011, https://leatherati.com/the-old-guard -classical-leather-culture-revisited-4fdc796aa25.

23. Tristan Taormino, *Opening Up: A Guide to Creating and Sustaining Open Relationships* (San Francisco: Cleis Press, 2008).

24. Christopher Ingraham, "Sex Toy Injuries Surged after 'Fifty Shades of Grey' Was Published," *Washington Post*, February 10, 2015, www .washingtonpost.com/news/wonk/wp/2015/02/10/sex-toy-injuries-surged-after -fifty-shades-of-grey-was-published/.

25. Julie Fennell, "'It's All About the Journey': Skepticism and Spirituality in the BDSM Subculture," *Sociological Forum* 33, no. 4 (2018): 1045–1067, https://doi.org/10.1111/socf.12460.

26. Rhonda N. Balzarini et al., "Demographic Comparison of American Individuals in Polyamorous and Monogamous Relationships," *Journal of Sex Research* (2018), doi: 10.1080/00224499.2018.1474333.

27. Balzarini et al., "Demographic Comparison."

28. Sarah Sloane, "Whole Hand Sex: Vaginal Fisting and BDSM," in *The Ultimate Guide to Kink: BDSM, Role Play and the Erotic Edge* by Tristan Taormino (Jersey City, NJ: Cleis Press, 2012).

29. Robin Bauer, "Transgressive and Transformative Gendered Sexual Practices and White Privileges: The Case of the Dyke/Trans BDSM Communities," *Women's Studies Quarterly* 36, no. 3/4 (2008): 233–253. Margot D. Weiss, "Working at Play: BDSM Sexuality in the San Francisco Bay Area," *Anthropologica* 48, no. 2 (2006): 229–245, https://doi.org/10.2307/25605313.

30. Weiss, "Working at Play," 239.

31. "Toxic Monogamy, Why Mono/Poly (and Poly) Is Hard," *Poly.Land*, October 31, 2016, https://poly.land/2016/10/31/toxic-monogamy-mono-poly-hard/.

32. Taormino, *Opening Up.*

33. Taormino, *Opening Up.*

34. Taormino, *Opening Up.*

35. Taormino, *Ultimate Guide.*

36. Dossie Easton and Janet W. Hardy, *The Ethical Slut: A Practical Guide to Polyamory, Open Relationships & Other Adventures* (Berkeley, CA: Celestial Arts, 2009).

37. Author interview with Stan Stanley.

38. Andie Nordgren, "The Short Instructional Manifesto for Relationship Anarchy," Anarchist Library, 2006, https://theanarchistlibrary.org/library/andie-nordgren-the-short-instructional-manifesto-for-relationship-anarchy.

39. Elisabeth Sheff, *The Polyamorists Next Door: Inside Multiple-Partner Relationships and Families* (Lanham, MD: Rowman & Littlefield, 2014).

40. Ana Swanson, "144 Years of Marriage and Divorce in the United States, in One Chart," *Washington Post*, June 23, 2015, www.washingtonpost.com/news/wonk/wp/2015/06/23/144-years-of-marriage-and-divorce-in-the-united-states-in-one-chart/.

41. Renee Stepler, "Led by Baby Boomers, Divorce Rates Climb for America's 50+ Population," *Fact Tank* (blog), Pew Research Center, March 9, 2017, www.pewresearch.org/fact-tank/2017/03/09/led-by-baby-boomers-divorce-rates-climb-for-americas-50-population/.

42. Steven P. Martin, Nan Marie Astone, and H. Elizabeth Peters, *Fewer Marriages, More Divergence: Marriage Projections for Millennials to Age 40* (Washington, DC: Urban Institute, 2014), www.urban.org/sites/default/files/publication/22586/413110-Fewer-Marriages-More-Divergence-Marriage-Projections-for-Millennials-to-Age-.PDF.

43. Jamie Ballard, "Millennials Are the Loneliest Generation," YouGov, July 30, 2019, https://today.yougov.com/topics/lifestyle/articles-reports/2019/07/30/loneliness-friendship-new-friends-poll-survey.

44. Barna, "End of Absolutes."

CHAPTER 8: TWO DOCTRINES FOR A GODLESS WORLD

1. u/church_on_a_hill, "Did the SSC post on Gender Imbalances and Offensive Attitudes inspire the Google SWE's Anti-Diversity manifesto?" Reddit post, August 6, 2017, www.reddit.com/r/slatestarcodex/comments/6rv2ib/did_the_ssc_post_on_gender_imbalances_and/.

2. Prachi Gupta, "Anti-Diversity Memo Writer Sues Google for Discriminating against Conservative White Men," *Jezebel*, January 8, 2018, https://jezebel.com/anti-diversity-memo-writer-sues-google-for-discriminati-1821888290.

3. George Packer, "No Death, No Taxes," *New Yorker*, November 20, 2011, www.newyorker.com/magazine/2011/11/28/no-death-no-taxes.

4. Emerson, *Selected Essays*, 58.

5. "Progressive Activists," in Stephen Hawkins et al., *Hidden Tribes: A Study of America's Polarized Landscape* (New York: More in Common, 2018), https://hiddentribes.us/profiles/progressive-activists.

6. Monica Anderson et al., "Activism in the Social Media Age," Pew Research Center, July 11, 2018, www.pewinternet.org/2018/07/11/activism-in-the-social-media-age/.

7. "The #MeToo Hashtag Has Been Used Roughly 19 Million Times on Twitter in the Past Year, and Usage Often Surges around News Events," Pew Research Center, October 11, 2018, www.pewresearch.org/fact-tank/2018/10/11/how-social-media-users-have-discussed-sexual-harassment-since-metoo-went-viral/ft_18-10-11_metooanniversary_hashtag-used-19m_times/.

8. Audrey Carlsen et al., "#MeToo Brought Down 201 Powerful Men. Nearly Half of Their Replacements Are Women," *New York Times*, last updated October 29, 2018, www.nytimes.com/interactive/2018/10/23/us/metoo-replacements.html.

9. Suzanna Danuta Walters, "Why Can't We Hate Men?," *Washington Post*, June 9, 2018, www.washingtonpost.com/opinions/why-cant-we-hate-men/2018/06/08/f1a3a8e0-6451-11e8-a69c-b944de66d9e7_story.html.

10. Anya Kamenetz, "Half of Professors in NPR Ed Survey Have Used 'Trigger Warnings,'" NPR, September 7, 2016, www.npr.org/sections/ed/2016/09/07/492979242/half-of-professors-in-npr-ed-survey-have-used-trigger-warnings.

11. Sam Sanders, "Upworthy Was One of the Hottest Sites Ever. You Won't Believe What Happened Next," NPR, June 20, 2017, www.npr.org

/sections/alltechconsidered/2017/06/20/533529538/upworthy-was-one-of-the
-hottest-sites-ever-you-wont-believe-what-happened-next.

12. Angela Nagle, *Kill All Normies: Online Culture Wars from 4Chan and Tumblr to Trump and the Alt-Right* (Alresford, UK: Zero Books, 2017), 43.

13. Robinson Meyer, "Why Are Upworthy Headlines Suddenly Everywhere?," *Atlantic*, December 8, 2014, www.theatlantic.com/technology/archive /2013/12/why-are-upworthy-headlines-suddenly-everywhere/282048/.

14. Lindsay Peoples, "Things to Keep You Warm and Dry at a Protest," *Cut*, January 13, 2017, www.thecut.com/2017/01/every-single-thing-you -need-to-bring-to-the-womens-march.html.

15. Emily Weiss (@emilyweiss), "#womensmarch us," Instagram photo, January 21, 2017, www.instagram.com/p/BPio7g2AwIi/?taken-by=emilywweiss &hl=en.

16. "One in Five Adults Have Attended a Political Protest, Rally or Speech," *Washington Post*, April 21, 2018, www.washingtonpost.com/page/2010-2019/ WashingtonPost/2018/04/06/National-Politics/Polling/release_516.xml.

17. "28 Students Respond to Donald Trump's Election," *Nation*, November 15, 2016, www.thenation.com/article/28-students-respond-to-donald -trumps-election/.

18. "28 Students."

19. Patrick Healy and Jeremy W. Peters, "Donald Trump's Victory Is Met with Shock across a Wide Political Divide," *New York Times*, November 9, 2016, www.nytimes.com/2016/11/10/us/politics/donald-trump-election -reaction.html.

20. Shane Bernard, "Ta-Nehisi Coates Ditched the Script and Kept It Real at This Marketing Conference," *Blavity*, November 9, 2016, https://blavity .com/ta-nehisi-coates-ditched-script-kept-real-hubspots-marketing-conference.

21. "The 1619 Project," *New York Times Magazine*, www.nytimes.com /interactive/2019/08/14/magazine/1619-america-slavery.html.

22. "1619 Project."

23. Andrew Sullivan, "America's New Religions," *New York*, December 7, 2018, nymag.com/intelligencer/2018/12/andrew-sullivan-americas-new -religions.html.

24. David French, "The Ferocious Religious Faith of the Campus Social-Justice Warrior," *National Review*, November 23, 2015, www.nationalreview .com/2015/11/religious-zealots-campus-social-justice-warriors/.

25. bell hooks, *Feminism Is for Everybody* (New York: Routledge, 2015), p. 117.

26. Emma Goldberg, "What's the Future of the Feminist Movement? 12 Leading Voices Respond," *Vice*, March 1, 2019, https://broadly.vice.com /en_us/article/zmayzx/future-of-feminism-roxane-gay-bell-hooks-longpath.

27. hooks, *Feminism*, 14.

28. Rituparna Som, "Is Self-Care an Act of Political Warfare?," *Vice*, January 30, 2019, www.vice.com/en_asia/article/nexbpz/is-self-care-a-political-act.

29. Peggy McIntosh, "White Privilege: Unpacking the Invisible Knapsack," National SEED Project, originally published 1989, https://nationalseed project.org/Key-SEED-Texts/white-privilege-unpacking-the-invisible-knapsack.

30. Mia McKenzie, "4 Ways to Push Back against Your Privilege," *BGD*, February 3, 2014, www.bgdblog.org/2014/02/4-ways-push-back-privilege/.

31. Sophia Stephens, "White People: This Is How to Check Your Privilege When Asking People of Color for Their Labor," *Everyday Feminism*, July 30, 2018, https://everydayfeminism.com/2018/07/white-people-this-is-how-to -check-your-privilege-when-asking-people-of-color-for-their-labor/.

32. Threads of Solidarity, "How to Compensate Black Women and Femmes on Social Media for Their Emotional Labor," *Everyday Feminism*, December 12, 2018, https://everydayfeminism.com/2018/12/how-to-compensate -black-women-and-femmes-on-social-media-for-their-emotional-labor/.

33. Jennifer Schaffer, "We Spoke to Lauren Chief Elk, the Woman Behind #GiveYourMoneytoWomen, About the Power of Cold Hard Cash," *Vice*, August 2, 2015, www.vice.com/en_us/article/8gkxd5/give-your-money-to -women-its-simple-284.

34. xoài phạm, "3 Reasons It's Irrational to Demand 'Rationalism' in Social Justice Activism," *Everyday Feminism*, March 25, 2016, https://everyday feminism.com/2016/03/why-rationalism-is-irrational/.

35. "Academic Invalidation of Lived Experience," *Brown Hijabi* (blog), February 27, 2015, https://thebrownhijabi.com/2015/02/27/academic -invalidation-of-lived-experience/.

36. Kaylee Jakubowski, "Stop Being So Attached!: A Beginner's Guide on Problematic Language," *Everyday Feminism*, February 3, 2014, https:// everydayfeminism.com/2014/02/guide-on-problematic-language/.

37. Katie Dupere, "5 Accidentally Transphobic Phrases Allies Use—and What to Say Instead," *Mashable*, October 18, 2015, https://mashable.com/2015 /10/18/transgender-ally-words/.

38. Sam Biddle, "Justine Sacco Is Good at Her Job, and How I Came to Peace with Her," *Gawker*, December 20, 2014, https://gawker.com /justine-sacco-is-good-at-her-job-and-how-i-came-to-pea-1653022326.

39. Clinton Nguyen, "An Attempted Suicide Forced a Tumblr Community to Open Its Eyes About Bullying," *Vice*, November 6, 2015, https:// motherboard.vice.com/en_us/article/3da838/an-attempted-suicide-forced-a -tumblr-community-to-open-its-eyes-about-bullying.

40. Sam Levin, "'Permit Patty': Woman Who Threatened Black Girl with Police Resigns from Cannabis Firm," *Guardian*, June 27, 2018, www.the guardian.com/us-news/2018/jun/26/permit-patty-san-francisco-police-black-girl -selling-water.

41. Cathy Young, "Standing Up to the Moral Outrage Industry," *Bulwark*, August 14, 2019, https://thebulwark.com/standing-up-to-the-moral-outrage -industry/.

42. Judith Shulevitz, "In College and Hiding From Scary Ideas," *New York Times*, March 21, 2015, www.nytimes.com/2015/03/22/opinion/sunday /judith-shulevitz-hiding-from-scary-ideas.html.

43. Richard Barbrook and Andy Cameron, "The Californian Ideology," *Mute*, September 1, 1995, www.metamute.org/editorial/articles/californian -ideology.

44. Barbrook and Cameron, "Californian Ideology."

45. Barbrook and Cameron, "Californian Ideology."

46. Mark Harris, "God Is a Bot, and Anthony Levandowski Is His Messenger," *Wired*, September 27, 2017, www.wired.com/story/god-is-a-bot-and -anthony-levandowski-is-his-messenger/.

47. Mark Harris, "Inside the First Church of Artificial Intelligence," *Wired*, November 15, 2017, www.wired.com/story/anthony-levandowski -artificial-intelligence-religion/.

48. Doug Bolton, "Russian Billionaire Dmitry Itskov Seeks 'Immortality' by Uploading His Brain to a Computer," *Independent*, March 14, 2016, www .independent.co.uk/news/science/dmitry-itskov-2045-initiative-immortality -brain-uploading-a6930416.html.

49. Kashmir Hill, "Silicon Valley's Young Tech Workers Are Betting That This 1960s Technology Will Let Them Live Forever," *Splinter*, March 2, 2016, https://splinternews.com/silicon-valleys-young-tech-workers-are-betting -that-thi-1793855142.

50. Elizabeth Segran, "Inside the Rationality Movement that Has Silicon Valley Buzzing with Positive Thinking," *Fast Company*, October 21, 2014, www.fastcompany.com/3037333/inside-the-rationality-movement-that-has -silicon-valley-buzzing-with-po.

51. Eliezer Yudkowsky, "12 Virtues of Rationality," 2006, http://yudkowsky .net/rational/virtues/.

52. Yudkowsky, "12 Virtues."

53. Linch Zhang, "Can the 'Secular Solstice' Become the Post-Ironic Celebration of Our Generation? One Game Designer's Foray into Redesigning Tradition," *HuffPost*, December 14, 2016, https://www.huffpost .com/entry/can-the-secular-solstice-become-the-post-ironic-celebration_b _58511263e4b0a464fad3e530.

54. Caroline McCarthy, "Silicon Valley Has a Problem with Conservatives. But Not the Political Kind," *Vox*, June 12, 2018, www.vox.com/first-person/2018 /6/12/17443134/silicon-valley-conservatives-religion-atheism-james-damore.

55. Ray Kurzweil, *The Singularity Is Near: When Humans Transcend Biology* (New York: Viking, 2005), 25.

56. Mark O'Connell, *To Be a Machine: Adventures among Cyborgs, Utopians, Hackers, and the Futurists Solving the Modest Problem of Death* (New York: Doubleday, 2017), 168.

57. Emily Chang, "'Oh My God, This Is So F—ed Up': Inside Silicon Valley's Secretive, Orgiastic Dark Side," *Vanity Fair*, January 2, 2018, www.vanityfair.com/news/2018/01/brotopia-silicon-valley-secretive-orgiastic-inner-sanctum.

58. Laurie Segall, "I Have a Fiancé, a Girlfriend and Two Boyfriends," CNN, January 28, 2015, https://money.cnn.com/2015/01/25/technology/polyamory-silicon-valley/index.html.

59. Segall, "I Have a Fiancé."

60. Melia Robinson, "A Silicon Valley Billionaire's Dream of a Floating Libertarian Utopia May Have Finally Been Killed," *Business Insider*, March 8, 2018, www.businessinsider.com/libertarian-peter-thiel-utopia-seasteading-institute-2018-3.

61. Quoted in Packer, "No Death."

62. Jay Yarow, "Google CEO Larry Page Wants a Totally Separate World Where Tech Companies Can Conduct Experiments on People," *Business Insider*, May 16, 2013, www.businessinsider.com/google-ceo-larry-page-wants-a-place-for-experiments-2013-5.

63. "Mobile Fact Sheet," Pew Research Center, June 12, 2019, www.pewinternet.org/fact-sheet/mobile/.

64. T. J. McCue, "57 Million U.S. Workers Are Part of the Gig Economy," *Forbes*, August 31, 2018, www.forbes.com/sites/tjmccue/2018/08/31/57-million-u-s-workers-are-part-of-the-gig-economy/.

65. "The Influencer Marketing Industry Global Ad Spend: A $5–$10 Billion Market By 2020," Mediakix, last updated March 6, 2018, https://mediakix.com/blog/influencer-marketing-industry-ad-spend-chart/.

66. Laura Geggel, "23andMe Is Sharing Its 5 Million Clients' Genetic Data with Drug Giant GlaxoSmithKline," *Live Science*, July 26, 2018, www.livescience.com/63173-23andme-partnership-glaxosmithkline.html.

67. Angelica LaVito, "Meditation App Headspace on Track to Double Corporate Clients, Bring Mindfulness to Work," CNBC, September 2, 2018, www.cnbc.com/2018/09/02/companies-are-turning-to-headspace-to-help-their-workers-meditate.html.

68. "Hackers Steal Data of 150 Million MyFitnessPal App Users," *Guardian*, March 30, 2018, www.theguardian.com/technology/2018/mar/30/hackers-steal-data-150m-myfitnesspal-app-users-under-armour.

69. Kopf, "Couples Now First Meet Online"; Ashley Carman, "Tinder Says It No Longer Uses a 'Desirability' Score to Rank People," *Verge*, March 15, 2019, www.theverge.com/2019/3/15/18267772/tinder-elo-score-desirability-algorithm-how-works.

CHAPTER 9: TWILIGHT OF THE CHADS

1. "Why BAPism, Why Now," *Froudesociety* (blog), February 11, 2017, https://froudesociety.wordpress.com/2017/02/11/why-bapism-why-now/.

2. Bronze Age Pervert, *Bronze Age Mindset* (self-published ebook, 2018).

3. Bronze Age Pervert, *Mindset.*

4. Bronze Age Pervert, *Mindset.*

5. Sten Morten, "4 Reasons Why Men Should Read Bronze Age Mindset," *Return of Kings*, June 15, 2018, www.returnofkings.com/179227/4-reasons-why-men-should-read-bronze-age-mindset.

6. Michael Anton, "Are the Kids Al(t)right?," *Claremont Review of Books*, August 14, 2019, www.claremont.org/crb/article/are-the-kids-altright/.

7. Rosie Gray, "Behind the Internet's Anti-Democracy Movement," *Atlantic*, February 10, 2017, www.theatlantic.com/politics/archive/2017/02/behind-the-internets-dark-anti-democracy-movement/516243/.

8. Ben Schreckinger, "The Alt-Right Manifesto That Has Trumpworld Talking," *Politico*, August 23, 2019, www.politico.com/story/2019/08/23/alt-right-book-trump-1472413.

9. Know Your Meme, s.v. "Black Pill," last updated March 18, 2019, 17:17, https://knowyourmeme.com/memes/black-pill.

10. Friedrich Nietzsche, *On the Genealogy of Morality*, ed. Keith Ansell-Pearson, trans. Carol Diethe (Cambridge: Cambridge University Press, 2007; Google Books, 2007), 27, https://books.google.com/books?id=wMzu8j4D1SYC&pg=PA27&lpg=PA27&dq=%E2%80%9Cimpotence+which+does+not+retaliate+is+being+turned+into+%E2%80%98goodness%E2%80%99;+genealogy+of+morals&source=bl&ots=ZvSGg48vOr&sig=ACfU3U2AuxV0xxqhl2oNGtyRJxx4ef2V5A&hl=en&sa=X&ved=2ahUKEwjFx_6YzaTmAhXF1FkKHTK5DK4Q6AEwAHoECAkQAQ#v=onepage&q&f=true.

11. Julius Evola, *Heathen Imperialism*, trans. Rowan Berkeley (France: Thompkins & Cariou, 2007).

12. Julius Evola, *Metaphysics of War* (Budapest: Arktos, 2011), 137–138.

13. Julius Evola, "Four Excerpts from *Pagan Imperialism: Fascism before the Euro-Christian Peril*," in *A Primer of Italian Fascism*, ed. Jeffrey Thompson Schnapp (Lincoln: University of Nebraska Press, 2000), 284.

14. Benito Mussolini, *The Doctrine of Fascism* (originally published by Ardita Publishers, Rome, trans. unknown), 1932, http://faculty.smu.edu/bkcarter/the%20doctrine%20of%20fascism.doc.

15. Michael Sebastian, "5 Ways You Can Revolt against the Modern World," *Return of Kings*, June 20, 2017, www.returnofkings.com/124659/5-ways-you-can-revolt-against-the-modern-world.

16. Steven Pinker, *The Blank Slate: The Modern Denial of Human Nature* (New York: Penguin, 2002), ix.

17. Christopher Dummitt, "Confessions of a Social Constructionist," *Quillette*, September 17, 2019, https://quillette.com/2019/09/17/i-basically -just-made-it-up-confessions-of-a-social-constructionist/.

18. Anti-Defamation League, "Mass Shooting in El Paso: What We Know," *ADL Blog*, August 4, 2019, www.adl.org/blog/mass-shooting-in-el-paso -what-we-know.

19. Mack Lamoureux, "YouTube Commenters Shift from 'Intellectual Dark Web' Fans to the Far-Right, Study Shows," *Vice*, August 29, 2019, www .vice.com/en_ca/article/pa7pvb/what-79-million-youtube-comments-can-tell -us-about-far-right-radicalization.

20. "Jordan B. Peterson," Quora, www.quora.com/profile/Jordan-B-Peterson /answers.

21. Jordan B. Peterson, "Q & A 2019 01 January," YouTube video, January 13, 2019, www.youtube.com/watch?v=mXPmLZRAPSo.

22. Rick Delafont, "Spurred by Censorship, Jordan Peterson Makes Pa- treon Alternative—Why Not Bitcoin?," *NewsBTC*, October 2018, www .newsbtc.com/2018/12/25/spurred-censorship-bitcoin/.

23. Tim Lott, "Jordan Peterson and the Transgender Wars," *Spectator*, September 20, 2017, https://life.spectator.co.uk/articles/jordan-peterson-and -the-transgender-wars/.

24. Cathy Newman, "Cathy Newman: 'The Internet Is Being Written by Men with an Agenda," interview with Nosheen Iqbal, *Guardian*, March 19, 2018, www.theguardian.com/media/2018/mar/19/cathy-newman-the-internet -is-being-written-by-men-with-an-agenda.

25. Jordan B. Peterson, *12 Rules for Life: An Antidote to Chaos* (Toronto: Random House Canada, 2018).

26. Peterson, *12 Rules*.

27. Peterson, *12 Rules*.

28. Peterson, *12 Rules*.

29. Peterson, *12 Rules*.

30. Peterson, *12 Rules*.

31. Peterson, *12 Rules*.

32. Peterson, *12 Rules*.

33. Nellie Bowles, "Jordan Peterson, Custodian of the Patriarchy," *New York Times*, May 18, 2018, www.nytimes.com/2018/05/18/style/jordan-peterson -12-rules-for-life.html.

34. Bowles, "Jordan Peterson."

35. Rob Henderson, "What Jordan Peterson Did for Me," *New York Times*, April 22, 2019, www.nytimes.com/2019/04/22/opinion/jordan-peterson -cambridge.html.

36. Bonnie Bacarisse, "The Republican Lawmaker Who Secretly Cre- ated Reddit's Women-Hating 'Red Pill," *Daily Beast*, April 25, 2017, www

.thedailybeast.com/the-republican-lawmaker-who-secretly-created-reddits
-women-hating-red-pill.

37. Bacarisse, "Republican Lawmaker."

38. Know Your Meme, s.v. "Millimeters of Bone," last modified October 29, 2017, 08:40, https://knowyourmeme.com/memes/millimeters-of-bone.

39. Zack Beauchamp, "Incel, the Misogynist Ideology That Inspired the Deadly Toronto Attack Explained," *Vox*, April 25, 2018, www.vox.com /world/2018/4/25/17277496/incel-toronto-attack-alek-minassian.

40. John Carver, "25 Painful Red Pill Questions Christians Need to Ask Themselves," *Return of Kings*, March 15, 2014, www.returnofkings.com /30716/25-painful-red-pill-questions-christians-need-to-ask-themselves.

41. Mike Cernovich, *Gorilla Mindset* (self-pub., Archangel Ink, 2015).

42. Nikhil Sonnad, "All the 'Wellness' Products Americans Love to Buy Are Sold on Both Infowars and Goop," *Quartz*, June 29, 2017, https://qz .com/1010684/all-the-wellness-products-american-love-to-buy-are-sold-on -both-infowars-and-goop/.

43. E. J. Dickson, "Are the Proud Boys Done or Are They Just Getting Started?," *Rolling Stone*, August 15, 2019, www.rollingstone.com/culture /culture-features/proud-boys-antifa-attack-trump-rally-2020-election -862538/.

44. Quoted in Nagle, *Kill All Normies*, 95.

45. Rachel Janik, "'I Laugh at the Death of Normies': How Incels Are Celebrating the Toronto Mass Killing," Southern Poverty Law Center, April 24, 2018, www.splcenter.org/hatewatch/2018/04/24/i-laugh-death-normies-how-incels -are-celebrating-toronto-mass-killing.

46. "Elliot Rodger: How Misogynist Killer Became 'Incel Hero,'" BBC, April 26, 2018, www.bbc.com/news/world-us-canada-43892189.

47. Rational Wiki, s.v. "Sargon of Akkad," last modified November 11, 2019, 00:43, https://rationalwiki.org/wiki/Sargon_of_Akkad#Relationship_with _the_alt-right.

48. Hatewatch Staff, "McInnes, Molyneux, and 4chan: Investigating Pathways to the Alt-Right," Southern Poverty Law Center, April 19, 2018, www .splcenter.org/20180419/mcinnes-molyneux-and-4chan-investigating-pathways -alt-right.

49. Anya Kamenetz, "Right-Wing Hate Groups Are Recruiting Video Gamers," NPR, November 5, 2018, www.npr.org/2018/11/05/660642531/right -wing-hate-groups-are-recruiting-video-gamers.

50. "Incels Hail Toronto Van Driver Who Killed 10 as a New Elliot Rodger, Talk of Future Acid Attacks and Mass Rapes [UPDATED]," *We Hunted the Mammoth*, April 24, 2018, www.wehuntedthemammoth.com/2018/04/24 /incels-hail-toronto-van-driver-who-killed-10-as-a-new-elliot-rodger-talk-of -future-acid-attacks-and-mass-rapes/.

51. Abigail Brooks, "Popping the Red Pill: Inside a Digital Alternate Reality," CNN, November 10, 2017, https://money.cnn.com/2017/11/10/technology/culture/divided-we-code-red-pill/index.html.

52. Roosh Valizadeh, "The Damaging Effects of Jewish Intellectualism and Activism on Western Culture," *Return of Kings*, May 4, 2015, www.returnofkings.com/62716/the-damaging-effects-of-jewish-intellectualism-and-activism-on-western-culture.

53. Nagle, *Kill All Normies*, 39.

54. Nagle, *Kill All Normies*, 33.

55. Sanjiv Bhattacharya, "The Battle for the Internet's Future," *Esquire*, January 25, 2014, www.esquire.com/uk/culture/news/a5597/hackers/.

56. Thomas Duff, "'I Will Carry Out an Attack against the Invaders': New Zealand Mosque Shooter Vowed to Massacre Muslims in Sick Blog Post a Day before the Attack," *Daily Mail*, March 15, 2019, www.dailymail.co.uk/news/article-6812241/I-carry-attack-against-invaders—shooters-social-media-post.html.

57. @aussie_bot, "Firstly. Has the accepted KEK, ancient Egyptian god of darkness, into their lives? Meme magic grows stronger each day, and soon KEK will return to smite the normies and bring about eternal chaos," Twitter, June 13, 2019, https://twitter.com/aussie_bot/status/1139080100320751617; "KEK," Me.Me, posted June 23, 2019, https://me.me/i/kek-kek-is-the-deification-of-the-primordial-concept-of-7aa91146f0fb4e409d7389b9e4ecf031.

58. Emma Stefansky, "Did Hillary Clinton Faint at This Year's 9/11 Ceremony?," *Vanity Fair*, September 11, 2016, www.vanityfair.com/news/2016/09/hillary-clinton-faints-911.

59. Quoted in Theødor, "Meme Magic Is Real, You Guys," *Tryangle*, November 11, 2016, https://medium.com/tryangle-magazine/meme-magic-is-real-you-guys-16a497fc45b3.

60. "The Smug Pepe Meme Sure Makes a Lot of Sense Now That Trump Has Won," *Truth about Pepe the Frog and the Cult of Kek* (blog), https://pepethefrogfaith.wordpress.com/smug-pepe-sure-makes-a-lot-of-sense-now-that-trump-has-won/.

61. Alex Krasodomski-Jones, "What Does the Alt-Right Do Now that 'God Emperor' Trump Won?," CNN, November 15, 2016, www.cnn.com/2016/11/14/opinions/what-next-alt-right-krasodomski-jones-opinion/index.html.

62. David Neiwert, "What the Kek: Explaining the Alt-Right 'Deity' behind Their 'Meme Magic,'" Southern Poverty Law Center, May 9, 2017, www.splcenter.org/hatewatch/2017/05/08/what-kek-explaining-alt-right-deity-behind-their-meme-magic.

63. Hatewatch Staff, "Flags and Other Symbols Used by Far-Right Groups in Charlottesville," Southern Poverty Law Center, August 12, 2017, www

.splcenter.org/hatewatch/2017/08/12/flags-and-other-symbols-used-far-right
-groups-charlottesville; Neiwert, "What the Kek."

64. @Cassandra, "Free Kekistan," YouTube video, April 15, 2017, www
.youtube.com/watch?v=5iA_6e4o9BQ.

65. John Fea, "Why Do White Evangelicals Still Staunchly Support
Donald Trump?," *Washington Post*, April 5, 2019, www.washingtonpost
.com/outlook/2019/04/05/why-do-white-evangelicals-still-staunchly-support
-donald-trump/.

66. @Saving You From Yourselves, "We Are the New Punk - Milo Yian-
nopoulus," YouTube video, October 10, 2016, www.youtube.com/watch?v=
2sf6acPHfAs.

67. Dale Beran, *It Came from Something Awful: How a Toxic Troll Army
Accidentally Memed Donald Trump into Office* (New York: All Points Books,
2019), xv.

68. Marcy Oster, "White Supremacists Have Murdered at Least 73 Since
Charlottesville, ADL Says," *Times of Israel*, August 9, 2019, www.timesofisrael
.com/white-supremacists-have-murdered-at-least-73-since-charlottesville-adl-says/.

69. "Why the 'Black Pill'?," *Freedom from the Gynocracy* (blog), https://
omegavirginrevolt.wordpress.com/why-the-black-pill/.

70. Ethan Jiang, "Blackpill Philosophy—A Closer Look at Incels," Medium,
August 23, 2018, https://medium.com/@ethanjiang4/blackpill-philosophy-a
-closer-look-at-incels-e49ede6a2f7e.

71. "Incels Hail Toronto Van Driver."

72. Jane Coaston, "The New Zealand Shooter's Manifesto Shows How
White Nationalist Rhetoric Spreads," *Vox*, March 18, 2019, www.vox.com
/identities/2019/3/15/18267163/new-zealand-shooting-christchurch-white
-nationalism-racism-language.

CONCLUSION: CLASH OF THE TITANS

1. Stetzer, "23 Easters Left."

2. "The Politicisation of White Evangelical Christianity Is Hurting It,"
Economist, February 28, 2019, www.economist.com/united-states/2019/02/28
/the-politicisation-of-white-evangelical-christianity-is-hurting-it.

3. Anna Pulley, "An Erotic Dinner Party Gave Me a Whole New Perspective on Sex," *Vice*, April 30, 2019, www.vice.com/en_us/article/mb8vvp
/erotic-dinner-party-deafness-sex.

4. Marianne Williamson, *The Law of Divine Compensation: On Work,
Money, and Miracles* (New Yorker: HarperOne, 2012).

5. Richards, "Want to Win Over Millennials and Gen Z?"

6. Christel J. Manning, "Gen Z Is the Least Religious Generation.
Here's Why That Could Be a Good Thing," *Pacific Standard*, May 6, 2019,

https://psmag.com/ideas/gen-z-is-the-least-religious-generation-heres-why-that-could-be-a-good-thing.

7. John Gramlich, "Young Americans Are Less Trusting of Other People – and Key Institutions – Than Their Elders," *Fact Tank* (blog), Pew Research Center, August 6, 2019, www.pewresearch.org/fact-tank/2019/08/06/young-americans-are-less-trusting-of-other-people-and-key-institutions-than-their-elders/.

8. Patrick J. Buchanan, "The Aggressors in the Culture Wars" (blog post), March 8, 2004, https://buchanan.org/blog/pjb-the-aggressors-in-the-culture-wars-583.

9. Steven D. Smith, *Pagans and Christians in the City: Culture Wars from the Tiber to the Potomac* (Grand Rapids, MI: Wm. B. Eerdmans, 2018).

INDEX

A

Rose Callahan

Tara Isabella Burton is a contributing editor at the *American Interest*, a columnist at Religion News Service, and the former staff religion reporter at *Vox*. She has written on religion and secularism for *National Geographic*, the *Washington Post*, the *New York Times*, and more, and holds a doctorate in theology from Oxford. She is also the author of the novel *Social Creature* (Doubleday, 2018).

PublicAffairs is a publishing house founded in 1997. It is a tribute to the standards, values, and flair of three persons who have served as mentors to countless reporters, writers, editors, and book people of all kinds, including me.

I. F. Stone, proprietor of *I. F. Stone's Weekly*, combined a commitment to the First Amendment with entrepreneurial zeal and reporting skill and became one of the great independent journalists in American history. At the age of eighty, Izzy published *The Trial of Socrates*, which was a national bestseller. He wrote the book after he taught himself ancient Greek.

Benjamin C. Bradlee was for nearly thirty years the charismatic editorial leader of *The Washington Post*. It was Ben who gave the *Post* the range and courage to pursue such historic issues as Watergate. He supported his reporters with a tenacity that made them fearless and it is no accident that so many became authors of influential, best-selling books.

Robert L. Bernstein, the chief executive of Random House for more than a quarter century, guided one of the nation's premier publishing houses. Bob was personally responsible for many books of political dissent and argument that challenged tyranny around the globe. He is also the founder and longtime chair of Human Rights Watch, one of the most respected human rights organizations in the world.

·　　·　　·

For fifty years, the banner of Public Affairs Press was carried by its owner Morris B. Schnapper, who published Gandhi, Nasser, Toynbee, Truman, and about 1,500 other authors. In 1983, Schnapper was described by *The Washington Post* as "a redoubtable gadfly." His legacy will endure in the books to come.

Peter Osnos, *Founder*